Register This New Book

Benefits of Registering*

- ✓ FREE **replacements** of lost or damaged books
- ✓ FREE **audiobook** – *Pilgrim's Progress*, audiobook edition
- ✓ FREE information about new titles and other **freebies**

www.anekopress.com/new-book-registration

*See our website for requirements and limitations.

LIGHT and TRUTH

The Old Testament

We enjoy hearing from our readers. Please contact us
at www.anekopress.com/questions-comments with
any questions, comments, or suggestions.

Light and Truth – The Old Testament
© 2023 by Aneko Press
All rights reserved. First edition 1868.
Revisions copyright 2023.

Please do not reproduce, store in a retrieval system, or transmit in any form
or by any means – electronic, mechanical, photocopying, recording, or
otherwise, without written permission from the publisher. Please contact us
via www.AnekoPress.com for reprint and translation permissions.

Unless otherwise indicated, scripture quotations are taken from the New American
Standard Bible® (NASB), copyright © 1960, 1962, 1963, 1968, 1971, 1972, 1973, 1975, 1977,
1995, 2020 by The Lockman Foundation. Used by permission. www.Lockman.org.

Scripture quotations marked (KJV) are from The Authorized (King James) Version.
Rights in the Authorized Version in the United Kingdom are vested in the Crown.
Reproduced by permission of the Crown's patentee, Cambridge University Press.

Cover Designer: J. Martin
Editors: Jon D. Fogdall, Ruth Clark

Aneko Press
www.anekopress.com
Aneko Press, Life Sentence Publishing, and our logos are trademarks of
Life Sentence Publishing, Inc.
203 E. Birch Street
P.O. Box 652
Abbotsford, WI 54405

RELIGION / Biblical Studies / Old Testament / General
Paperback ISBN: 978-1-62245-952-0
eBook ISBN: 978-1-62245-953-7
10 9 8 7 6 5 4 3 2
Available where books are sold

LIGHT and TRUTH

The Old Testament

Bible Thoughts and Themes

HORATIUS BONAR

Contents

Preface ix

Ch. 1: The Old and New Creation..1

Ch. 2: The Link Between Being and NonBeing.......................................4

Ch. 3: A Happy World 8

Ch. 4: The Sin, the Sinner, and the Sentence 12

Ch. 5: Man's Fig Leaves..16

Ch. 6: Expulsion and Reentrance...19

Ch. 7: The Blood of Sprinkling and the Blood of Abel.........................23

Ch. 8: The Way of Cain..27

Ch. 9: The Man of Rest 31

Ch. 10: Going Out and Keeping Out..35

Ch. 11: The Shield and the Recompense...39

Ch. 12: Liberty and Service...43

Ch. 13: The Day of Despair...46

Ch. 14: The Blood of Deliverance 49

Ch. 15: How God Deals with Sin and the Sinner..................................53

Ch. 16: The Fire Quenched...56

Ch. 17: The Vision from the Rocks..60

Ch. 18: The Doom of the Doublehearted..63

Ch. 19: Be Not Borderers 68

Ch. 20: The Outlines of a Saved Sinner's History.................................71

Ch. 21: Divine Longings over the Foolish 75

Ch. 22: What a Believing Man Can Do..78

Ch. 23: Song of the Putting Off of the Armor 82

Ch. 24: The Kiss of the Backslider..86

Ch. 25: The Priestly Word of Peace..90

Ch. 26: Human Anesthetics..94
Ch. 27: Spiritual and Carnal Weapons 98
Ch. 28: Divine Silence and Human Despair.. 101
Ch. 29: Jewish Unbelief and Gentile Blessing.. 104
Ch. 30: The Restoration of the Banished.. 107
Ch. 31: The Farewell Gift... 111
Ch. 32: God's Dealing with Sin and the Sinner....................................... 115
Ch. 33: God Finding a Resting Place... 119
Ch. 34: The Moriah Group.. 122
Ch. 35: Diverse Kinds of Conscience 126
Ch. 36: The Soul Turning from Man to God... 130
Ch. 37: Man's Dislike of a Present God 133
Ch. 38: True and False Consolation... 136
Ch. 39: Gain and Loss for Eternity 139
Ch. 40: Man's Misconstruction of the Works of God............................. 143
Ch. 41: The Two Cries and the Two Answers.. 147
Ch. 42: The Knowledge of God's Name.. 151
Ch. 43: Deliverance from Deep Waters... 154
Ch. 44: The Excellency of the Divine Lovingkindness........................... 157
Ch. 45: The Sickness, the Healer, and the Healing 161
Ch. 46: The Consecration of Earth's Gold and Silver 164
Ch. 47: The Gifts of the Ascended One... 167
Ch. 48: The Speaker, the Listener, the Peace.. 170
Ch. 49: The Believing Man's Confident Appeal...................................... 173
Ch. 50: The Love and the Deliverance... 176
Ch. 51: The Sin and Folly of Being Unhappy 179
Ch. 52: The Book of Books 183
Ch. 53: The Secret of Deliverance from Evil.. 186
Ch. 54: The Voice of the Heavenly Bridegroom...................................... 190
Ch. 55: The Love That Passes Knowledge 193
Ch. 56: The Vision of the Glory 197

Ch. 57: Man's Extremity and Satan's Opportunity 201
Ch. 58: The Day of Clear Vision to the Dim Eyes 204
Ch. 59: The Unfainting Creator and the Fainting Creature 207
Ch. 60: The Knowledge That Justifies 211
Ch. 61: The Heritage and Its Title Deeds 215
Ch. 62: The Meeting between the Sinner and God 219
Ch. 63: God's Love and God's Way of Blessing 222
Ch. 64: Divine Jealousy for the Truth 226
Ch. 65: Divine Love and Human Rejection of It 230
Ch. 66: God's Desire to Bless the Sinner 234
Ch. 67 The Resting Place Forgotten 237
Ch. 68: The Day That Will Right All Wrongs 241
Ch. 69: The Glory and the Love 245
Ch. 70: False Religion and Its Doom 249
Ch. 71: No Breath, No Life 252
Ch. 72: Every Christian a Teacher 255
Ch. 73: Work, Rest, and Recompense 258
Ch. 74: Human Heedlessness and Divine Remembrance 262
Ch. 75: Lies, the Food of Man 265
Ch. 76: The Love and the Calling 268
Ch. 77: The Anger and the Goodness 273
Ch. 78: Darkness Pursuing the Sinner 277
Ch. 79: Jerusalem, the Center of the World's Peace 280
Ch. 80: Jerusalem and Her King 284
Ch. 81: Looking to the Pierced One 288
Ch. 82: The Holiness of Common Things 291
Ch. 83: Wearying Jehovah with Our Words 294
Ch. 84: Dies Irae (Day of Wrath) 298

Horatius Bonar – A Brief Biography 303
Other Similar Titles 307

Preface

"All the rivers run into the sea, yet the sea is not full," said the wisest of the wise. We might add to this, and say, "All the rivers come out of the sea, yet the sea is not empty." All the good books in the world have, more or less directly, come out of the Bible, yet the Bible is not empty. It is as full now as it was when it was first written. Let us not be afraid of exhausting it.

There is only one book that bears such study. Let us be thankful that our world does contain such a book. It must be superhuman, supernatural. Blessed be God that there is at least one thing thoroughly superhuman and supernatural in this world. There is something that stands out from and above "the laws of nature," something visible and audible to link us with Him whose face we do not see and whose voice we do not hear. What a void there would be here if this one fragment of the Divine, now venerable, both with wisdom and age, were to disappear from our midst. Or what is the same thing if the discovery were to be made that this ancient volume is not the unearthly thing that men have deemed it to be, but, at the highest estimate, a mere fragment from the great block of human thought – perhaps, according to another estimate, a mere relic of superstition.

"Bring the Book," said Sir Walter Scott, upon his deathbed to Lockhart. "What book?" asked Lockhart. "What book?" replied the dying novelist. "There is but one Book." Yes, there is but one Book, and one day we will know it, when that which is human will pass away (like the mists from some Lebanon peak), and leave that which is divine to stand out and to shine out alone in its unhidden grandeur.

God is recalling humanity to the Book now that was written for it. By the very attacks made on it by enemies, as well as by the studies of its friends, He is bringing us back to this one volume as the light shining in a dark place. He is asking us to take ourselves to it so that we may know the past, the present, and the future.

Let us read it, let us study it, let us love it, let us reverence it.

It will guide, it will cheer, it will enlighten, it will make wise, it will purify.

It will lead us into all truth. It will deliver us from the fermenting errors of the day. It will save us from the intellectual dreams of a vain philosophy, from the corrupted taste of a sensational literature, from the baseless novelties of spiritual mysticism, from the pretentious sentimentalisms of men who soar above all creeds and abhor the name of "law," from Broad Churchism, and High Churchism, and no Churchism. It will lead us into light and love, into liberty and unity, imparting strength and gladness.

This Book is the *Word* of God. It contains the words of God, and it is the *Word* of God, the thing that God has spoken to man. Being the *Word* of God, that which it contains must be the *words* of God.

Each word of God is true, and is as divine as it is true. But are there not various readings, so that at times we are uncertain as to which is the authentic word? Yes, but these cases are few, and doubtful cases do not invalidate those that are not doubtful, the latter of which compose more than nine tenths of the Bible. The doubtful readings make us far more secure as to all the rest. There are various readings in Homer and Cicero, but the occurrence of these does not prove that the rest are not really the very words of Homer and Cicero.

But are there not words of wicked men, indeed, even of Satan himself, in the Bible? How can I say that it contains nothing but the words of God? I did not say this. But I say that even the words of the wicked are inserted in it by God for a wise purpose. In interpreting such words we are to consider what that purpose is, so that taking the passage as a whole we will extract the truth of God from it and even discover also how the words of the ungodly are made to illustrate the truth of God. No word is set down in the Bible except by the authority of God. This is our security and joy.

But are there not variations in the narratives, as in Kings and Chronicles, as in the Gospels, even as in the very words said to have been spoken at our Lord's baptism? Yes, variations, but not inconsistencies. The Holy Spirit introduced these variations for the purpose of bringing out all the aspects of the scene. These variations from the exact original words are not by chance or without a purpose. The Spirit was the author of the original words, and He is also the author of the variations. Does He not have the right to vary His own words when He sees fit, and when He varies them should He be accused of inaccuracy? Should the fact of the variations be used as an argument against the verbal inspiration of Scripture, as a proof that the original words were not worth the exact reporting? If the variations were a *contradiction*, the reasoning would hold good; but since this is not alleged, the accusation falls to pieces. For it is a pure absurdity to deduce from a *variation* the same conclusions as from a *contradiction*. It is as arbitrary as it is absurd to deny a writer the liberty of setting his own words in different lights, indeed, even to base upon the fact of his doing so a charge or a suspicion that he never spoke or wrote any such words at all. So long as we can show that we have *divine authority for the variations,* we do not need to shrink away from acknowledging these, or suppose that the consequences of such an acknowledgment must be a relinquishment of the full inspiration of Scripture. Suppose I am arguing with a friend concerning something that I did and said. Am I not at liberty at one time to cite my original words, and at another time to vary them so as to make a point with them or add force to my argument? And because I explain myself this way in varying language, should it be said that I never really used the very words, or that it is of no consequence to know whether the words were really mine, when the very object of the discussion is to get at the original words and their true meaning? Yes, we have divine authority for the variations in the different narratives. Having that, we have divine security for words of Scripture, *just as if there had been no variation at all.* This becomes all the stronger when it happens, as is admitted in the present case, that the aim of the writer is really to present the varying truth to us, that he can have no object in misrepresenting it or misreporting himself, even that his character is such as to place himself above all suspicion, both in regard to truthfulness and wisdom.

I take this Book, then, as "the one Book," the Book of God, as truly such as Calvin's *Institutes of the Christian Religion* or Hooker's *Of the Lawes of Ecclesiastical Politie* are the books of men. And why men should write books for their fellow man, and God not write one Book for His creatures to tell them of Himself, I do not understand. It seems to me the most natural of all things. The utter silence of God to the creatures that He has made would surely be so unnatural as to be incredible. That God should *speak* is what we might expect; that He should be *mute* is beyond all belief. That He should speak in words of His own choosing is what we should desire above all things, for then we would know that His thoughts were really presented to us. That He should speak in words of man's choosing (if such a thing could be), is altogether undesirable and unlikely. For then we would not know whether the language and the thought were in the least coincidental, or, even that we should feel that we had gotten an incorrect and untrustworthy volume, that we had been cheated and betrayed, that instead of bread we had gotten a stone, and instead of an egg we had gotten a scorpion.

The pages that follow are an attempt to bring out, as briefly as possible, the thoughts of God, as contained in the words of His Book. It is with light and truth that we must handle that Book. The old Latin poet says, *Verborum vetus interit aetas* (Words die of old age), but the divine volume, with its true words, like the light that is its emblem, remains, forever perfect, and forever young.

Edinburgh, November 1867.

Chapter 1

The Old and New Creation

Genesis 1

Only faith can read this chapter correctly, because its record goes back beyond human history, because we do not have the authority of testimony nor experience for its statements. We have only the bare *word of God* (Hebrews 11:3). These prehistoric annals of earth are the region of *faith,* quite as much as those posthistoric annals given in the Apocalypse. It is by *faith* that we understand that the worlds were framed by the word of God. For faith has to do with the unseen both behind and before us. This chapter contains the substance of our creed concerning God as the Creator.

1. *The Creation.* It comprises the whole of what we call the universe, and all that it contains, visible or invisible, *the heavens and the earth* (Genesis 1:1). This universe was *created.* It did not create itself, nor did chance create it, nor did it exist eternally. Its Creator was God. It was not *a* god, but the one living and true God, who calls Himself *El, Elohim,* and *Jehovah.* Its Creator was the Word of God, the Son of God, the second person of the Elohim or Godhead (John 1:2; Colossians 1:16). This was *in the beginning,* that is, the indefinite past, the far past. It was then that the things that we see now were made, not out of preexisting materials, or things that do appear, but out of nothing.

2. *The Chaos.* It was shapeless and unfilled, without form and void. It was not properly "the earth" or "the world." *The fulness thereof* (Psalm 89:11 KJV) had not come yet. Whether this chaos was the *first* state or a *later* condition, that of fall and punishment in connection with the apostasy of angels, we do not say. Here, however, earth lies before us in chaos. How long, we do not know. This chaos was one of *darkness,* which covered the whole face of the abyss, or the deep. How this could be, except in connection with a sinning race, is not easily seen. For *God is Light, and in Him there is no darkness at all* (1 John 1:5).

3. *The Life.* The Spirit of God moved upon (or brooded like a dove over) the face of the waters. These waters were everywhere; the globe was fluid, but the waters were dead. The fluid mass had no vitality in it. It was like the lifeless bodies of the valley. The Holy Spirit came upon them, and the power of the highest overshadowed them; *life* was imparted, the deep was enlivened, or, as Milton writes, "made pregnant." This Spirit, then as now, came from Him *who has the seven Spirits of God* (Revelation 3:1) – the Son of God, the Creator, for *in Him was life* (John 1:4). The enlivening Spirit is with Him. *The life was manifested* (1 John 1:2; cf. Psalm 104:30).

4. *The Light.* God spoke. The light came following the life. For it is not first light then life, but first life then light. *The life was the Light of men* (John 1:4). Christ *the life* was *the Light* of the World. It was God, the Son, who commanded the light to shine out of the darkness. It needed only a word, nothing more.

5. *The Order.* There has been confusion up to this point – mixture. Sky and earth, light and darkness, air and water, everything is commingled. Every element needed is there, but they are mixed up with each other, and so are useless. As to the air, earth, and water, there must be *division.* The landmarks of each must be set. As to light and darkness, there must be *alternation:* day and night, sunrise and sunset. All must be in perfect *order:* no one interfering with its fellow, but each left free to work its own work in the development of a glorious universe.

6. *The Beauty.* It is no longer *without form* (Genesis 1:2 KJV). It is now coming into shape in all its different features, and all is beautiful. *"By His breath the heavens are cleared"* (Job 26:13). It is by degrees or stages that this beauty is drawn out, yet it does come. The blue heavens, the translucent atmosphere, the sparkling stars, the bright sun, the waxing and waning moon, the green earth, the blossoming trees, the manycolored flowers – everything is beautiful. For He who formed them is Himself the fountainhead of all beauty, the perfection of perfection, the infinitely lovable One. We were made to love "the beautiful" in the creature, how much more in the Creator! He has made everything beautiful in its season and He has given us minds capable of appreciating and admiring it all; but it is He Himself who is altogether excellent, the sum as well as the source of all beauty. He claims admiration and love for Himself, as the infinitely glorious One.

7. *The Fruitfulness.* Valley, plain, hill, and field are all fruitful. They bring forth their shrubs and fruit trees, their corn, and their abundance of everything that is good for food, as well as pleasant to the eye. It is a *fruitbearing* earth. Barrenness is unknown. Man and beast are there, fish and fowl are there; all kinds of life, intelligent or unintelligent are there. It is not mere beauty or order that satisfies God, but fruitfulness. It is fruitfulness He asks from us. We are ourselves a part of His fruitful earth, as well as its lords. In both aspects, He asks for fruitfulness. He comes to us daily *seeking fruit* (Luke 13:7 KJV).

8. *The Goodness.* He gazed on it and pronounced it all very good. Each part of it was good. The whole *was very good* (Genesis 1:31). It is good in every sense: good in the sense of beauty; good in the sense of promoting benevolent and loving ends; good in the sense of earth and sea, hill and valley, river and forest, all mutually helping each other. All is goodness! Yes, a marvelous whole of unutterable goodness. Death is not here, nor ferocity nor warfare. Everything is good, very good. The earth is full of the goodness of the Lord. God delights in His handiwork. And though it is much marred and defaced, it still exhibits its original excellence. But it will do so more gloriously in the times of the restitution of all things when there will be the new heavens and new earth wherein dwells righteousness. *Behold, I make all things new* (Revelation 21:5 KJV).

Chapter 2

The Link Between Being and NonBeing

Then God said. – Genesis 1:3

This first chapter of Genesis, in many places, prefixes the name *God* to what is said or done, so that there is no mistake as to the speaker or the doer, and that God Himself may be prominently presented to us in His divine personality. We read, *God created, God made, God saw, God separated, God called, God placed, God blessed, God formed, God planted, God took,* and *God commanded.* But the most frequent phrase here is *God **said*** (emphasis added). As it is written elsewhere, *He **spoke,** and it was done* (Psalm 33:9, emphasis added); *[He] **commanded** the light to shine out of darkness* (2 Corinthians 4:6 KJV, emphasis added); *the worlds were prepared by the **word** of God* (Hebrews 11:3, emphasis added); *[He] upholds all things by the **word** of His power* (Hebrews 1:3, emphasis added).

God's *word* is then the one medium or link between Him and creation. Creation is in one sense *immediate* – the result of direct power. In another sense, it is *mediate,* as accomplished by the intervention of speech. How far this mode of statement is a condescension to man's weakness, we will not say, but the frequency with which it is repeated shows what stress God lays on it. There was evidently an intervention of something corresponding to human speech, if, indeed, the actual words were not spoken just as they are set down. Between the "nothing" and the "something" – nonexistence and creation – there intervenes only the *word*. But after that, many other agencies come in, animate or inanimate – second causes, natural laws and processes – all unfolding the great original authorization. It is only as in connection with it that these laws and processes have any power at all. The power or energy of the original *word* still lasts, still vibrates through the universe, still keeps creation in motion, and still preserves the sequences and orderliness of all created things above and beneath.

He is the sovereign Speaker and the sovereign Worker. Everyone and everything is under His authority. He says to this creature, "Go," and it goes, and to another, "Come," and it comes. He sits on His throne commanding the universe.

It is that same word that is still acting, as effective and as potent as at the start. Why does the sun still move and shine? Not merely because of a word spoken some thousands of years ago, but also because that word is still operative and energetic. We read the original *God said* in every revolution, in every sunrise and sunset. *By His word the present heavens and earth are being reserved* (2 Peter 3:7). Vitality, growth, beauty, and fruitfulness are indications not of a past power, but of a present energy, a continuation of the original impulse, or rather of the very same original impulse still prolonged and working. *"My Father is working until now"* (John 5:17).

When the Son of God was here, He acted this way in doing His miracles. He spoke and it was done: *"Lazarus, come forth"* (John 11:43); *"Young man, I say to you, arise!"* (Luke 7:14); *"Little girl, I say to you, get up!"* (Mark 5:41); *"Be opened!"* (Mark 7:34). It was a *word* that was still the medium. And in His case, we see the wholeness, for He was *the Word* (John 1:1). But there is the same wholeness in the first creation, for He was Himself the Creator. It was He who spoke the creating word at first. His words are the words of authority and power.

This God (and this Son of God) still speaks to us. He does not keep silent, though our outer ears hear no sound.

1. *He speaks to us in creation.* This earth and these heavens are the echo of His voice. God speaks to us in each part of His handiwork. It is not "nature's voice," as men say. It is the true, authentic voice of God. He

speaks each day to us and is never silent. As He spoke at first, and the universe heard His voice, so He speaks to us now. Will we hear or not?

2. *He speaks to us in the Word itself.* This Book embodies His words. Creation is the visible embodiment of His power and wisdom. It is the result of His words. His power came forth in speech as a channel or medium. This Book of His is, in a different way, the effect of His speaking. It is His written wisdom and power. *There* is His voice to us. The thunder and tempest are His loud voice of grandeur. The sunshine and the gentle breeze are His still small voice. But deeper, clearer, keener, softer, and still more penetrating than all of these is His Word. Men speak of the Bible being the *thoughts* of God, but not His *words*. As if you could speak of a certain piece of music apart from the notes that compose it, or of the sea apart from the drops that make it up; as if you might say that creation embodied the general purpose of God, but not any minute or special designs. That Book is what it is because it contains the *words* of God. To our outer ear God speaks to us, and through our outer ear to our inner man. For it is through the Word, and in connection with it, that God communicates with us. That Word revives: *Your word has revived me* (Psalm 119:50). That word produces faith: *Faith comes from hearing* (Romans 10:17). That Word strengthens, comforts, heals, nourishes, and revives. It gets into contact with each part of our souls and works its own work there. And it does this because it is *divine.* No human words could be trusted to work the work in a human soul so unrestrictedly. It is not eloquence, poetry, nor argument, but something more than all these together. It is something peculiar and indescribable, which man could not have formed, and which he cannot understand, that makes it so suitable for the soul of a foolish and sinful man.

3. *He speaks to us in providences.* Let us listen reverently to everything that happens, and we will recognize a divine voice and divine words in everything. No providence is mute. No sorrow, joy, sickness, recovery, nor calamity, public or private, is mute. *God said* sounds out from all of them. By them God is pursuing us at every step, and constantly stretching out His hands to a disobedient and denying race. How articulate, how eloquent are the daily events of the most common life on earth.

Yet we close our ears! Day unto day utters speech, yet we will neither interpret nor listen!

4. *He speaks to us by His Sabbaths.* I mention this especially because of its connection with the creation. Each Sabbath is to us a silver trumpet speaking directly from God. It gives no uncertain sound. It speaks of grace, love, and rest. It is God's weekly invitation to the weary. He who would take from us our Sabbaths would silence the voice of God.

That is how God speaks to us. Yet deeper than all these is a divine and irresistible voice speaking to our inner man. Not separate from the Word, yet still distinct – the direct, sovereign, almighty voice of God by which the new creation is formed. Thus it is that out of many people hearing the same sermon, or reading the same Bible, some believe and some do not believe. As in the old creation, so it is in the new: it is God that is the speaker and the worker. *"Behold, I am making all things new"* (Revelation 21:5). The new creating words come from His lips to souls dead in sin.

What noble and mighty things are words! Through them we wield the mind of our fellow man. We cannot operate on dead matter through them, as God can, but we can on living souls. What a responsibility is on us for our words! What a danger and sin there is in idle or evil words. Let our words always be true and holy.

Chapter 3

A Happy World

Genesis 2

What a poem, what a picture the first chapter was! Unrivaled in magnificence. The work that was done and the words that describe it are both of God. Now we get some details of the work.

1. *Its completion.* Thus, the heavens and earth were finished, and the whole host or array of everything that they contained. God finishes what He begins. He leaves nothing imperfect. And He delights to speak of it as finished. So with creation, so with the tabernacle, so with the temple, and so with the great work on the cross. *"It is finished!"* (John 19:30). So at the close of time. *"It is done"* (Revelation 21:6).

2. *The rest.* The seventh day saw the work done. Up until then it had been continuous work. Now it is rest. God rests. Creation rests. The morning stars begin their song, and the sons of God their shout. What *rest* means to Him who *does not become weary or tired* (Isaiah 40:28), we cannot say. It means more than mere cessation from work. God's *rest* must be as real a thing as His joy and His love, though what it is we cannot say. He calls it *rest*. It must be something in Him exactly corresponding to what rest is in us. The day on which He rests He *blesses*. *Blessing* with Him is not merely a word. It must be a day more abounding with blessing to us and to creation than the rest. More blessing flows

out on that day. There are deeper things in this than we think. One day we will learn that neither earth nor man could have done without this day of blessing. Invisible blessing flows out from it even to those who are profaning it. God sanctifies it, sets a fence around it, and makes it a holy thing, like the altar when sprinkled with blood. He has done this because He *rested*, and because He *will rest*. It is the Sabbath, the rest day. Will we not love the name?

3. *The details* (verses 4-6). God graciously summarizes and gives us a glimpse of the process of creation. All plants and herbs were His handiwork; they did not come about by chance, nature, nor man. Until now the ground was unfilled and rain had not fallen. But now God intercedes. He covers earth with a refreshing mist and He creates man. Probably the state of the atmosphere then was such as to produce mist instead of rain. It may be that this was the state of things up until the flood. How wonderful are His works. In wisdom He made them all, the finished and the unfinished!

4. *Man's formation.* Man is said to be *formed,* to be *made,* and to be *created*, all by God and out of the dust. His origin is partly of earth and partly of heaven. His body is from beneath, his soul is from above. God breathes the *breath of life* (Genesis 2:7) into him, and he becomes a living soul. Thus, his body is *made* or *formed,* but his soul is *created*. The first Adam was made a living soul, the last Adam a life-giving spirit. The first man is of the earth – earthy, the second man is the Lord from heaven. *In him we live, and move, and have our being* (Acts 17:28 KJV). We are His offspring.

5. *Man's dwelling* (verses 8-15). God plants a garden for him, in a region that He names Eden (meaning "delight"). This garden is the eastern part of Eden, later called Paradise. He stores it with everything that is beautiful and fruitful: a tree of life and a tree of knowledge. Down from the heights of Eden there flows a river that waters the garden, and then it divides into four streams, in four directions, each flowing through some sizeable land. Thus, the garden is doubly watered by the mist and the river. It is a dwelling fit for man, and worthy of God. *God is not ashamed to be called their God* (Hebrews 11:16), seeing that He

has provided for them such a habitation. Man is to keep and tend this habitation. It needs his care, yet the care is slight. No sweat of the face, no anxious toil. Easy and pleasant labor! Such is the love of God.

6. *The test* (verses 16-17). A right to every tree but one! Large scope and free welcome to every tree but that tree of knowledge. Herein is love. Yet here is a link fastening man to God. Man is not to be allowed to go at-large, without anything to remind him of God or divine law or divine sovereignty. Even in this pleasant garden God's authority must be acknowledged. You will and you will not, you may and you may not. These are the formulas in which God presents His authority and lays down a test of obedient love. Here is love on the largest scale of generosity. Here is obedience reduced to the smallest possible point. Liberty is as wide as possible, restraint is almost nothing. One little piece of selfcontrol.

7. *The helper* (verse 18). Man cannot do it alone; it is not his nature. Doing it alone cannot exist with his happiness. He will not need much to remove the gloom of solitude. One companion will do. God forms this one for him – a helper – taken not out of the dust, but out of himself. Not out of his head, as if superior; not out of his feet, as if inferior; but taken out of his side, where his heart lies. His equal in one aspect, yet he is the head. He is the first Adam who is the representation of the second Adam, out of whose wounded side, when He slept the sleep of death, His Eve – the church – was brought; the offspring of His heart, the object of His love – altogether *one*.

8. *The purity*. Naked, yet not ashamed. This is holiness, the perfection of innocence. No fear, no blush, and nothing to hide. They can look to one another without shame. They can look up to God without fear, for *sin* is not there. It is sin that gives an evil conscience. It is sin that spreads blushes on the face. Conscious guilt – how this makes one hang his head! Let us learn:

   1. *That evil is not of God.* God creates nothing sinful. Sin comes from the creature, not from the Creator. Sin comes from beneath, not from above.

2. *That God's works in connection with earth and man are those of love.* He made the world and its fullness so excellent, because He loved man. God is love.

3. *That God loves holiness.* He made man holy, because He is holy, and He loves what is holy. He loves to see holiness in the world that He has made. He will see it again when all things are made new.

Chapter 4

The Sin, the Sinner, and the Sentence

Genesis 3

The first two chapters gave us creation's perfection. Like a newly finished statue, there it stands. The chisel has given its last touch. The sculptor is satisfied, pronounces it very good, and rests. All is fair. Earth is like heaven.

But now the descent begins. The steps are no longer upward, but downward. Creaturehood cannot stand alone. The moment that it is left to itself it totters, it falls. It must be joined to the Creator before it can stand. The fall is the first step towards this everlasting union, in virtue of which creation is to become infallible.

1. *The tempter.* Outwardly the serpent, inwardly the devil, thus called *the serpent of old* (Revelation 12:9; 20:2); thus the apostle Paul says, *as the serpent deceived Eve* (2 Corinthians 11:3), and *so that no advantage would be taken of us by Satan* (2 Corinthians 2:11). This is the first demoniacal possession. Afterwards we read that the devils entered the herd, that Satan entered Judas, and that he filled the heart of Ananias. In speaking to man, he must use some fleshly form. Thus, by means of the serpent he communicates with man.

2. *The temptation.* The tempter makes use of the *testing tree,* and points to it as a mark of restraint and tyranny. His goal is to separate Adam

and Eve from God, and to produce the evil heart of unbelief that would make them depart from the living God. For this end he suggests doubts on three points: (1) *God's goodness* – in prohibiting the tree, (2) *His faithfulness* – in fulfilling His threats, and (3) *His truthfulness* – in deceiving them as to the real nature of the tree. Having gotten Eve to listen, he leads her on, and then flatly contradicts God: *"You surely will not die!"* (verse 4).

3. *The bait.* The tempter uses faulty logic: (1) *Negative* – *"You surely will not die!"* and (2) *Positive* – *"You will be like God, knowing good and evil"* (verse 5). The first was to remove the dread of danger, the second to lead her on. Knowledge! Knowledge like that of God! Intellectual ambition – this is man's first snare, and it will be his last. Worship of intellect and genius. Human supremacy in mind. Progress! Not in the knowledge of *God Himself* (Satan does not dare promise *that*), but of good and *evil*. Does not this imply that *evil* is, in itself, a strange attraction? To know *evil*, man will do and dare as much as to know good. Evil is in his eyes an empire of boundless range, to whose utmost limits he would willingly penetrate, thus his love of the "sensational." The opening of the eyes to see afar off, whether into space or time, or the substance of things, is an irresistible bait. What will man not do to obtain a wider range of vision?

4. *The success.* The tempter triumphs. Woman, "the weaker vessel," yields. She falls, and in falling, she drags her husband down. Three things win her over: (1) *The tree was good for food* (verse 6). Why then not eat of it as of all the rest? Yet for this she had only Satan's word. But the *lust of the flesh* (1 John 2:16) prevailed. (2) *It was a delight to the eyes* (verse 6). It looked good, and the *lust of the eyes* (1 John 2:16) prevailed. (3) *It makes wise.* It is the tree of knowledge. She wants to be wise, and she will not wait for God's time, nor take it in God's way, but in her own, or rather the devil's. *Wisdom* is the devil's bait; wisdom apart from the only wise God – apart from Him who is the wisdom of God. What harm is there in wisdom? he still says. So with this dishonesty he leads men into knowledge where God is not, into literature where God is not, and where Christ is unknown.

5. *The shame.* The first feeling that arises after the sin is the feeling of being unfit to be seen. Unfit to be seen by anyone, even by one another. Unfit for the sun to shine upon. A covering or darkness is their only refuge. Now they know what nakedness is. The "virus" of the forbidden tree has shot through them, and the sense of disobedience clouds their conscience. They know now for the first time the distinction between their attractive and unattractive parts – the clean and the unclean. They take the nearest and the broadest leaf and twist it over them. Here it is simply *coverings;* in later days it became *ornaments* as well.

6. *The dread.* How should we look on God, or how should God look on us? God comes down, and they flee, as far off as possible, into the cover of the trees. Their fig leaves were more for themselves than for God. They dare not face Him. They dread His anger. O folly! To hide from God! Yet man has always done so. Doing his deeds in darkness or when alone, which he would not do in the light or before the others, is the same feeling as here.

7. *The trial.* God summons them. They come forth and stand at His bar. He questions them and brings out their whole guilt step-by-step. They blame each other, they blame God, they blame the serpent. But they sullenly admit the deed. Poor excuses! What can assuage sin? What will God accept as mitigation? They are guilty on their own admission. This is the verdict.

8. *The sentence.* Each of the guilty parties receives judgment: (1) *The serpent.* As the instrument he is cursed, and as the representative of the Devil, he is cursed. One greater than the serpent is here. In this curse on the serpent, God reveals His love to the sinning race, and tells them that instead of cursing the victim, as no doubt Satan expected, He means to take His part against Satan – to raise up a deliverer, the Son of the woman, who, though not without wounds, will destroy man's Enemy. The man with the bruised heel is to be the bruiser of the serpent's head. (2) *The woman.* No curse, but still a chastisement, a memorial of her sin. As the first in sin, she is to be in subjection. Though through childbearing she is to be the source of blessing, this very thing will be done in sorrow to remind her of her sin. (3) *The man.* No curse on himself, but on the ground for his sake. Fruitfulness in evil is the doom of the soil. Sorrow and death, toil and sweat are the doom of man. Yet these after all are earthly. They do not separate him from the love of God.

9. *The man's faith.* He names his wife according to the promise: *mother of all the living* (verse 20), not of the dead; mother of him who is the living One, the resurrection and the life. Adam believed God and was justified. He accepted God's testimony to the coming Messiah as the living One, though born of her who had brought in death, and he became a partaker of life eternal.

10. *God's clothing for man.* Coats of skins – those skins of the slain sacrifices, provided by God Himself – were better and more durable than the fig leaves. They were types of heavenly garments and preindications of the source from which that clothing was to come – of the materials of which that clothing was to be composed, namely, the life and death of *the Lamb of God who takes away the sin of the world* (John 1:29). This was what the Lord meant when He said, *"Bring out the best robe and put it on him"* (Luke 15:22); and what Paul meant when he said, *Put on the Lord Jesus Christ* (Romans 13:14).

Yes. The Son of God has come to clothe us! He has provided the garments, and He puts them on. They are fair and goodly, washed white in His own blood, and glorious as the sun. He asks us to take them. Indeed, He pleads with us to allow Him to put them upon us. *"I advise you to buy from Me gold refined by fire so that you may become rich, and white garments so that you may clothe yourself, and that the shame of your nakedness will not be revealed"* (Revelation 3:18).

Chapter 5

Man's Fig Leaves

They sewed fig leaves together and made themselves loin coverings. – Genesis 3:7

They are alone, yet they are ashamed. They are in Paradise, yet they are ashamed. It is conscience that is making them blush. It not only makes cowards of them, but it also works shame and confusion of face. They are ashamed of themselves, their nakedness, and their recent doings. They cannot look one another in the face after their disobedience and recriminations against one another. They cannot look up to God now. Possibly too they shrink from being in view of the serpent who beguiled them. The feeling of happy innocence is gone.

They must be *covered*. This is their feeling, the dictate of conscience. The eye must not see them, neither the eye of God nor of man. The light must not shine on them, the eye of the sun must not look on them, and the fair flowers and trees of Paradise must not see their shame. They love darkness rather than light. Covering is what they seek – covering from every eye. Thus, shame and guilt are inseparable. "I must be covered" is the sinner's first feeling – "from the eye of God and man, even from my own. They cannot look on me, nor I on them!"

So far, they are right. But now they go wrong. Their mistake was twofold: (1) that they could cover themselves, and (2) that they could be covered with materials from vegetable nature. Let us look at these.

1. *Man thinks he can cover himself.* He does not know the greatness of the evil. He does not calculate on the penetration of the allseeing eye. He sets to work and makes himself a covering, and he says this will do. He has no idea of what sin is, what the sinner needs, or what God requires. Each sinner has his own way of covering himself. He weaves his own web, whatever may be the substance of which it is composed. He wishes to be his own coverer, the maker of his own clothing. He thinks he can do it himself. He has no idea that it is utterly beyond his power. He trusts the skill of his own hands to provide the clothing that will hide his shame from the eye of God and man. He thinks it an easy thing to deal with shame, fear, conviction, and conscience. He will not believe that these can only be dealt with by God. This is the last thing that he will admit. He will try a thousand plans before accepting this. He will make and try on many kinds or sets of clothing before committing himself to what God has made. The unbelieving man's whole religious life is a series of plans and efforts for stitching clothing for himself with which to appear before God and before men; indeed, with which he hopes to appear before the judgment seat. It is with this manmade, selfmade clothing, this earthmade, priestmade, or churchmade religion, that he robes himself. With this he soothes his conscience. With this he quiets his fear. With this he removes the feeling of guilty shame. He can do all that is needful himself, or at the most with a little help from God.

2. *Man thinks he can cover himself with leaves.* He supposes that what will hide his shame from his own eye will hide it from God's eye. That even such a frail covering as the foliage of the fig tree will do. He has no thought of anything beyond this. He thinks that the fig leaf will do. What more do I need? But he is mistaken. The fig leaf will not do, broad and green as it may be. But why will it not do?
    1. *Because it is man's device, not God's.* That which covers sin and renders the sinner fit to draw near must be of God, not of man. Only God has the right. Only God can prescribe to man how he is to draw near. What then is empty, unbiblical ritualism but a religion of fig leaves?
    2. *Because it is simply for the body, not the soul.* It does not relieve the conscience, satisfy the guilty spirit, or cover the whole man. It is

utterly insufficient. It could not remove one fear, quiet one pang of remorse, or make the man feel tranquil in the presence of God.

3. *Because it is composed of life, not death.* That which is to cover man's sin and deliver him from the sense of shame must be something that has had the life taken out of it. The green fig leaf will not do. It is no better than Cain's sacrifice – the fruit of the ground. The only thing that can relieve the sinner from guilt and shame is *atonement*. The only atonement is by blood. For *without shedding of blood there is no forgiveness* (Hebrews 9:22). Therefore, the only sufficient covering must be one connected with atonement: one that represents death, one that tells of the payment of the righteous penalty and the removal of the righteous condemnation. The fig leaf spoke of life, not of death; of the blessing, not of the curse. It had nothing in it that told of propitiation or substitution; nothing that spoke of God's anger turned away by means of the endurance of that anger by another.

The truths taught here are not a few. They are of profound importance.

1. *Man's own devices for covering sin are useless.* They may be easy or difficult, cheap or costly. They are still vain. They profit nothing. The covering is narrower than a man can wrap himself in. They are all fig leaves!

2. *Man's devices all turn upon something that he himself must do, not on what God has done.* Man misses the main point of importance. This was not wonderful in Adam, to whom nothing had been revealed. It is amazing in us now because God has announced that He has done everything through Christ.

3. *Man's devices assume that God is such a one as himself.* He can conceal himself from his fellow man. Therefore, he thinks he can cover himself so that God will not see him. He supposes that that which conceals him from a human eye will conceal him from a divine eye.

4. *Man's devices all trifle with sin.* Man does not fathom sin's depths of malignity in God's sight. He assumes that it will be easily forgiven and forgotten. He overlooks its evil, its hatefulness, its eternal desert of woe. What are fig leaves as a protection against the wrath of God or the flames of hell?

Chapter 6

Expulsion and Reentrance

So He drove the man out; and at the east of the garden of Eden He stationed the cherubim and the flaming sword which turned every direction to guard the way to the tree of life. – Genesis 3:24

We may safely conclude that this solemn act on the part of God is not separate from, or in contradiction of, the previous promises of grace, but is in fulfillment of it – embodying an illustration or exposition of it. As generally interpreted, it stands alone and speaks wholly of judgment, not of grace. But read correctly, it anticipates the apostle's statement: *For the wages of sin is death, but the free gift of God is eternal life in Christ Jesus our Lord* (Romans 6:23); or if there is nothing about it that is apparently stern or terrible, it amounts to nothing more than that in the epistle to the Hebrews: *The Holy Spirit is signifying this, that the way into the holy place has not yet been disclosed while the outer tabernacle is still standing* (Hebrews 9:8).

1. *The expulsion.* The holy dwelling that was so specially made for man can no longer be his abode. He has sinned it away. He is not to be cast out of earth or even out of Eden, but he must leave Paradise so that God may testify to the evil of sin. But the simple fact of his being left on earth – indeed, in Eden – is a proclamation of God's forgiving love.

1. *The Expeller.* It is God himself, He who made Paradise for man and set man in it! *He* expelled him. The expulsion and the introduction are the acts of the same Being.

2. *The expelled.* It is *man* – no, **the man**. The same man as mentioned before. The man so newly made, so greatly loved – made in God's image, to represent Him and to serve Him!

3. *The expelling.* The word is a strong one – driving out by force, as the nations of Canaan. In verse 23 we read that *the Lord God sent him out,* but man would not go. So He is compelled to force him out! It is forcible ejection from a forfeited abode.

Paradise was the place of God's dwelling with man, and now either God or man must leave. If God leaves, man is hopeless. If man leaves, his place is still kept open for him by God. Even in the expulsion God shows His grace, His long-suffering, His unwillingness to leave man or man's earth. He still desires to have a habitation here. *"This is My resting place,"* He says (Psalm 132:14).

2. *The guard.* This was a sword – or rather, **the** *sword,* the sword of fire, or the flame of the sword. It was the sword that turned around every which way, perhaps encircling Paradise with a flaming belt. It was the sword spoken of in Joshua 5:13; 1 Chronicles 21:16, 27; Psalm 45:3; Isaiah 34:5-6; Ezekiel 21:5; and Zechariah 13:7. It was placed not simply to bar entrance, but also to inflict death on everyone who would attempt to enter. It was *the veil,* but it was more. It told that the holiest was not opened and that until God withdrew the barrier it was death for the sinner to enter. What more efficient, more terrible fence could there be? Sword and fire in one! God's sword and fire – revolving, in life and power – making access an impossibility. Living fire or fiery life! It is the shekinah in the form of a sword, as elsewhere in the form of a pillar, according to the purpose to be served. O man, can you reenter Paradise without God's permission? Can you open the barred gate? Can you remove or quench the sword of fire? You cannot. There is one that shuts and no man opens, that kindles and no man quenches. Only He can open who closed the gate. Only He can quench the fire who kindled it. It is He who said, *"Awake, O sword, . . . against the man, My*

Associate" (Zechariah 13:7). That sword is quenched in the blood of Jehovah's person; the gate is open, the access unchallenged and free!

But the special objective of this fence was to protect the way to the Tree of Life, which was in the midst of the garden. The eating of this tree was to preserve man's immortality. As the common fruit of the garden was to uphold him against the wear and tear of each day, so the Tree of Life had in it special virtue. It is no more inconsistent with man's immortality to say this than to say that he needed other food to maintain his life. It was *in the midst* (Genesis 2:9), as the most conspicuous and most accessible place, marking its importance and preeminence among the trees of the garden. The preservation of man's immortality was now no longer a desirable thing. Besides, it was forfeited. He was taught that there was immortality in store for him, but not through that tree. It must be reached through death. It must be the immortality of resurrection. His being banned from the Tree of Life was the preliminary or preparatory step to his being taught this wonderful lesson that would evolve in time. Man will one day approach the Tree of Life (Revelation 2:7), but not now! Death lies between him and life. Death is the gate of life; resurrection is our hope.

3. *The new occupants.* The cherubim now are set where man was. These are doubtless *symbolic* things, such as those of gold in the tabernacle; or, if having the semblance of life, they are like those spoken of in Ezekiel and Revelation, which are still symbolic, not real beasts or living creatures. Their appearance (earthly animals), their position on the mercy seat, their being one with the mercy seat, their being sprinkled with blood, and the song they sing in Revelation all tell us that they are redemption symbols. Symbols proclaiming that man and man's earth with all its creatures is redeemed and glorified. Man is reintroduced into Paradise, higher than that from which he was driven out, the paradise of God. These cherubim in the earthly Paradise are said to *dwell* there. Not "set," but "made to tabernacle" there. They are placed there as in a dwelling to indicate man's future restoration to the abode he had lost. The sight of them is good news to Adam. He and his seed are to be restored after all. They are not always to be banished; not always to worship at the gate or stand upon the threshold. They are to reenter and partake of the better tree in the better paradise.

The way is now opened; the sword withdrawn; the invitation unrestricted and unconditional. A new and living way! Let us draw near! Outside is condemnation, inside is pardon; outside is death, inside is life and immortality. There is no barrier now, no veil, no hindrance, no distance, and no uncertainty. The blood is shed and sprinkled. Through death, life has come. The tomb becomes the gate of life. Why do we stand outside as if the sword of fire was still there, or as if the veil was not torn in two? Why hesitate, tremble, or doubt, when everything is plain, and when God Himself is calling us to enter in? *Let us therefore come boldly unto the throne of grace* (Hebrews 4:16 KJV). *Let us draw near with a true heart and in full assurance of faith* (Hebrews 10:22 KJV). Let us not linger on the threshold, but go in at once. The blood that has been shed on earth and accepted in heaven is that which emboldens us to approach with confidence, not reckoning it possible that we can be sent away empty.

Chapter 7

The Blood of Sprinkling and the Blood of Abel

He said, "What have you done? The voice of your brother's blood is crying to Me from the ground." – Genesis 4:10

And to Jesus, the mediator of a new covenant, and to the sprinkled blood, which speaks better than the blood of Abel. – Hebrews 12:24

This cry of Abel's blood reminds us of the *"How long?"* of the martyrs (Revelation 6:10), and of the injured widow's *Avenge me* (Luke 18:3 KJV). It was a cry from the ground where it had been hidden from every eye but God's eye. A cry to God. A cry that brought down a curse.

The *sprinkled blood* is, first of all, the blood that was sprinkled in the tabernacle, which, with all its imperfections, spoke better things than Abel's blood. But it is especially the blood of the Lamb of God as sprinkled on the conscience, in believing.

In one aspect the cry of Christ's blood is the same. For it is that blood that now rests on Israel. Through it the long curse has come upon the nation. But still this is not the direct and proper meaning or application of the blood. It speaks of better things than that of Abel.

1. *It speaks of love, not hatred.* It was to Cain's hatred, a brother's hatred, that Abel's blood bore witness. The *sprinkled blood* speaks of a brother's love – the love of Christ, the love of Him who loved us and washed us from our sins in His own blood. It is truly of love that the blood so loudly and explicitly speaks. Thus it speaks of better things than that of Abel, for it speaks both of a father's and a brother's love. "God is love" is its message. Of the love that passes knowledge it bears witness to us – love unto death, love stronger than death.

2. *It speaks of grace, not of wrath.* Because of Abel's blood, God was angry. It was divine wrath that spoke out in His words to Cain. But it is divine grace and mercy that speak in the blood of Christ. The *sprinkled blood* appeases God and draws out grace. It says, *Where sin increased, grace abounded all the more* (Romans 5:20). Grace abounding over divine wrath and human sin; riches of grace; exceeding riches of grace; *for the grace of God has appeared, bringing salvation to all men* (Titus 2:11). These are the voices that come from it to us.

3. *It speaks of forgiveness, not condemnation.* The blood said, *"Father, forgive them"* (Luke 23:34). It was not condemning blood. He who heard of it and believed God's testimony to its meaning and effect was thereby assured of forgiveness. The blood showed the true basis and the true way of pardon – pardon through the condemnation of another; pardon through the blood-shedding, for the blood-shedders themselves; righteous, true, holy, unchangeable, eternal pardon. No condemnation. No, it gave justification through the great transaction on the cross.

4. *It speaks of comfort, not of terror.* Abel's blood was dreadful to everyone who saw it – full of terror to the murderer, alarm to his conscience, remorse to his spirit. Not so with this better blood. Its voice is comfort. It soothes the sinner's terrors. It does not lessen the seriousness of his sin; yet it speaks to him to let him know that the blood-shedding that brings him in guilty, and deserving of a murderer's death, assures him at the same time of the removal of all his fears. It is indeed nobler, richer blood, the blood of God, and so brings on the shedder more awful guilt. Yet by its appeasing nature, its

atoning power, it announces, with divine certainty, the deliverance from the infinite danger under which they who had shed it had brought themselves.

5. *It speaks of peace come, not of peace gone.* The blood of Abel said, "Peace is gone. Peace has forsaken the earth. It has left man and the families of man." Everything is now hatred, strife, murder, and separation between man and God, between man and man, and between brother and brother. The blood of Jesus tells us that peace has returned. He is our peace. His blood has brought it back to earth. He has made peace by the blood of His cross. It has come! It has come down from heaven. Heaven and earth are meeting. God and the sinner are being reconciled. There is still hope for man. We do not need to despair, as if peace had fled away forever.

6. *It speaks of the blessing, not of the curse.* Abel's blood spoke wholly of the curse. It brought the curse on Cain and on the earth. It doubled the curse that Adam's sin had brought to the world. Christ's blood blesses and does not curse. Its voice is the voice of blessing. It means blessing in every drop. It meant blessing when it was first shed, and it still means blessing. There is no curse in it, except to those who reject it. In it is the fullness of eternal blessing, blessing such as the sinner needs – the removal of the entire curse for soul and body.

7. *It speaks of nearness, not of distance, between man and God.* Reconciliation, friendship, communion, nearness – all these are contained in it. *You who formerly were far off have been brought near by the blood of Christ* (Ephesians 2:13). No separation, darkness, or uncertainty of relationship, but recemented union on the basis of a purged conscience and an everlasting righteousness. Every hairbreadth of the distance that sin had produced is forever swept away. Perpetual nearness! Eternal fellowship! This is our portion, secured to us by the righteous removal of all that intervened between us and God – either on God's side or ours.

8. *It speaks of the purged, not of the pricked and despairing conscience.* Abel's blood spoke to Cain's conscience. It must have been a perpetual pricking and wounding. Christ's blood speaks of purging, healing, and

soothing. No more conscience of sins! A conscience purged from dead works to serve the living God! Every wound in it healed; every trouble laid to rest; every shadow resting over it dispelled. Not despair, but hope.

9. *It speaks of life, not of death.* Abel's blood seemed to seal the death of the race. Brother murders brother – what is to be the end of this? But Christ's blood speaks of life, the reversal of the sentence by the payment of the penalty. There was no life through the word and death of Abel. There is life through the blood and death of the Son of God. Life from the dead is the voice of the blood; life to the slayers of the Prince of Life. The voice from the cross was one of life: *"I give eternal life to them"* (John 10:28). The voice from the tomb was the same: *[God] made us alive together with Christ* (Ephesians 2:5).

10. *It speaks of restoration, not of expulsion.* It was Abel's blood that made Cain a fugitive and vagabond. Christ's blood brings us back from our wanderings, restores us to Paradise, delivers us from exile, and gives us possession of the paradise of God, the heavenly city, and the new heavens and earth wherein dwells righteousness. It is the blood of the Son of God that makes us friends, children, heirs of God, and joint heirs with Christ.

Let us receive God's testimony to this blood, this better blood, this blood of the everlasting covenant. The reception of this divine testimony is life, peace, and holiness.

Be warned against the rejection of this testimony and trampling on this blood. It is blood which, when sprinkled on the soul, saves, but which, when not sprinkled, condemns. It will sink the rejector to the lowest hell.

Chapter 8

The Way of Cain

Then Cain went out from the presence of the Lord.
– Genesis 4:16

Not as Cain, who was of the evil one and slew his brother. And for what reason did he slay him? Because his deeds were evil, and his brother's were righteous. – 1 John 3:12

Woe to them! For they have gone the way of Cain, and for pay they have rushed headlong into the error of Balaam, and perished in the rebellion of Korah. – Jude 1:11

As *the way of Cain* is spoken of by the apostle Jude, especially the way of the last days, let us inquire what it was. It was evil, not good. He is an open and defiant sinner, and in him sin takes its full swing. He is the first child of the fall, and the offspring of the fallen. He is not a common transgressor. He runs no ordinary career of wickedness. He rushes to the extremity of evil. He is given as a beacon, yet as a true specimen of man, of the human heart even in the most favorable circumstances. He came into the world not like Adam, fullgrown, but as a child, and therefore with the least possible amount of evil in him. He is the child of believing parents; for Adam showed his faith by calling his wife, and Eve showed hers by the way in which she received her firstborn. He had a most godly brother and was one of a devout household; brought up within sight of Paradise, and from childhood taught the knowledge of the true God, and the woman's seed. He was not exposed to outward temptation. He had no companion in sin. He walked the broad way alone. He was warned, no doubt, about the serpent and his seed. God spoke directly to him more than once. He had every possible advantage, in the absence of evil and the presence of good. Much might have been expected from him, yet he turns his back on God, Paradise, the altar, the sacrifice, and on all that is good and blessed.

But let us see more specially what the apostle calls *the way of Cain*.

1. *It is the way of unbelief.* Cain is the first specimen of an *unbelieving man*. His parents were sinners, but they believed. His brother was a sinner, but he believed. Cain is not an atheist, nor an altogether irreligious man. He acknowledges God and brings his fruits to the altar. But he brings no lamb, no blood, nothing that speaks of death. He comes with no confession, no cry for mercy. He sees no need of the woman's seed, no danger from the serpent, no preciousness, and perhaps no truth in the promise of the serpent's crushed head or Messiah's bruised heel. He takes Satan's side against God, not God's side against Satan; for all unbelief is a siding with Satan against God. God is not to him the God of grace, nor the woman's seed the Savior of the lost. He has a religion, but it is selfmade, a human religion, something of his own – without Christ, blood, or pardon. The love of God to him is mere indifference to sin. Rejection of God's religion, and of His Messiah – this is *the way of Cain*.

2. *It is the way of apostasy.* He turns his back on God and will have none of Him. He is not like one of our dark heathens, ignorant of the true God. He knows Jehovah and has heard His voice, but he turns away. He is an apostate (the first apostate) from the religion of his father, a scorner of the Messiah. He wants a Messiah of his own – "a Christ that is to be." Not God's Christ, but man's. From what small beginnings apostasy springs.

3. *It is the way of worldliness.* Having forsaken his father's God, he makes a god to himself. That god is the world. He goes far from Paradise, builds a city, becomes a thoroughly worldly person. He becomes the father of

the inventors of all curious instruments, and he leads the everswelling crowd in its race of worldliness and vanity with the cry, "Onward, onward; progress, progress." They eat and drink, marry and are given in marriage. Everything about Cain is of this present evil world. In our age what a spirit of worldliness is abroad; often not open wickedness, but simply worldliness, so absorbing the soul as to draw it down from the region of *the world to come* (Hebrews 2:5).

4. *It is the way of hatred.* He begins with envy of his brother, goes on to hatred, and ends in murder. He is especially jealous of his brother's having found favor with God. Yes, it is strange, that though he would have none of God for himself, he cannot bear that his brother should have it. It is not the love of man or woman, but of God that is the cause of the first jealousy and the first murder. He hates God even more for loving his brother. He even hates Abel for being loved of God. He cannot lay hands on God, as he would gladly do, but he lays hands on His favorite and takes his revenge. Yes, the way of Cain is the way of envy, jealousy, hatred, and murder!

5. *It is the way of Goddefiance.* He pretends. He wipes his bloody weapon and his bloody hands, saying, "What have I done?" He lies, he pretends, and he hides his doings from God. He has lured his brother into a lonely field and slain him, thinking that no one would rescue him and no one would see. He acts as the liar and the hypocrite in the very presence of God. The way of Cain is the way of hypocrisy, falsehood, and defiance of God. God asks him about his brother. His answer is not only a lie, but also a brazen-faced piece of irreverence: *"Am I my brother's keeper?"* (Genesis 4:9). Thus, he mocks God and utters the language of irreverence and defiance: "He is Your favorite; why don't You keep him? I never pretended to keep him." Here mingled fear, shame, audacity, and defiance are manifested. He would gladly deny the deed but he does not dare to. He trembles and would gladly conceal it. He puts on a defiant air and attitude, as if to brave it out before the allseeing One!

Such is the way of Cain! Note his doom:

1. *Despair.* No cry for mercy, but merely, *"My punishment is too great to bear!"* (Genesis 4:13). So it is in other ages. The sinner's despair

of mercy, or complaint against God for making his punishment so heavy, is the repetition of Cain's offense and his doom. Why should a sinner despair on this side of hell? There is forgiveness to the uttermost; grace reaching far beyond the extremity of human guilt.

2. *Banishment from God.* He goes out from the presence of God, as if he could no longer bear that. He must get away from Paradise, the birthplace of the race, the old seat of worship. But what is this to the eternal banishment? Cain has no rest, moving to and fro without hope or aim, a fugitive and a vagabond, seeking rest and finding none. Sad curse! Yet this is nothing to eternal wandering!

3. *Disappointment.* He himself was his mother's disappointment, for she thought she had gotten the manchild. So is he a disappointment to himself. From first to last, we see in him a disappointed man, trying everything, succeeding in nothing. Building cities, roaming from place to place to soothe his conscience and fill up his heart's void. But in vain!

4. *Fruitless worldliness.* He is the heir of a barren world, for the whole world is his. He is possessor of a soil made unfruitful by a brother's blood; tilling and sowing, yet not reaping. A weary man, toiling for that which is not bread; trying to wring water out of the world's dry sands and broken cisterns. Such is the career of thousands. Fruitless worldliness. A life of vanity; a soul utterly void; a being wholly wasted.

Chapter 9

The Man of Rest

Lamech lived one hundred and eightytwo years, and became the father of a son. Now he called his name Noah, saying, "This one will give us rest from our work and from the toil of our hands arising from the ground which the Lord has cursed." – Genesis 5:28-29

This is the utterance of *faith*. It is the voice of a believing man that we hear in Lamech's words. Lamech speaks because God had spoken to him. It is not mere parental yearning. It is not mere selfish weariness crying out under toil. It is not the expression of a dark and vague hope. It is faith speaking out the revelation that God had made to it regarding creation's deliverance, and it is the first indication we have as to the removal of the curse as to the rest and consolation.

It is a *double* prophecy. By this I do not mean a doubtful or a conditional prophecy. There is no such thing as a conditional prophecy. If it be prophecy, it is not conditional. If it be conditional, it is not prophecy. A *double* prophecy is one that takes in two events, persons, or places in one description – the near and the far – predicting *both,* while seeming to predict only *one.* Like David, in Psalm 72, points both to Solomon and to a greater than Solomon; and as Isaiah points to the Babylon of his day and Babylon the great. The prophet sketches a scene or person immediately before his eye, but in language that indicates that a far-greater is coming. The near or miniature sketch is drawn so as to bring out the full features of the larger and more distant.

So is it here with Lamech. God reveals to him the future of two persons and two things: (1) his own son, and a far-greater, of whom his son was but the shadow; and (2) the alleviation or removal of earth's curse, partially under Noah, fully under the greater-than Noah. There are two remarkable prophecies before the flood. The *first* is that of Enoch concerning Messiah's coming with His saints to destroy the wicked. This was a double prophecy, relating both to the flood and to the judgment at the Lord's coming. The *second* is that of Lamech concerning the *rest* of the saints (2 Thessalonians 1:7 KJV) and the removal of the curse. Let us look into this second prophecy.

1. *The curse on the ground.* When man sinned, the first stroke of the curse fell. It had now lasted about fifteen centuries, unabated. It was something real. Its results were both barrenness in what was good and fruitfulness in evil. The whole creation groaned. The blight and sadness were felt everywhere. It was a record of human sin, God's visible testimony to the greatness of the first sin – the *one* sin of primary disobedience. *"Cursed is the ground because of you"* (Genesis 3:17). It is not yet removed. Creation is still subject to vanity. Corruption, mortality, decay, and death are here. It has been a long curse, yet it is the memorial of a *single* sin.

2. *Man's toil and weariness.* The whole verse breathes weariness and heaviness of spirit – almost despair. The world was growing more wicked and more luxurious. It was increasing in population. Men were not allowed to eat flesh, nor to kill animals except for sacrifice. These animals, increasing rapidly, would require immense pasturage. Man's toil would increase greatly. It would become quite oppressive and overwhelming. He did not know what to do, nor which way to turn. Toil, toil, toil! This was his daily lot. In the sweat of his face, he was made to eat his bread. The curse on the ground did not grow lighter, and his labor grew heavier. What with barrenness in good and fruitfulness in evil, it demanded endless labor of him and weariness. He groaned under it along with a groaning creation. He was compelled to sympathize with the groaning and laboring creature. Such should be our feeling. Our toil may not be quite so oppressive. We

do not depend as much on our toil. The tools of art and the permission to eat animal food have alleviated our labors. But still creation groans, and man eats his bread by the sweat of his face.

3. *Man's longing for comfort.* The words of the verse are those of the worker looking for the shadow, and longing for rest. These patriarchs were aged men – some nearly a thousand years old. One thousand years of toil! What a life! If threescore and ten is so wearisome to some, what would one thousand be? Lamech, when he uttered these words, was one hundred and eightytwo. Surely, he had known toil and weariness beyond what we can do! Do we wonder that he longed for comfort, that he sighed for rest, and that he breathed out these deep longings for deliverance? Are we not longing too? Is toil so sweet that we wish for its continuance? Or is rest so terrible that we do not desire it and say, "How long?"

4. *Man's expectation of deliverance.* He knew that the condition of earth was not hopeless. He would gather from the first promise that God meant, at some time or other, to undo the curse. And while he sympathized with the groaning and toiling of creation, he joined in its *earnest expectation* (Romans 8:19 KJV). He sustained himself under his toil by the expectation of rest. He was not satisfied to remain forever toiling and sweating. It was part of his creed to look for rest, to grasp the coming consolation. Man labored and was heavy-laden, but he heard the voice of the true Noah saying, *"Come to Me, all who are weary and heavy-laden, and I will give you rest"* (Matthew 11:28).

5. *Man's expectation was connected with one individual to be born in due time.* Lamech had been taught by God to expect something in connection with his son, whom he named Noah, in consequence of this expectation. And in his time relief was granted – the alleviation, though not the removal, of the curse and the toil: (1) Noah received a confirmation of the first blessing given to Adam before he fell. (2) In his time man's life began to be shortened. (3) Permission was granted to kill animals and eat their flesh. (4) Special attention was directed to husbandry, when *Noah began farming* (Genesis 9:20). These partial

alleviations given in connection with Noah were figures of the complete deliverance of creation in connection with a greater-than Noah; in the day of the Son of Man, the day of the manifestation of the sons of God, of those of whom Enoch prophesied, *"The Lord came with many thousands of His holy ones"* (Jude v. 14).

Thus we anticipate the deliverance of creation, the removal of the curse in the day of the Son of Man, when He will say, *"Behold, I am making all things new"* (Revelation 21:5). The greater-than Noah is at hand, and with Him the manifestation of the sons of God, and with that, the rest that remains for the people of God: the times of the restitution of all things, when barrenness will be exchanged for fruitfulness, and the wilderness will rejoice and blossom as the rose. For *according to His promise we are looking for new heavens and a new earth, in which righteousness dwells* (2 Peter 3:13). Seeing, then, that we look for such things, what kinds of people we should be in all holy conversation and godliness!

Chapter 10

Going Out and Keeping Out

Now the Lord said to Abram, "Go forth from your country, and from your relatives and from your father's house, to the land which I will show you; and I will make you a great nation, and I will bless you, and make your name great; and so you shall be a blessing; and I will bless those who bless you, and the one who curses you I will curse. And in you all the families of the earth will be blessed." So Abram went forth as the Lord had spoken to him; and Lot went with him. Now Abram was seventyfive years old when he departed from Haran. - Genesis 12:14

Thus begins the story of Israel's calling as a nation. Like the great rivers of earth, it has a small beginning – one individual; a Chaldean of Ur; an idolater of Mesopotamia; with no recommendation or worthiness; a genuine specimen of God's electing grace, and of divine sovereignty, as well as of the power of the Holy Spirit.

So far as it appears, God had not personally intervened from Noah's time up to this time. The only kind of intervention was that at Babel. Now He comes forth out of His silence and darkness. He speaks. Indeed, He appears. He appears as *the God of glory* (Acts 7:2), or "God of the glory." The shekinah reappears, and out of it God speaks to Abram. The frequent use of the words *the Lord* **appeared** *to Abram*

(Genesis 12:7; 17:1, emphasis added), in connection with Stephen's reference to the glory in Acts 7:2, alludes to this mode of revelation.

1. *The command.* It is sovereign and authoritative. It is explicit and uncompromising. It does not wait on our will or choice. It leaves no room for hesitation on our part. *"Go forth"* are Jehovah's words to Abram. They refer to *one single* transaction, about which there can be no mistake. And lest there should be any mistake, the three things to be left are specified: *country, relatives,* and *father's house.* The getting out is to be complete and decided. It is also to be *immediate* – no waiting, lingering, nor preparing. Get out at once. This command is even more authoritative from its not specifying the place to go to. He was not to concern himself with that. The *terminus a quo* (starting point) was quite explicit; not so the *terminus ad quem* (destination). The latter was of little significance in the meantime. It would eventually come to light. It was on the simple command of Jehovah that he was to act; putting himself blindfolded into the hands of God. All that Abram was to know of his route or destination was this: *"The land which I will show you."* Thus, he was completely shut in and shut up to obedience.

2. *The promise.* It is as directly from God as the command is, so that he can no more doubt the one than the other. It relates wholly to the future – much of it to the future of far ages. Yet it is a very explicit and blessed promise, for the fulfillment of which he had the divine truthfulness and unchangeableness. *God, who cannot lie* (Titus 1:2), who does not repent – this is the God both of the command and the promise. He gives both. Let us accept both, not separating the one from the other. In this promise God comes forth strikingly as the doer of the whole: *"I will show," "I will make,"* and *"I will bless."*

Everything is of the Lord and of no one else: (1) a land – though unknown, (2) numbers, (3) blessing, (4) honor, (5) fountain of blessing, (6) the occasion of blessing or cursing, and (7) the blessedness of the whole earth in Him. These are large promises! Glorious blessings! They include everything that Abram needed for eternity as well as at that time. This gives a vision of Messiah and His glory, as well as of all earth under Him, for Abram is to be *heir of the world* (Romans 4:13).

3. *The obedience. Abram went forth as the Lord had spoken to him* (verse 4). *Abraham, when he was called, obeyed,* says the apostle (Hebrews 11:8). God called, he complied. He did not argue, linger, hesitate, or look back. He set out at once. He did not know where he was going, not a step of the way or anything of the land. He had no earthly counselor or guide. Only the God of glory – Jehovah in His shekinah – went before him, as in the pillar of cloud. Everything connected with this obedience was supernatural and divine. Jehovah broke his earthly ties; enabled him to triumph over earthly affections; made his face like a flint against all opposition; and took him by the hand and led him out. Here we have obedience in its simplest, purest form – believing, trusting obedience. *God has spoken.* That is his answer to all suggestions from without or within. *God has spoken.* That cheers and gladdens him. He could not mistake the voice – either its meaning or where it came from. That was enough for him. We do not need to ask if this was the time of his conversion. It probably was. It was the day of God's power to him. It was what Christ's words were to the sons of Zebedee or to Zaccheus. God spoke and the Holy Spirit carried the message to the inner man. He was turned from dumb idols to serve the living God. He became *heir of the righteousness which is according to faith* (Hebrews 11:7). He became Messiah's ancestor, yet a trophy of Messiah's power.

There are some striking texts in subsequent Scriptures that derive much light and purpose from this scene. They are the following:

1. Psalm 45:10. *Listen, O daughter, give attention and incline your ear: Forget your people and your father's house.* God thus speaks to His chosen ones – the bride of Christ. Thus He speaks aloud to an unheeding world. *"Listen, that you may live"* (Isaiah 55:3). Oh, listen now – turn your back on the world; turn your face to Jesus!

2. Matthew 16:24. *"If anyone wishes to come after Me, he must deny himself, and take up his cross and follow Me."* Christ's command is as explicit as that to Abram. *"Come after Me."* Come at once! Come now! Deny self and come! Deny yourself and take up your cross! Whatever hinders, come!

3. 2 Corinthians 6:17a. *"Come out from their midst and be separate."* Here the words are remarkably like those addressed to Abram.

The command is, therefore, *"Come out . . . be separate, . . . do not touch."* The promise is like it: *"I will welcome you. And I will be a father to you, and you shall be sons and daughters to Me"* (2 Corinthians 6:17b-18). God speaks to us and says, *"Come out."*

4. Revelation 18:4. *"Come out of her, my people."* In one aspect this is the most like Abram's call, for it is a call out of Babylon. It suits these last days well. Come out of Babylon! Come out of every false church, every city of idols, and every refuge of lies! Come out! Do not say, "I will stay, but will worship the true God inside." No! Come out! This is God's command!

Chapter 11

The Shield and the Recompense

After these things the word of the Lord came to Abram in a vision, saying, "Do not fear, Abram, I am a shield to you; your reward shall be very great." – Genesis 15:1

The full meaning of this *word of the Lord,* which *came to Abram in a vision,* can only be understood by reference to the events narrated in the preceding chapter. Never had such an unequal battle been waged as between Abram and these mighty kings. With his 318 servants he had pursued, conquered, and spoiled thousands, perhaps tens of thousands. Truly he put his life into God's hand, and with marvelous courage encountered the peril. On the back of this, God comes to him with, *"I am a shield to you."* He had, moreover, given up the spoil to others, reserving nothing for himself. Then God comes in with His words: *"Your reward shall be very great."* He had done both of these in simple *faith,* having no previous command, promise, or assurance of success. God, having thus tested his faith, comes to him with a blessed word of assurance, speaking to him in a vision, and calling him by name. Let us observe:

1. *The word of cheer.* *"Do not fear, Abram."* It is God who speaks. He calls Abram by name, as one on familiar terms with Him. No doubt Abram recognized the comforting voice and cheering words. How frequent

throughout Scripture are the divine *fear not*'s. How ready God is to utter them, even as a father to his trembling child. To Isaac He said, "**Do not fear,** *for I am with you*" (Genesis 26:24, emphasis added). To Jacob He said, "*I am God, the God of your father;* **do not be afraid** *to go down to Egypt*" (Genesis 46:3, emphasis added). Frequently to Israel He said the same words: "**Do not be afraid** *or tremble at them, for the Lord your God is the one who goes with you*" (Deuteronomy 31:6, emphasis added); "**Do not fear,** *for I am with you*" (Isaiah 41:10, emphasis added). And in many cases, as here, He names the name of him whom He is cheering: "*Do not be afraid,* **Zacharias**" (Luke 1:13, emphasis added); "*Do not be afraid,* **Mary**" (Luke 1:30, emphasis added); "*Do not be afraid,* **Paul**" (Acts 27:24, emphasis added). God takes for granted that His servants may have cause for fear, that at times their hearts may fail them due to external fightings and internal fears: sorrows, storms, dangers, burdens, troubles, and enemies. To meet and counteract the influence of these upon the soul, He says, *"Do not fear."* Yes, it is God, our God, who speaks this way. He knows our frame and remembers that we are dust (Psalm 103:14). He knows the world in which we live and remembers that everything is adverse and hostile. He knows that Satan rages, and that his legions are all abroad. He knows that the spirit may be willing, yet the flesh is weak (Matthew 26:41; Mark 14:38). And so He says to us, "Do not fear, be of good cheer." Thus Jesus spoke on earth, and thus He still speaks from heaven.

2. *The word of security.* "*I am a shield to you.*" This is truly a divine form of expression, full of force and point. God does not say, "I shield you," but, "*I am a shield to you.*" This latter is far stronger than the former; just as the expression, *He Himself is our peace* (Ephesians 2:14) is far stronger than "He gives us peace," or "He is our righteousness" is stronger than "He justifies us," or "He is our treasure" and is stronger than "He makes us rich." Here God proclaims *Himself* to be Abraham's shield. So is He the shield of everyone who is Abraham's seed.

The past, the present, and the future are all included in this.

1. *I* **was,** *or have been, your shield.* He had been so in Abraham's case, memorably and marvelously so in the recent conflict with these

invaders from the East. Had God not been both sword and shield to him, how could he have ventured into, or come safely out of, such a conflict with such superior forces? He has been that to us, as every day of our past lives has testified, a perpetual and impenetrable shield.

2. *I am your shield.* It is not the past alone that is witness to this protection. It is still continued. Each day we *need* the shield, each day we *have* it. Each day brings up a new battlefield and a new enemy, a new danger and a new assault. But God is our perpetual shield. All around us, above and beneath us, our complete suit of armor, our high tower. This is our daily security.

3. *I will be your shield.* Abraham dwelt among enemies, with dangers on every side. He was a stranger in a strange land, without a friend except God. He gets the assurance of perpetual protection. No evil will attack, no weapon will prosper, no enemy will overcome or wound him. God says to His church, "I will be your shield." Her dwelling is among enemies; she is a lily among thorns, a sheep among wolves. The world is against her, hell is against her. If God were to permit it, she would be swept from earth in an hour. She has no might, no skill against such an array of deadly foes. Her sufficiency, her security, is only in God. He is her shield. Not only does He *defend* her, but He is also her shield. Yes, each of us may say, "God is my shield, I am safe; I can defy the world, I can shake my hand at hell. I will be more than a conqueror through Him that loved me. Safe now, safe in days to come, safe in conflict, safe in evil days, safe in sorrow or in joy, safe on a sickbed or a deathbed, safe forevermore. God the Lord is my sun and shield. Who will make me afraid?" This is more than even the *shield of faith* and the *breastplate of righteousness* (Ephesians 6:16, 14). It is a divine shield and breastplate, behind which I am absolutely and entirely secure. Jehovah Himself stands between me and danger. His omnipotence surrounds me. Am I not safe forever?

3. *The word of recompense.* Abraham had given up everything and left Chaldea. He had refused to lay his hand on the spoil of the invaders whom he had defeated. He had parted with everything of earth. Now

God comes in and promises to make up for all by giving *Himself*. He does not say, "I will recompense you," but, "I *am* your recompense." How powerful are the words? I am: (1) your reward, (2) your great reward, and (3) your exceedingly great reward. How full and rich are these words of promise! Here is *present* reward, and there is *eternal* reward. God does for us *exceeding abundantly above all that we ask or think* (Ephesians 3:20 KJV). Not pardon; we have that already. It is far beyond that. Not salvation; it is far beyond that. Not heaven nor glory; it is far beyond these. It is God Himself, He whom the heaven of heavens cannot contain! *He* is our reward – He – *Himself*!

In all this we find:

1. *Strength for work and duty.* What encouragement, comfort, and invigoration is here! How can we tire in well-doing or shrink from peril? Jehovah is our shield and recompense.

2. *Motive for selfdenial and selfsacrifice.* We are called to these. But God gives more than a command or call; He presents us with a motive – protection and everlasting recompense. Should we grudge the surrender, seeing the reward is so great?

3. *A reason for calmness and steadfastness.* God is with us. We are on His side. He is on ours. It is *His* work that we are doing. It is *His* battle that we are fighting, not our own. Let us not be ruffled nor moved. Let no opposition, provocation, vexation, defeat, nor triumph of evil annoy us. Our shield is the Omnipotent. Our reward is the fullness of God Himself.

Chapter 12

Liberty and Service

"Let My people go, that they may serve Me." – Exodus 8:1

Thus God spoke of Israel in Egypt, commanding deliverance for them. It was a word of *power*, like *"Let there be light"* (Genesis 1:3). Reluctant Pharaoh was compelled to let go of his grasp. The command was irresistible.

God adds His reason for the command and its authoritativeness: *"That they may serve Me."* He did not need to give a reason, yet He does so. He justifies His claim upon them and against Pharaoh. God's authority over men is an infinitely reasonable one. He makes no claim regarding which even our own consciences do not justify Him. He has a claim on us, and no one else can compete with this. He says to us, "You must serve *Me*." He says to them who held them in bondage, "*They* must serve *Me*." The length, strength, and apparent justice of other service cannot be considered when God puts in His claims.

It is in this way that Christ speaks with respect to His church, His elect; the Holy One of Israel in respect to His Israel. He speaks to His enemies and theirs; to those who hold them in bondage, the Pharaohs of the world, to Satan: *"Let My people go, that they may serve Me."* It is out of earthly bondage into heavenly liberty that He calls us, from the bondage of Satan to the liberty of Christ. It is both to a divine service and a divine liberty that we are called. These are the two things, and they are inseparable. Not liberty for its own sake, but liberty for the sake of service; not service without liberty, but service as the result of liberty. Liberty and service conjoined. Not the one without the other, but hand in hand. Freedom is a noble thing, yet its value consists in the position in which it places us for service.

But what I especially notice here is the order of the two things – first liberty, and then service, implying that service is impossible without liberty. There may be Egyptian service – such service as will satisfy the gods of Egypt, without liberty, but not such as will please the God of Israel. There may be selfrighteous service, mechanical service, pharisaical service, the service of the outer man, without liberty, but not the glad service of the soul.

1. *We are in bondage.* Our natural condition is one of bondage. We are born in Egypt, not in Canaan; born in a prison; born with the fetters on our limbs; born slaves. Our wills are in bondage; our faculties are in bondage; our affections are in bondage; our whole souls are in bondage.

There is no free motion or free action of any part of us. Everything is constraint. We act under the sense of terror, for a reward, or to obtain pardon. We do nothing freely or purely. Work done in chains is no work at all. Work done in order to purchase liberty is not acceptable work.

2. *We were made for liberty.* Israel was not made for Egypt, nor Egypt for Israel. So we were not created for bondage and the prison house. God made man both upright and free. His whole being – faculties and affections and will – were made free, truly free, with no constraint upon them except the glad constraint of love. God did not create us as bondslaves. Liberty is the proper, the normal condition of the creature.

3. *We cannot serve God without liberty.* We may do some things without liberty. The body can labor in a prison with fetters, but the soul must be *free* in order to serve – free in all its parts so that nothing is done by constraint, but willingly. Other services may be performed in any way – for wages or under threat – but God's service must be performed *freely* in every way. We must be free in order that we may serve. It is not service in order to have liberty, but liberty in order to serve. This is

God's order. Whoever disregards it or inverts it is a servant of whom the Master cannot approve – whose service He rejects. Indeed, his is no servant at all. Until we are free, we cannot serve. He that is not free cannot perform any duty correctly, no true work for God.

4. *Christ calls us to liberty.* He came to open our prison doors, to bring us out of the house of Egypt. He came to break our chains, and to make us wholly free. He has stated the matter this way: (1) The Son will make us free, implying that the liberty comes directly from Himself. (2) The truth will make us free, teaching us that it is through the truth that He gives us the liberty. *He* liberates. *His truth* liberates. *His Spirit* liberates. With our chains broken by His touch, our souls receiving His truth, and ourselves filled with the spirit of liberty, we go forth as freed men to serve God. In the bondage of unpardoned sin, in the anxiety of uncertainty as to our relationship, we cannot serve God. It is not true service, happy service, loving service, or acceptable service. We must be let go so that we may serve.

Have you been set free? Are you walking in liberty? Has the gospel brought its peace in to you? Is the Spirit of adoption teaching you to say, *"Abba! Father!"* (Romans 8:15)? You say you are endeavoring to serve God, but in what spirit? In love or in dread? In gladness or in terror? In light or in gloom?

Chapter 13

The Day of Despair

"Make supplication for me." – Exodus 8:28

Pharaoh is brought down from his haughtiness. He had earlier scoffed at both Moses and his God. Now he is humbled – indeed, only for a season – yet he is humbled. He confesses Jehovah; he becomes a petitioner to Moses and to his God. Is this the Pharaoh that said, *"Who is the Lord"* (Exodus 5:2)? How he has come down from his pride!

What brings him down? It might be: (1) true repentance, (2) cunning, or (3) terror. It is only the last of these that is here at work, and his impressions pass away with the terror. He does not care anymore about God than he did before, but he would gladly be delivered from these judgments. Now let us look beyond Pharaoh.

1. The sinner's day of prosperity. There is such a thing as prosperity even in this fallen world. Prosperity for the wicked – *Behold, these are the wicked; and always at ease, they have increased in wealth* (Psalm 73:12). They are not in trouble as other men. They revel in pleasure, they roll in wealth, they are decked with honor. Everything goes well with them. They say, "Tomorrow will be like today, and more abundant." The sinner sits at ease and puts away the thought of trouble. He basks in sunshine and laughs at storms. He sails onward with favoring breezes and believes that there will be no shipwreck, no adversity for him!

2. *The sinner's day of trouble.* No prosperity lasts forever, nor is it even lifelong or half a lifetime. Then the clouds gather, the tempest breaks, the waves wash over the vessel, and it becomes a wreck. Sometimes it is one long day of trouble, after as long a day of peace. Sometimes it is the succession, at brief intervals, of joy and sorrow, light and darkness, health and sickness, prosperity and adversity. *Each man has his day or days of trouble.* Let this be thoroughly pondered and taken to heart. Care will come; distress will come; sickness will come; death will come; weariness will come. The sky will darken; the smile will vanish; the night will fall. These are *certainties,* O sinner, and perhaps very near. You cannot ward them off. Wise precautions cannot ward them off, nor powerful friends, nor prudent friends, nor healthy regulations; no, these will not help. God's Word, God's purpose, will break through all these and lay you low. You will find out what it is to be in the hands of the living God. He will deal with you. He is dealing with you now by His goodness. Tomorrow He may be dealing with you in severity and sore displeasure.

3. *The sinner's helplessness.* He does not know what to do. He once thought he was strong, but now he feels he is weak, unable to contend against his ills. The current is too strong. He cannot swim against it. His foes are numerous; his difficulties great; his friends fail; his conscience awakes; his heart trembles. What can he do? He is utterly helpless, and in his helplessness, he turns coward.

4. *His remembrance of God.* Up to now God had not been in all his thoughts. Now he says that only God can help him. Man cannot help him; devils cannot; angels will not. Perhaps God will. He remembers his longdespised God. So, in danger, the sinner cries. In shipwreck and in the plague, he cries.

5. *His dread of God.* He does not go straight to God. If he does, it is in despair. He trembles before Him, afraid to look up. He is overawed, overpowered by a sense of God's greatness. *It is a fearful thing to fall into the hands of the living God* (Hebrews 10:31 KJV). God is to him the most terrible object of all, yet he cannot but take himself to Him in some way. He is undone anyway. Perhaps this dreadful God, who is more powerful than these evils, may help him.

6. *His appeal to God's people.* Once he despised, hated, and shunned them. Now he goes to them with, "Pray for me." What a different man a saint seems now! He has something to say to God, and that is a great thing for a despairing sinner. He has influence at court. So he goes to Him. How often has the stricken, afflicted sinner had these words wrung from him: "Pray for me."

O sinner, look forward to your day of darkness. Prepare for it now. It is coming. How dreadful to be overtaken by it unprepared.

O sinner, go to God now, straight to God. Not to Moses, nor to any saint, but at once to God. Go, with all your sins, burdens, and trials. Go now! He will receive you and bless you.

The day is coming when another cry will be heard, when you will cry on rocks and hills, and all in vain. O *seek the Lord while He may be found* (Isaiah 55:6)! We do not know when Jesus Christ, the great Judge, will come. He may come soon. Earth is growing old. Its sin is heavy upon it. *Your* sin adds to the load. It will soon be too heavy to bear. Then the vengeance comes. God's longsuffering is great but will not last forever. The great day approaches. *He that shall come will come, and will not tarry* (Hebrews 10:37 KJV). Get up and get ready! Get up and watch!

Chapter 14

The Blood of Deliverance

"It is the Lord's Passover." – Exodus 12:11

We first notice:
1. *The name given here to the ordinance.* The Lord's, or Jehovah's, Passover. This reminds us of our New Testament feast, so like in name: *the Lord's Supper* (1 Corinthians 11:20). Both belong to the Lord. Both were instituted by Him. Both referred to Him. The Passover and the Supper have no meaning without Him. He is the Alpha and the Omega of both. *The Lord* is Christ's New Testament name, but it is also His Old Testament name. It is He, the Son, the Messiah, that is spoken of so often there under the name *the Lord*. Therefore, we rest our belief on the fact that Christ is God, not so much on the fact that the names of God are applied to Christ, as on this greater fact, but that the names of Christ are applied to God. It was of Him that Eve said, *"I have gotten a manchild with the help of* **the Lord***"* (Genesis 4:1, emphasis added). It was of Him that Enoch spoke, *"Behold,* **the Lord** *came"* (Jude v. 14, emphasis added). It is of Him we read: *Then* **the Lord** *said, "My Spirit shall not strive with man forever"* (Genesis 6:3, emphasis added); **the Lord** *was sorry that He had made man on the earth* (Genesis 6:6, emphasis added); **the Lord** *said to Noah* (Genesis 7:1, emphasis added); **the Lord** *said to Abram* (Genesis 12:1, emphasis added); for He who appeared to

Saul also appeared to Abraham. So in regard to the Passover, ***the Lord spoke to Moses and to Aaron*** (Exodus 6:13, emphasis added).

2. *The persons to whom this ordinance was given. To Moses and to Aaron.* In almost all other places we read, *The Lord spoke to **Moses*** alone (emphasis added). Here it is specifically to both – to him who was king in Jeshurun, and to him who was Israel's high priest. They were the representatives of the nation of kings and priests, even Israel; and representatives also of the church, the higher and truer *royal priesthood* (1 Peter 2:9), to whom the Lord's Supper was to be given. To us then, as the true Moses and Aaron, kings and priests, the Lord's Supper is given. It is the banquet of Jehovah's royal priesthood. To us as such He says, "Eat, drink. *Do this in remembrance of Me*" (1 Corinthians 11:24).

3. *The place where it was given.* It was in the land of Egypt. It was a feast *in* Egypt, and yet not *of* Egypt. It did not consist of Egyptian food. It spoke of deliverance *from* Egypt, and yet it was first to be observed *in* Egypt. It told of Egypt, and it told of Canaan. So it is with the Lord's Supper. It is *in* the world, yet not *of* the world. It is given *here,* observed *here,* yet it points away from here. It reminds us of our heavenly inheritance.

4. *The institution itself.* It consists of two parts, according to how the writer of Hebrews divided it (Hebrews 11:28): (1) the feast (the Passover), and (2) the sprinkling of blood. Let us examine these.

   1. *The feast.* What is it?

      a. *In itself.* It is a lamb, without spot; a lamb roasted; with unbroken bones; with bitter herbs; eaten in haste with staff in hand.

      b. *Symbolically.* It is commemoration; it is testimony; it is nourishment; it is repentance; it is strength.

   Such is the Supper of the Lord. It is a feast. The food is the Lamb of God. The bread and wine speak to us. The Lord's Supper is full of meaning. It is commemoration, testimony, and nourishment. *My flesh is meat indeed* (John 6:55 KJV). Man eats better than angels' food. *"Take, eat"* (Matthew 26:26) are the gracious words of the divine provider.

2. *The sprinkling of blood.* The feast and the blood must go together. The one hangs upon the other. It is not simply blood, but *sprinkled blood* that we find in the Passover, the blood of the Lamb on which we feast. What then does this blood proclaim? What is it? What does it mean? There is *life* in question. For wherever the blood comes in, the question of life and death comes in. Here there is then the giving of life for life. It is not *cleansing* that is the special importance of the Passover blood, though indirectly that may come in. It is something else. Let us see what it is.

   a. *It is the blood of separation.* That blood was sprinkled on doorpost and lintel. By this sprinkling of blood, Israel was separated from Egypt. The difference between them was marked by the blood. Those people in our day who deny the blood would obliterate the distinction between the church and the world. Hatred of the blood has been the mark of the world since the days of Cain. Love for it and trust in it is the characteristic of the church of God from Abel downward. Israel dwells alone, isolated by the blood.

   b. *It is the blood of protection.* "When I see the blood I will pass over you" (Exodus 12:13). That blood was Israel's shield. There seems a twofold kind of protection – the blood warding off the destroying angel and making him *pass over,* and God Himself (attracted by the blood) passing over as a defender between Israel and the angel (Isaiah 31:5). God says, *"When I see."* The blood is ever before *Him. We* do not see it. It is outside – beyond our vision – shed eighteen centuries ago. But God sees it, and that is our security. We think upon the blood that God sees, and we feel secure.

   c. *It is the blood of deliverance.* It not merely protected *in* Egypt, but it also delivered *out of* Egypt. It was this blood that saved: *"I have given Egypt as your ransom"* (Isaiah 43:3). There is death for Egypt, but life for Israel. Pardoned and set free, Israel turns her back on the land of bondage. That blood was the opening of her prison doors. It is still the blood that sets us free! Freedom through the blood is what we preach.

d. *It is the blood of doom.* It was doom to Egypt. It did not merely say that God is for Israel, but that He is also against Egypt. Indeed, there is death for Egypt, for Jehovah's enemies. It is still the blood that condemns. For everyone who is not under its shield, there is only death! It seals the sinner's death! The wrath of God abides on him. The blood that would have saved, now dooms.

Chapter 15

How God Deals with Sin and the Sinner

Leviticus 4:27-35

We have here: (1) The *sinner*. He is one of the common people; *anyone* (verse 27); whosoever. (2) The *sin*. It is one of ignorance. He is not aware of it; conscience did not take cognizance of it; he has forgotten it. (3) The *remedy*. It is a sin offering. This can only make it pass as completely from God's memory as it has passed from his own. (4) The *atonement*. It is by blood, through the intervention of the priesthood. There is no atonement without the blood of a substitute. (5) The *connection*. It is between the sinner and the atonement. He lays his hands on the sacrifice for a twofold reason: to identify himself with it and to transfer his sin to it. He says, "Let this stand instead of me; its life and death for my life and death." (6) The *forgiveness*. The sin passes away. There is no condemnation. It is instantaneous, complete, and perpetual pardon.

Such was the symbol. Full and expressive – revealing to us atonement and pardon through the one great sacrifice. Let us see what this old sin offering teaches us.

1. *What God thinks of sin*. It is something that must not be slighted. It is infinitely hateful, calling for condemnation and wrath. There is nothing light or trivial about it. It is not to be jested with, transiently frowned upon, or forgotten in a day. It calls for special marks of wrath. It is the abominable thing that He hates.

Its beginning is wrath and death. Its end is hell. As *He* thinks, so does He wish *us* to think. What do you think of sin? What is your opinion of its nature, its evil, and what it deserves?

2. *How He deals with it.* He does not despise nor forget it. He deals with it as a Judge. He estimates it as a Judge. He condemns it as a Judge. He inflicts punishment as a Judge. This must be either executed on us personally or on our substitute. Condemnation must be proclaimed. The penalty must be executed.

    a. *He condemns sin.* He gave the law to condemn sin. He set up the cross to condemn it more. *The soul that sinneth, it shall die* (Ezekiel 18:4 KJV). *The wages of sin is death* (Romans 6:23).

    b. *He provides a Sin-Bearer.* He does not leave us to do this, but does it Himself. He not only appoints the sin offering, but He also provides the victim. His Son – the Word made flesh – He is the appointed Sin-Bearer, divine and human in His constitution, perfect in all respects, sufficient for the great undertaking, able to bear wrath without being consumed.

    c. *He transfers the guilt.* *The LORD hath laid on him the iniquity of us all* (Isaiah 53:6 KJV). *The chastisement of our peace was upon him* (Isaiah 53:5 KJV). He who has the right to retain or transfer the guilt, transfers it to a substitute.

    Thus, then, He has provided the atonement. His appointed High Priest has made the atonement. This atonement is now a past fact. It is done. The sin offering has been brought. The blood has been shed. The propitiation has been accomplished. God has done it all, without man's help, desire, or concurrence. Nothing more is needed now in the shape of atonement for the guiltiest. No more blood, no more fire, no more endurance of wrath. It is all done! Nothing can be added to it or taken from it. Love is now free to flow out.

3. *How He deals with the sinner.* He bids him to come for pardon, and assures him of getting it at once, freely, on the ground of the provided atonement, and simply as a sinner. His objective is to connect the sinner with the propitiation. As long as they remain

separate, there is no resulting benefit to man from the shed blood. He provides thus for the connection of the sinner.

a. *He issues a declaration* concerning His own free love, His goodwill to men, His willingness to pardon any sinner. *"God so loved the world"* (John 3:16). *God, being rich in mercy, because of His great love with which He loved us* (Ephesians 2:4). Thus we have God's own assurance of a personal welcome to each of us – as we are. We do not make the welcome personal by our prayers or feelings. We avail ourselves of an already existing personal welcome to each sinner – as a sinner.

b. *He issues a testimony* to the completeness of the atonement. He raised up His Son from the dead as the *visible* testimony. But besides this, He has in various ways given full testimony as to the sufficiency and suitableness of the atonement.

c. *He issues a promise* of forgiveness to everyone who will receive this testimony. *"It will be forgiven him"* (Leviticus 5:13) is His promise to everyone who thus believes. Therefore, forgiveness becomes a matter of certainty to everyone who connects himself with the divine sin offering.

Perhaps you say, "I see that God has provided a propitiation, that this is complete and available for me, but how am I to be so connected with it as to obtain the pardon?" Everything depends on this connection being established, for without it there is no pardon. Now, how did the Israelite connect himself with the sin offering? He simply took the lamb, brought it to the priest, and said, "Let this stand for me," laying his hand on it and thereby transferring all his guilt to it. So we, by receiving the testimony and the promise, connect ourselves with the divine atonement. We go to God saying, "Let this life and death be for my life and death." We consent to be dealt with on the footing of another, not our own, and immediately the personal exchange takes place. He gets all our evil; we get all His good. Our demerit goes to Him; His merit comes to us. We take the royal grant of life and righteousness through the life and death of another. Pardon is secured and should be a thing as sure and as conscious to us as to the Israelite after he had brought the sacrifice and had seen it laid on the altar.

Chapter 16

The Fire Quenched

"Fire shall be kept burning continually on the altar; it is not to go out." – Leviticus 6:13

This was one of God's special commandments to Israel, and no doubt has a special meaning both to them and to us. For He does not speak random words. His trumpet does not utter an uncertain sound. He says only what He means, and He means everything He says. His words are profoundly real – more so than those of the deepest thinker of any age, and far more enduring. For they are eternal words, embodying eternal truths. The fire, altar, sacrifice, and tabernacle have all passed away, but *the truth* embodied in these remains forever. It is for *our* instruction as truly as for Israel's.

1. *The fire.* Fire in general is the symbol of wrath. It is sometimes the figure of purifying. More commonly, though, it is the figure of anger, divine anger – anger on account of sin; for in no other connection do we ever read of divine anger. No personal affront, whim, anger, partiality, or ill humor – none of these – are ever connected with God's wrath. Only sin! The history of *fire* in Scripture is very instructive. It begins in Paradise and ends in the last chapter of Revelation. There is the flaming sword, the fire of the sacrifice, the fire of Sodom, the fire of Egypt's plagues, the fire of the pillar, the fire of Sinai, the fire of Korah, the fire enveloping

itself in Ezekiel, the unquenchable fire, the fire that accompanies Christ's second coming, the fire of apocalyptic judgment, the lake of fire, the fire that comes down from heaven that is to consume the ungodly. These are some of the memorable allusions to fire in Scripture. Most of these are connected with the shekinah or visible symbol of the divine presence, inferring that it is from that presence that the fire proceeds, even from God Himself. Thus God infers most solemnly that there is such a thing as *wrath*. Yes, there is wrath, now hidden, one day to be revealed; wrath that the wicked treasure up against the day of wrath. God is not too benevolent, too merciful, to be angry. If there is no anger in God, the Bible utterly deceives us and a very large portion of it, is quite unmeaning, or rather *false*. The expulsion from Paradise, the flood, Sodom, sacrifice, pain, death, sorrow, the law, the cross, the unquenchable fire – these are very plain indications of *wrath* – wrath against sin; wrath for the *punishment*, not merely for the deliverance or warning of the sinner. All the ills that flesh is heir to are originally and in their proper interpretation (however overruled) expressions of *divine anger*. How terrible for a sinner to be confronted with an angry God! How hateful a thing *sin* must be to excite that anger; to be the *one* thing that provokes His wrath.

2. *The altar.* The word means the "place of sacrifice." It was elevated, implying that what was placed on it was lifted up to be presented to God. There was but *one* altar of sacrifice – one spot for the sinner to meet God. It was the most essential part of the tabernacle and the temple. Without it there could be no place of worship for a sinner. A sinner can only worship at an altar, can only meet God there. Why? Let us see. There are two things very prominent and visible about the altar: the fire and the blood. The fire is the symbol of wrath. The blood is the symbol of the effects of that wrath, in the infliction of punishment. Thus while the altar proclaimed wrath, it also proclaimed wrath appeased in consequence of the deserved punishment having been inflicted. Condemnation and pardon were thus fully expressed; hatred of sin, yet love to the sinner: unavoidable justice, inexhaustible grace. No sin is pardoned without first being punished (either in person or by a substitute). No debt is canceled without being fully paid. A just God and a Savior; not only a Savior *through* a just God, but also a Savior *because of* a just God. Thus the altar was:

1. *The place of condemnation.* There God condemned the sinner and his sin. Condemnation was the first thing the altar exhibited and proclaimed.

2. *The place of confession.* The sinner comes, not to hide, nor to explain away, excuse, nor to deny, but to confess his sin.

3. *The place of pardon.* The pardon is the result of the condemnation – the condemnation of the substitute or surety. First condemnation, then confession, then pardon: free, large, and irrevocable.

4. *The place of meeting with God.* The *one* spot on which God and the sinner can meet. Only over *blood,* only over *death,* can the great business of salvation be transacted, and the great question of pardon be settled between the sinner and God. Only there is it lawful or honorable for God to meet with the sinner. Only there is it safe or comfortable for the sinner to meet with God. There the great reconciliation takes place.

The cross is the altar. At the cross we meet with God, and God meets with us. There we learn our condemnation and our deliverance, our death and our life. There we confess, and there we are freely forgiven. There we know what sin is and what grace is! *Our God is a consuming fire* (Hebrews 12:29), yet God is love.

The fire upon this altar was peculiar in many respects.

1. *It was kindled by God.* At first it was lit directly from heaven – from the shekinah glory. It was God's own fire.

2. *It was fed with the fat of the sacrifices.* The peace offering is specially mentioned in connection with this, as if that which ratified the peace was that which satisfied the fire.

3. *It was never to go out.* Once kindled, it was to burn always. It needed no rekindling. It was kindled by God, but fed and kept up by man. In the case of the lost, the fire of God is eternal and unquenchable. In the case of the saved, it is only quenched because it is exhausted in and by Him who, as the eternal One, endured the wrath of eternity during His brief life on earth. Good news to sinners! *The fire is quenched.* There is one who has borne wrath

for sin. He who accepts that one wrathbearing is personally delivered from it all. But he who rejects it and tries to bear the wrath himself must reap what he sows and bear it forever.

There is only one tabernacle, one altar, one fire, one sacrifice, one Priest! Not two ways of approaching God, or two ways of pardon – only one! He who accepts and uses that one way is safe. He who tries another way must perish forever. Yes, there is but one cross, one Christ, one Savior. But He is sufficient. *Christ is all, and in all* (Colossians 3:11).

Chapter 17

The Vision from the Rocks

"As I see him from the top of the rocks." – Numbers 23:9

It was of Israel and Israel's glory that the false prophet of Pethor spoke. He stood upon the top of Moab's barren rocks and gazed down on the happy nation whom God had delivered from Egypt, had brought through the desert, and was about to lead into the land flowing with milk and honey. It was with wonder, perhaps with envy too, that Balaam looked on the many tents beneath him.

So, from this desert land and these desert hills, we gaze upon the church on her way to Canaan, about to be settled in the blessed land and the Holy City. And when we gaze, what do we see?

1. *The ruggedness of the land of our present stay.* It is the region of hostility as well as barrenness. This is not our rest. These dark mountains are not our home. We may pitch our tents among them for a season or climb to the top to gaze around us. But they are not a dwelling place for us. We may look on Canaan from Pisgah, but Pisgah will not do for a home. Nebo lies close to Pisgah, and Nebo tells of death, not of life – mortality is here. This is the land not of Israel, but of Moab, and its gods are Baal, not Jehovah. We could not abide here.

2. *The glorious land.* Far away now, but still visible, still beautiful. It is the paradise of God. It is the new Jerusalem, the city that has

foundations. The new heavens and new earth, wherein dwells righteousness. The vision gives us a wonderful contrast between what we are and what we will be, making us long for the day we enter it.

3. *A people delivered from a present evil world.* Once in bondage, now free; once groaning under oppression, now in the service of a heavenly Master and heirs of the world to come; the Red Sea crossed, now between them and their persecutors as an iron wall. Forgiven and redeemed, with their backs to Egypt, and their faces to Jerusalem. *"A people saved by the Lord"* (Deuteronomy 33:29).

4. *A people sustained by Jehovah Himself.* Theirs is the hidden manna, the water from the struck rock. Jehovah feeds them. Jehovah gives them the living water. It is not man but God who cares for them. Everything that they have they owe to Him who has delivered them. They feed on angels' food; indeed, even better! The very bread of God; on Him whose flesh is meat indeed, whose blood is drink indeed.

5. *A pilgrim band.* They are strangers on the earth. This is not their home. Their city is not here. Their loins are wrapped, their staff is in their hand, and they are hastening onward. No sitting down, no taking ease, and no folding of their hands. Forward, still forward, is their watchword! Theirs is a pilgrimage, not a pleasure tour. They must not delay.

6. *A people bought with a price.* Their ransom has been blood, and they are not their own. Another life has died for theirs. They have been plucked from death and the grave, because another has died and risen for them. They belong to that other, not to themselves, the flesh, nor the world.

7. *A people loved with an infinite love.* The banner that is over them is love. The song they sing is love: *To Him who loves us* (Revelation 1:5). It is a love that surpasses knowledge; a love without bound or end; a love that is eternal and divine. All around and above them is love – the love of Father, Son, and Holy Spirit. They are the monuments of love; the witnesses of love – free love, forgiving love, redeeming love; love beyond that which angels

know. A love that constrains them, purifies them, urges them forward, and gladdens all of their way.

8. *A people preparing to pass over to the fair land.* It is within sight; a few days, perhaps less, will bring them into it. Their journey is nearly done. Their toil and weariness will soon be exchanged for rest and glory. And *now salvation is nearer to us than when we believed* (Romans 13:11). From the top of the rocks they can see Jerusalem, Olivet, and Bethlehem. They get glimpses of the whole outstretched land. It is a land of plenty, where they will hunger no more, neither thirst anymore. It is a land of light where there is no night; a land of blessing where there is no curse; a land of gladness where sorrow does not come; a summer land where the frosts of winter do not chill; a calm, sunny land where storms do not vex and shadows do not fall; a land of health where the inhabitant will not say, "I am sick"; a land of peace where the war trumpet never sounds; a land of life where corruption and mortality do not enter and where death and the grave are unknown; a land of union where broken ties are all reknit and broken hearts are all healed. *"For the Lamb in the center of the throne will be their shepherd, and will guide them to springs of the water of life; and God will wipe every tear from their eyes"* (Revelation 7:17). Jesus reigns there. There we reign with Him.

Chapter 18

The Doom of the Doublehearted

They also killed Balaam the son of Beor with the sword. – Numbers 31:8

Balaam had taken the field against Israel – against a people whom he had pronounced blessed – whom he had pronounced invincible both by earth and hell. Yes, *Balaam the son of Beor* – he, and not another of the name – rushes on the studs of the Almighty's armor. *He defies Israel and Israel's God!*

But he fails. He would gladly have cursed Israel, but he could not. He counseled Moab to seduce Israel by temptation, and his device succeeded too well. He now fetches his last stroke, in vain. He perishes inferiorly. He is slain with the sword that he had defied.

Such is the end of the backslider; of one who knew the truth but did not do it; who once said, *"Let me die the death of the upright, and let my end be like his!"* (Numbers 23:10). It was certainly not the end he prayed for, yet it was the end to which his whole life had been headed. He reaped what he sowed, and in him *God [was] not mocked* (Galatians 6:7). He died as he lived, in fellowship with Moab, yet persuaded in his heart that Israel was the beloved of the Lord, and that Jehovah was God. His life had been with Midian, and so was his death. His grave is with the unclean. He passes from earth with no one to soothe his deathbed and close his eyes; none to lament for him or to build his monument. A sad end of a life of halting and indecision, and resistance of the Spirit, defiance of conscience, rejection of light, and wretched covetousness. He loved the wages of unrighteousness, and he certainly received his reward.

Let us see what he wanted and how he failed. How ambitious he was, yet what a life of utter failure and disappointment was his. He would gladly have risen, but he sunk. He would gladly have been rich, but he lost everything. What a wasted life! Yet it was the life of one who knew to do better things but did not do them; who knew that the world was vanity, yet followed it; who knew that Israel's portion was the best, yet chose that of Moab; who knew the true God and the true Messiah, but preferred the idolatries of Israel's enemies. He saw Him from the top of the rocks, but that was all. He got a passing glimpse of the cross, but no more. It was everything that he saw of the way of life before he plunged into death and woe.

1. *He wanted to serve two masters.* These were the same that the Lord later designated as God and wealth. He wanted not to offend either one, but to please both. He was like Issachar crouching between two burdens. But it would not do. He failed. Such is the certain failure of everyone who makes a similar attempt. *"You **cannot** serve God and wealth"* (Matthew 6:24; Luke 16:13, emphasis added). He *loved* the one master – wealth; and he *dreaded* the other – God; but he would gladly do the will of both. He could not afford to lose the favor of either. Miserable life! More miserable death! The life and death of one whose whole career was one long attempt to do the bidding both of God and the devil.

2. *He wanted to earn two kinds of wages.* The wages of righteousness and the wages of unrighteousness (2 Peter 2:15) were both in his eyes. He would gladly have the pay of both God and the devil. He was unwilling to do or say anything that would deprive him of either. He was as cautious and cunning as he was covetous. He would not work without wages. He would work for a hundred masters if they would only pay him well. How like many socalled "religious" men among us.

3. *He wanted to do two opposite things at the same time.* He wished both to bless and to curse. He was willing to do either, so long as it would serve his interests. The only question he had was, "Would it pay?" If the

blessing would pay, he would take it; if the curse would pay, he would take it. If both would pay, he would take both of them. Both blessing and cursing were alike to him, confessing and denying the true God, worshipping Baal or Jehovah; it did not matter if *by this craft [he could] have [his] wealth* (Acts 19:25 KJV). So it is with many among us. If keeping the Sabbath will pay, they will keep the Sabbath; if breaking the Sabbath will pay, they will break the Sabbath. These are true Balaams – without principle, without faith, and without fear!

4. *He wanted two kinds of friendship.* He would gladly be friends with everybody. Perhaps he was timid of those whom Scripture calls *cowardly* (Revelation 21:8). Perhaps, also, he was ambitious, and sought great things for himself wherever these could be obtained (Jeremiah 45:5). He certainly had before him *the fear of man [that] brings a snare* (Proverbs 29:25), and the love of man's commendation that brings no less of a snare. He *dreaded* Israel's God, of whom he knew much, but he also dreaded Moab's gods, though whether he really believed in them we do not know. Made up of these contradictions, and acting not by faith but by unbelief, he tried to secure the friendship of everyone whom he counted great, whether in heaven or on earth. He shut his eyes not only to the sin but also to the *impossibility* of such a course. He did not see that the friendship of the world is the enemy of God, and that whosoever will be the friend of the world must be the enemy of God.

5. *He wanted to have two religions.* He saw religion to be a paying concern, a profitable trade, and he was willing to accept it from anybody or everybody, to adopt it from any place if it would raise him in the world and make his fortune. Perhaps he thought all religions were equally right or equally wrong, equally true or equally false. He would rather not offend any god if he could help it. He would make concessions to "religious prejudices" of any kind if the prejudiced people would only help him. He was like Erasmus of old, whom a German writer thus describes: "Erasmus belongs to that species of writers who have all the desire to build God a magnificent church; at the same time, however, not giving the devil any offence, to whom, accordingly, they set up a neat little chapel close by, where you can offer him some touch of

sacrifice at a time, and practice a quiet household devotion for him without disturbance." Such was Balaam. He wanted to have two gods and two religions.

But this double service, double friendship, and double religion would not do. He could make nothing by them. They profited him nothing either in this life or in that life to come. His end was with the ungodly, his portion with the enemies of Israel. And for his *soul*, where could it be? Not with Israel's God, or Israel's Christ, or in Israel's heaven. He reaped what he sowed.

He was a good specimen of multitudes in these last days. An educated and intelligent man, shrewd and quickseeing, of respectable character, high in favor with the rich and great, a *religious* man, too, after a fashion, not unsound in creed so far, for he acknowledges Jehovah as the true God. But he is fond of the world, fond of money, and fond of promotion. He is one that would not let his religion stand in the way of his advancement; who could pocket all scruples if he could pocket a little gold along with them. He is hollow of heart, but with a fair outside. He is just an Erasmus, not a Luther, Calvin, Knox, confessor, nor martyr. His worldly interests are the main thing to him. He would rather not risk offending God, but yet he would not like to lose Balak's rewards and honors. He would rather not take up his cross, nor deny himself, nor forsake all for his God. Religion with him is not just a thing to be suffered for – at least if he can help it.

So it is with multitudes among us. They want as much religion as will save them from hell and not an atom more. The world is their real God; gold is their idol. It is in wealth's temple that they worship. Love God with all their heart? They don't so much as understand the meaning of such a thing. Sacrifice riches, place, honor, and friends to Christ? They scoff at those things as madness.

Oh, be on the side of God completely. Don't trifle with religion. Don't mock God and Christ. Do not love the world. Be religious in your inmost soul. Don't mistake sentimentalism for religion, or a good character for the new birth. You may go very far and yet not be a Christian. You may follow Christ in *some* things, but if not in *everything*, then what is your following worth? This world *or* the world to come – that is the alternative, not this world *and* the world to come. Christ, *all* or *nothing*. The soul more precious than worlds, or utterly worthless.

No middle ground; no halfdiscipleship; no compromise. No! *The friendship of the world is enmity with God* (James 4:4 KJV). *"Come out... and be separate"* (2 Corinthians 6:17). The new birth, or no religion at all.

Look to your end! *What* is it to be? *Where* is it to be? *With whom* is it to be? Anticipate your eternity. Is it to be darkness or light, shame or glory? Oh, make sure, make sure!

Do not sear your conscience by praying Balaam's prayer: *"Let me die the death of the upright."* What will that get for you? It is the *life* of the righteous that God is calling you to lead, and He will take care of your death. Decide. Do not hesitate, or else your life will surely be a wretched life and you will have a still more wretched death. What will gold, purple, or honor do for you when you lie down to die, or rise up to be judged?

Chapter 19

Be Not Borderers

"Go in and possess the land." – Deuteronomy 10:11

Israel passed through many changes in their history, but here we have their earthly history's termination – the possession of the land. They were bondspeople, wanderers, outsiders, and borderers. However, they were not to remain as such. They were to possess the land. Here their earthly history, which began with Abraham, ends. Let us learn from this something about ourselves and our history.

1. *We are not to be without a land.* We are to have a country and a city. When we are in the world, we have these in a certain way, but they are all carnal. They pass from us and we from them. The world's cities and possessions will not do for us. They cannot fill us, satisfy us, nor abide with us. Therefore, even when we are in the world, we are truly strangers; we are landless, cityless, and homeless. And after we have come out from the world, we are strangers, though not as before; for a land, a city, and a home have been secured for us. Sinners, God offers you the better Canaan!

2. *We are not to be dwellers in Egypt.* The house of bondage is not for us. Pharaoh cannot be our king. We must, like Moses, refuse to be called the sons of Pharaoh's daughter. We must go out, not

fearing the wrath of the king, and counting the reproach of Christ as greater riches than Egypt's treasures.

3. *We are not to be dwellers in a barren land.* The wilderness may do for a day, but not for a permanent abode. Ishmael may have the desert, Israel must have the good land – the land flowing with milk and honey.

4. *We are not to be borderers.* To be out of Egypt is one step, to come up to the borders of Canaan is another, but that is not to be all. We are not outsiders, never crossing the boundary; nor borderers, belonging to neither region, ever crossing and recrossing the line, as if we had no wish to stay or had no portion in the land. The borderlands are not for the church, nor for anyone calling himself a Christian, an Israelite indeed.

5. *We are to go in and possess.* Out of Egypt, out of the wilderness, across the borders, into the very heart of the land – Judah's hills, Ephraim's vales, Issachar's plains, Manasseh's pastures, Naphtali's lakes, and Zebulun's fertile reaches. We go in and take possession, leaving all other lands and regions behind. It is the Godchosen, Godgiven land. Let us enter it. It is rich, goodly, and wellwatered. Let us possess it. Not merely survey it or pitch our tents in it, but also build our houses there, to dwell in it forever.

What I gather especially from our text is that we are not to be *borderers*. Not just not Egyptians nor Ishmaelites, but also not *borderers*. The place to which God invites us is the land, the kingdom, and the city. Just now, of course, it is but the *promise*, for the kingdom has not come yet. But I speak of the promise as if it were the thing itself, for the promise is God's, not man's.

There are many *borderers* in our day; halfandhalf Christians; afraid of being too decidedly or intensely religious. They are not Egyptians, and they are not perhaps quite outsiders, for they occasionally seem to cross the line and take a look at the land from some of its southern hills. But they are *borderers*. They have not boldly taken up their abode in the land. They have not entered in nor possessed it. They are vacilators, worshippers of two gods, trying to secure two kingdoms, and laying up two kinds of treasures. Let me speak *of* and *to* these. Why should you not be borderers?

1. *It is sin.* It is not merely your misfortune, it is also your guilt. That halfheartedness and indecision is about the most sinful condition you can be in. Borderer, you are a *sinner;* you are a sinner because you are a borderer!

2. *It is misery.* You cannot be happy in that halfandhalf state. You don't know *what* you are, nor *whose* you are, nor where you are going. You are not sure of anything good, only of evil. You were dying in that state – you were cut off *on the borders.* You are lost. Does not that thought make you truly wretched?

3. *It is danger.* You think perhaps that because you have gone a little way that everything is well, or at least that you are out of danger. No! The danger is as great as ever. If you were to die on the borders – only almost a Christian – you are as sure of hell as if you had died in Egypt.

4. *It is an abomination to God.* It is an insult to Him. It says that you do not care for Him or His goodly land. That halfheartedness is abominable to God. It is like Laodicea, or perhaps worse. Borderer, beware of provoking and insulting God.

5. *It is loss to yourself.* Even now, you will lose a lot. You might be so happy! If decided and sure, you might have such peace! And then the prospect of such a land! What a loss! Yes, your own interests as well as God's honor demand decision. It is such a goodly, glorious land! It is so foolish and so cowardly to hold back. Oh *decide.* Do not be a borderer anymore. Enter in and possess the land at once!

Chapter 20

The Outlines of a Saved Sinner's History

"He found him in a desert land, and in the howling waste of a wilderness; He encircled him, He cared for him, He guarded him as the pupil of His eye." – Deuteronomy 32:10

We might take this figuratively of Abraham in Chaldea or of Israel in Egypt, but Moses is speaking literally of the Sinaitic wilderness and of Israel there. No sooner had they crossed the Red Sea than they became wanderers in the desert. God found them there. He came to them. It was truly a desert land, without bread, water, dwellings, or cities. It was all heat, barrenness, danger, and terror. He met them, came to them, took their hand, and became their guide (Deuteronomy 1:31, 33; Nehemiah 9:19). By day and night He kept and led them for forty years. He taught, protected, and watched them, as if they had been the most tender part of the most tender member of His body. Such was Israel's story, until He brought them to Canaan, and such is that of every Israelite. Indeed, such is that of every saved sinner from his first arousing until he enters into the joy of his Lord. Consider:

1. *The sinner in his native country.* That land of his birth is a desert waste. It is the far country into which the Prodigal Son went, the world where everything is evil. It is a barren land, without comfort, safety, friends, or kindred. No living bread to feed his famished soul.

No fountain of living water to quench his thirst. No peace, rest, nor gladness. No shelter from the wrath to come. He is wretched and empty; a poor wanderer of the desert, a man without a home.

2. *The sinner found by God* (Jeremiah 2:2). The three parables of our Lord bring this out: the lost sheep found by the shepherd, the lost silver coin found by the woman, and the lost son found by his father. It is not the sinner that seeks God, but God that seeks the sinner. When God comes, He finds him in the land of barrenness, famine, and danger. He finds him in his sin and wretchedness; a child of wrath, an heir of hell. He goes in quest of him, seeks him, and saves him. By convictions, terrors, disappointments, a sense of need, and weariness – by these He pursues him from valley to valley, and from refuge to refuge. Not by these only, but also by a thousand such things great and small. Each believer, as he looks back, reminds himself of this: *"He found [me] in a desert land, and in the howling waste of a wilderness"* (Deuteronomy 32:10). Ask all of them and they will tell you this. Ask Abraham, Moses, Manasseh, Zaccheus, and Paul. Ask the Corinthians and the Thessalonians. They will all tell you the same story: *"He found [me] in a desert land";* "He chose me, sought me out, found me, called me, sent from above, *took me,* and *drew me out of many waters* (2 Samuel 22:17; Psalm 18:16). I was a lost sheep, but He found me! A prodigal, but He found me!" Some He found in childhood, some in youth, some in adulthood. Yet everyone the same in the end.

3. *The sinner under God's care.* The finding is not the ending, but the beginning of God's dealing with him, which from first to last is all marvelous – the display of wisdom and love.

   a. *Guidance.* No place needs a guide like the desert. One gets utterly bewildered in its intricacies and labyrinths of rocks and plains. He who finds Him knows this, and takes Him under his guidance, so that at every turn, every step, he will be sure of being in the right way indeed. God often brings him into circumstances in which there can be no help except in Himself.

The desert is pathless and the sinner is ignorant. There are false guides, uncertain ways, as well as darkness and enemies. Therefore, God leads us! By His Word, His providence, His rod, His hand, and His eye; by joys and sorrows, prosperities and adversities; by the footsteps of the flock; by hedging up our way; by denying us our own will. He "leads us about"; not directly, but with many a winding and apparent backturning; with many stages and unlikely bypaths. He does not take us at once to Canaan, but leads us about, for wise purposes of grace and discipline and purifying; for the manifestation of Himself and the overthrow of Satan. What a leader! Whatever are the entanglements, briars, thorns, and darkness, He will guide us. Onward, still onward, to the city of habitation; we come up out of the wilderness leaning on the beloved. We pray, *Let Your good Spirit lead me on level ground* (Psalm 143:10).

b. *Instruction.* One of His first instructions is, *"Learn from Me"* (Matthew 11:29). The sinner needs His teaching – divine, not human teaching – as to what sin is, as to himself, as to God, to Christ, the cross, the love of God, the grace of Christ, and the glory to be revealed. God teaches these to us. Every day and hour are teaching times. He who has found us is the One who has compassion on the ignorant.

c. *Protection.* He comes at once under the shadow of the divine shield, so that he is kept by the power of God, *preserved in Jesus Christ* (Jude v. 1 KJV). No enemy prevails, no weapon injures, no evil comes near; he is made more than conqueror. How careful God is of the newfound one! How sensitive about the injury done to him, as if it were done to Himself, to the apple of His eye! What a guardian, what a protector do we find in God! The sun will not strike by day nor the moon by night, nor will the sand of the desert blow into our eye.

O men of earth, are you still wanderers? Lost, unguided, uninstructed, and unprotected? What will the desert do for you? Will it be an equivalent to Canaan and Jerusalem? God pursues you, appeals to you, seeks to win you, asks you, "Have I been a wilderness to you?" He calls! In every way, and by every agency; by the gospel, by the law, by a sense of need, by sorrow, by pain. He calls – He pursues! Oh, do not flee from Him any longer. Let Him overtake you today!

Chapter 21

Divine Longings over the Foolish

"Would that they were wise." – Deuteronomy 32:29

These are the words not of anger, but of love, of disappointed affection, of a sorrowful friend, of a tenderhearted father, of an earnest, gracious, and longsuffering God. In them God yearned over Israel. In them He still yearns over us. In them we learn the attitude in which God is standing over us, always stretching out His hands to a disobedient and arguing people.

1. *God's desire to make us wise.* He is the infinitely wise God. He longs to make us partakers of His wisdom. He has no pleasure in our ignorance. Indeed, it excites His compassion as much as His displeasure. He knows the preciousness of wisdom, and He loves to not see us without it. He wishes us to be wise. Why then does He not make us wise, seeing that He is as powerful as He is wise? I cannot explain this whole puzzle. It is mysterious. Only let us remember that: (1) He is sovereign as well as loving. (2) Wisdom, from its very nature, cannot be *forced*. (3) The power of a human will for evil, for resistance both to wisdom and to love, is very great, far greater than can be supposed from the feebleness of the creature in whom it is. We cannot disentangle the whole knot, but we know from His own words that He desires sincerely and

honestly to see us wise. What else can our text mean, *"Would that they were wise."* Is not this good news? God desires to make you wise! *If any of you lacks wisdom, let him ask of God* (James 1:5).

2. *Man's unteachableness.* The wish to be wise and the unwillingness to be taught is one of the many strange contradictions of humanity. The search for wisdom and the rejection of it when God presents it is a spectacle – strange, but not quite unaccountable. For the wisdom man searches for is wisdom of his own selecting; it is wisdom without God, it is wisdom that will not contradict his propensities and lusts, it is wisdom reasoned out by himself and according to himself the credit of discovery. Submission to divine instruction is what he especially dislikes; liberty to take or reject God's instruction is what he claims for himself, and the present age is developing man's unteachableness to the full. He claims to be his own teacher, and to be the judge of the wisdom that he is to receive. He insists that his own reason, his own conscience, and his own moral sense will sit in judgment on all that is presented to him. The *authoritative* presentation to him of any doctrine he holds to be inconsistent with his liberty, and therefore even when he receives the doctrine thus presented, he rejects the authority on which it comes. He may receive the truth, but it is because his own reason has proved it or accepted it, not because God has offered it. He would have his faith to stand in the wisdom of man, and not in the power of God.

3. *God's provision for our becoming wise.* He has not left us to gather wisdom at random, nor contented Himself with the mere expression of a wish that we should be wise. He has given substantial proof of His sincerity in this thing. He has provided:

   a. *The lesson.* This Book of His contains that lesson. It is full, varied, complete, and simple. It is a lesson for learned and unlearned, for Jew and Greek, for rich and poor – the same lesson for everyone. In this one Book is written the lesson of lessons; the lesson which, when learned, removes darkness, ignorance, and anxiety, and gives light, peace, health, and an eternal salvation.

b. *The school.* It is the school of Christ. For our first step is to become His disciples, to accept Him and His rules for the guidance of our studies. *"Make disciples of all the nations"* (Matthew 28:19) was His commission. So we enter His academy, we enroll among His scholars. This discipleship is the first step to wisdom; it is the renunciation of the false schools of the world, of man, and of philosophy; and it is the submission of our whole man to the regulations of this school.

c. *The discipline.* It is not simply pouring in information that is required. The mind, the soul, and the conscience must be so disciplined and prepared as to receive it correctly. Various is this discipline, this training. Hardship, sorrow, trial – all kinds of chastisement are required in order to suit us for the reception of the wisdom. In this divine school all of these are brought into use, daily use, to make us receptive, pliable, teachable, and submissive.

d. *The Teacher.* He is the Holy Spirit. Sometimes we are said to "learn of Christ" and to "learn of the Father," but the Spirit is the special teacher; *"He will teach you all things"* (John 14:26); *"Who is a teacher like Him?"* (Job 36:22). His teaching is perfect, irresistible, yet not miraculous; gradual, natural, yet supernatural. He teaches us out of that Book that He has inspired.

Thus God yearns over us, grieving at our ignorance, mourning over our unteachableness, offering to teach us and to make us wise. Thus pitying us, He provides for us; leaving us inexcusable if we remain untaught. *"Would that [you] were wise,"* He says to each one of us, and He says it sincerely. Let us place ourselves entirely in His hands for instruction, for light, and for blessing. All He asks is that we enroll ourselves as His scholars and submit to His teaching. In His infinite compassion and love He implores us to be wise.

Chapter 22

What a Believing Man Can Do

Then Joshua spoke to the Lord in the day when the Lord delivered up the Amorites before the sons of Israel, and he said in the sight of Israel, "O sun, stand still at Gibeon, and O moon in the valley of Aijalon." So the sun stood still, and the moon stopped, until the nation avenged themselves of their enemies. Is it not written in the book of Jashar? And the sun stopped in the middle of the sky and did not hasten to go down for about a whole day. There was no day like that before it or after it, when the Lord listened to the voice of a man; for the Lord fought for Israel. – Joshua 10:12-14

There are several miracles referred to in Scripture in connection with the sun. When the sun was darkened in Egypt (Exodus 10:21); when *the light of the sun will be seven times brighter* (Isaiah 30:26); when the shadow went back on the stairway of Ahaz (Isaiah 38:8); when the sun was darkened at the crucifixion (Matthew 27:45); when the sun will become *black as sackcloth* (Revelation 6:12); and when it will *scorch men with fire* (Revelation 16:8). But this is the most extraordinary of them all, indeed, of all the miracles of the Bible. It is quiet and beneficial; it is conservative, not destructive; it restrains but does not injure. It is not like the flood or the plagues of Egypt, desolating and deathdealing; nor like the Red Sea, Sinai, or Jordan; nor like the descending fire on

Carmel. It is simply a stoppage of creation's movements, restraining the descent of the two great lights, making day a little longer. It does not look like a miracle, for there is no change in the sun, moon, sky, or earth; yet it is this "no change" that is the greatest of all miracles. *There was no day like that before it or after it, when the Lord listened to the voice of a man* (Joshua 10:14). The time had not come when they should have no more need of the sun.

The thing was done in a moment, without premeditation or preparation. It was not by fasting and prayer, or an appeal to God, as in the miracles of Moses and Elijah. It was by a *command,* a word, addressed directly to the sun and moon. It was as if Joshua was assuming the Creator's authority. Joshua's command of faith, uttered in simple confidence in God; the word of *one* man; the word of a man in sympathy and fellowship with God. O with confidence in God, what can you not accomplish? Joshua is a man of like passions as we are, yet he speaks to the sun and it stands still!

It is not only a very extraordinary miracle in itself, but it is also a very *manifest* one. It was not done in a corner, but was open to the eyes of all. That long, long day in Palestine would doubtless be remembered forever. It could not be hidden. It was in one respect a helpful miracle; in another, indirectly, destructive; for it enabled Israel to overthrow their enemies; and in such a ruin, God is glorified. It was, we might say, a very *superfluous* miracle. Why not enable Joshua to cut short the work, or send the lightning or the earthquake? God does not always economize His forces, His gifts, or His treasures. He sometimes loves to show how He can lavish His fullness – how He can be, as men say, *extravagant.* How completely a much lesser miracle would have served the purpose! Yet He does not grudge this, in answer to the word of one of His saints. It seems stupendous and superfluous to us – for the one stoppage of the sun (or earth) includes so many other stoppages and the putting forth of an amount of power absolutely inconceivable. We can measure the amount of power put forth in severing the Red Sea or the Jordan River, but the restraining of sun and moon involves an amount of power beyond all calculation or conception.

1. *Familiarize your minds with a great miracle like this.* Do not try to lower it or diminish it or empty it of the supernatural. Take it

for what it is stated here to be. God means what He says. He does not exaggerate. Take it for what it is.

a. *It will enlarge your thoughts of God.* He is seen in this miracle as infinitely great and powerful; able to restrain sun and moon in a moment. We need to have our thoughts elevated, expanded, and greatened. It is with a great God that we have to do. Alpine or Grampian magnificence declares His greatness, but this far more. In days when man tries to make himself look great and to think of himself as powerful, it is well to remember the greatness of Jehovah.

b. *It will increase your reverence.* Reverence for God comes, in part at least, from what we see of His power and majesty. We must be steeped in such views of God as this miracle gives us, so that we may be delivered from flippancy and frivolity in dealing with God – in prayer and praise. Are we sufficiently reverential? Are we bowed down in spirit before this mighty God?

c. *It will give you a true insight into the true supernatural.* The tendency of the age is to disbelieve the supernatural; to assume that man occupies the whole space of being and that beyond what he sees, hears, and feels, there is nothing – no room for angels or spirits, no room for God, no room for agencies apart from known forces and ascertained laws. The Bible is full of the superhuman and supernatural. In studying it we are delivered from *superstition,* which is the supernatural of the *fake,* and we are taught the world of faith, which is the supernatural of the *true.* For faith deals with the *true* supernatural, the divine supernatural. It is *the evidence of things not seen* (Hebrews 11:1 KJV).

2. *Have faith in God.* Here is a miracle so great that we can hardly ask for a greater one. Therefore, we ought to say, "Is there anything too difficult for God?" It cherishes faith and expectation. It shows what God is willing to do for people like us. Let us not be staggered by the greatness or difficulty of any work or the power of any enemy. What if we needed a miracle? If not a visible miracle, yet something as great? Is not God willing to do it for us? There

is still power, still love. He still takes part with His Israel against their enemies. Let us be trustful, believing, and brave. *If God be for us, who can be against us?* (Romans 8:31 KJV). What can faith not do? What can unbelief not mar? Have faith in God. Not in self, man, schemes, societies, organizations, churches, money, intellect, science, or progress, but in *God*. Let us be Joshuas. Let us show what one living man, armed with the living Word, can do with the living God!

Chapter 23

Song of the Putting Off of the Armor

"O my soul, march on with strength." – Judges 5:21

This is one note of the warrior's song, a note loud and glad. It is the exulting cry of victory; the song of triumph; victory and triumph when the battle was not merely for Israel but also for God. It is the song of Deborah and Barak; a song inspired by the Holy Spirit; a song of earth, yet doubtless responded to in heaven; the song of the putting off of the armor; the song of one who was *strong in the Lord, and in the power of his might* (Ephesians 6:10 KJV).

We might suppose it was uttered by Abraham on returning from the slaughter of the kings; by Moses when he saw Pharaoh overthrown; by Joshua when he embarrassed Amalek; by David when he killed Goliath; or by Israel in the latter day (Isaiah 14:3-4). It is the song of one who, out of weakness, had been made *strong in the Lord, and in the power of his might*.

We might suppose it to be Christ's song of triumph when He died, with *"It is finished!"* on His lips; or still more when He rose again from the dead; or still more *when he ascended up on high, [leading] captivity captive* (Ephesians 4:8 KJV).

We might take it as the song of the apostles on the day of Pentecost, when, *"not by might nor by power"* (Zechariah 4:6), they saw three thousand saved, and as the song of the apostles wherever they went preaching the gospel in Ephesus, Corinth, Colossae, or Rome. That wonderful gospel, proving itself mighty in their hands to the pulling down of strongholds and the overthrow of enemies. Surely it was Paul's when he said, *I have fought the good fight* (2 Timothy 4:7).

We might take it as the church's song in the day of her coming triumph over all her enemies, over Antichrist, over Babylon, over Satan; when caught up into the clouds, or standing on the sea of glass: *"O my soul, march on with strength."*

It must be ours: (1) daily; (2) especially at certain seasons and emergencies; (3) in the end, like Paul; and (4) hereafter throughout eternity, as we look back upon the past and understand more fully our own helplessness, as well as the greatness of the powers arrayed against us. How often will we find ourselves repeating, even in the new Jerusalem, the song of the ancient prophetess: *"O my soul, march on with strength."*

1. *Our warfare.* It is "a good warfare," or more exactly, "a glorious warfare." It is against enemies within, around, and beneath; against self, the flesh, and the world, but especially, the principalities and powers of evil. *Fight the good fight of faith* (1 Timothy 6:12). It is *our* battle. It is *God's* battle. It is the *church's* battle, for we are but one of a mighty army of warriors. It is a warfare from which we cannot escape, except by deserting Christ's ranks, for there is no discharge in this war. It is a *constant* warfare. It is a *lifelong* warfare. It is earnest and terrible; no child's play; no mere sound or name, but an intense reality. Nowhere outside of Scripture do we find it better described than by Bunyan in his book *The Pilgrim's Progress.* He knew the reality and painted it well. Our life is then a warfare – a warfare that enters into everything, because at every step our great adversary stands to bar our progress, and to prevent us from glorifying God in each part and transaction of life. You complain of the power of sin. Well, fight! You complain of the difficulty of believing. Well, fight!

2. *Our weapons.* We need to be armed, both for defense and offense, fully equipped in every instrument of battle. No halffurnished soldier can fight a battle like this. There must be no broken swords, no rusted spears, and no shattered helmets.

    a. *What our weapons are not.* They are not carnal – earthly, self-made, nor manmade. They are not the weapons of science, philosophy, or human intellect. These are of no benefit against sin, the flesh, or Satan.

    b. *What they are.* They are divine and heavenly, forged and hammered on no earthly anvil. They are Godmade and Godgiven. They are complete, both for attack and defense. Sword, shield, sandal, helmet – everything that is needed in this warfare and described by the apostle in Ephesians 6 is provided for us. No man loses this battle for lack of offered armor.

3. *Our strength.* We need power to use the provided weapons. Not the weapons without the power, nor the power without the weapons, but both together. *Be strong in the Lord and in the strength of His might* (Ephesians 6:10). Our sufficiency is of God. All of our strength is in the Lord. What are sword and shield to paralyzed limbs? We need strength – divine strength for divine armor. The fullness of Him to whom all power is given is at our disposal. There need be no lack of strength to us in this warfare.

4. *Our victory.* It is no vain warfare this battle of ours; no idle battlefield. We go forth to *win*! Yes. Our eye is fixed on victory from the outset. We are assured of triumph from the moment we draw the sword. We are made more than conquerors. How often are these words sounded in our ears: *"To him who **overcomes**"* (Revelation 2:7, emphasis added). We aim at daily victory – we aim at final victory – such as that of Paul. Fight and conquer. Let us anticipate the warrior's song: *"O my soul, march on with strength."*

5. *Our recompense.* Everyone that wins has their rewards, but some victories are harder to win, and some are more or less complete. And there is a difference in the degree of reward. The seven rewards promised to the seven churches are *representative* rewards. They represent seven different kinds or degrees of glory set before the conqueror. Yet the least reward is unutterably excellent, worth all the struggle, sacrifice, and sorrow.

Brethren, let us fight! Let us aim at victory, at complete and perfect victory. Let us covet a high reward. Let us be ambitious for no common crown. Our great Captain speaks to us, *"Behold, I am coming quickly, and My reward is with Me"* (Revelation 22:12). We do not know how soon He may appear. And He comes with the crown of righteousness, the crown of glory in His hand for His own. If we suffer, we will also reign with Him.

Chapter 24

The Kiss of the Backslider

Orpah kissed her motherinlaw, but
Ruth clung to her. – Ruth 1:14

In this book we have the Gentile sheltering the Jew, and the Jew in return inviting the Gentile to partake of Israel's land and blessing. Moab receives Judah and feeds him in the day of famine (as the prophet later says, *"Let the outcasts of Moab stay with you"* (Isaiah 16:4)), and Judah bids Moab welcome to his better portion. Israel's famine first sent Israel to Egypt for food. Israel's persecution drove Israel's true Son – the Messiah, the Son of David – to seek protection in Egypt. So now we see Naomi leaving Bethlehem, passing over the rugged hills of Judah, crossing the Dead Sea, and settling in the land of Moab, until the calamity ended. Whether it was faith or unbelief that led her to flee from Bethlehem, we cannot say. It was faith that led her to return. It is as a believing woman that we now find her leaving her exile to seek her own land again, though at that time she did not know that the Messiah was to come from her line.

She sets out with her two daughtersinlaw, after a sojourn of ten years in Moab. They travel onward for a little way until they come to some particular spot – perhaps the shore of the Dead Sea, which they must cross. There Naomi tests them, and there the difference comes out between the two. It is this difference that we will now examine.

THE KISS OF THE BACKSLIDER

The difference is brought out in Orpah's kissing and Ruth's clinging. There was great resemblance up to a certain point. Both were Moabites, related by marriage, if not by birth; both were attached to Naomi up to a certain point; both were linked to Bethlehem by their marriage; and both were going out with Naomi to dwell in Judea. There were many points of likeness between the two. It will be profitable to notice these. There are many Orpahs among us, but few Ruths; many Balaams, many Demases, many who follow for a while, and then go back and no longer walk with the Lord.

1. *Orpah and her kissing.* There are many kinds of kissing spoken of in Scripture, some evil and some good. There is the murderer's kiss – that of Joab (2 Samuel 20:9), the harlot's kiss (Proverbs 7:13), the kiss of the enemy (Proverbs 27:6), the kiss of idol worship (Hosea 13:2), the flatterer's kiss (2 Samuel 15:5, Absalom), and the traitor's kiss (Luke 22:48). These, however, have nothing in common with Orpah and her kiss. Then there is the kiss of affection (Genesis 50:1, Joseph), the kiss of homage (1 Samuel 10:1, Samuel), the kiss of reconciliation (2 Samuel 14:33), the kiss of meeting (Luke 15:20, the Prodigal Son), and the kiss of parting (Acts 20:37). In some of these we find Orpah's kiss. It was the kiss of affection and the kiss of parting. So far it was good and not evil. But we must consider its meaning in the circumstances. Everything depends on that. It meant that:

    a. *She was not prepared to leave Moab.* The ties between her and it were still unbroken, though for a time they were loosened a little. Moab was still Moab to her – the home of her kindred, the center of her affections, the dwelling place of her gods. Thus, millions are not ready to leave the world, though often in some measure they are broken from it. They cling to their old haunts of vanity, foolishness, pleasure, lust, or literature. They cannot think of forsaking these. Indeed, they soothe their consciences with the argument that it would not be right to break off from all of these. To them the world is still the world: attractive and excellent. They cannot think of crucifying it, or themselves to it. They have been born in it, lived in it, and their friends are in it. Why should they leave it? Their hearts are still here, their treasure is here. They linger in it, though at times they feel the necessity of leaving it. What would life be to them without the novel or the ballroom, the theater, the merry assembly, the banquet, the revelry, the folly, the wine cup, or the song?

 b. *For the sake of Moab, she was willing to part with Naomi*. She was not without longings after Naomi and her city, her kindred, and her God. But her old longings and ties kept her back, and in the end they prevailed. Yet she wished to part in peace, to bid a decent farewell to her motherinlaw. She kissed so that she might *not* cling. Her kiss was a farewell. A farewell to Naomi, her land, and her God. Do we not have many Orpahs? They would gladly have both Israel and Moab. They would rather not part with either. Their heart is divided. They would gladly cast in their lot with God's people and obtain their inheritance. They are not scoffers, not openly godless, and not reckless pleasure seekers, but they are halfandhalf, or rather, not so much. They would be religious up to a certain point – to the point when a choice must be made – and then their heart speaks out. They give up Christ and turn back to the world. Yet they do so quietly, as it were, and kindly. They kiss at parting, but will that kiss help them? Will God accept the kiss as an excuse for turning back, or as a substitute for the wholehearted service that He desires? What does that kiss mean now? What will it stand for in the great day of the Lord? It is certainly not the kiss of Judas, but it is the kiss of the *cowardly and unbelieving* (Revelation 21:8).

2. *Ruth and her clinging.* Orpah kissed, but Ruth clung. Orpah kissed so that she might not cling. Ruth clings silently, and without show or demonstration. She does not linger nor halt. Moab is behind her, Israel is before her, and Naomi is at her side. Her choice is made. She does not falter, either in heart or in step. Before her are Judah's hills, behind her lies Bethlehem; she presses forward. Jehovah must be her God, and Jehovah's land her heritage. Nothing will come between. She forgets her kindred and her father's house. What are Moab's hills, cities, temples, or gods? Jehovah, God of

Israel, is now her God forever. Here is clinging; here is decision; here are faith and love; here is the undivided heart.

It is this that God still looks for. He will accept nothing else. Not half a heart nor half a life. Not Orpah's kiss, but Ruth's clinging. He wants *decision*. He abhors vacillation and compromise. If you prefer Moab, then go dwell there, enjoy its pleasures, and worship its gods. If you choose Israel, then pitch your tent there, and take Jehovah for your all. It is a mean and poor thing to divide yourself between the two. Be decided, brave, manly, and determined. *Do you not know that friendship with the world is hostility toward God?* (James 4:4). Do not love the world. Love the world to come. Love Him who is Lord and King of that coming world. *"Come out . . . and be separate, . . . and do not touch what is unclean"* (2 Corinthians 6:17).

Indecision will profit you nothing. Even in its gentlest and kindliest form, it is hateful to God. It will not satisfy you, it will not satisfy God. You cannot have a whole *world* and a whole *Christ*. Half of the world and half of Christ is equally an impossibility. Alliance with the world and alliance with Christ is out of the question. You cannot drink the cup of the Lord and the cup of devils. Beware of carnal fascinations and snares. Beware of pleasures and vanities. Do not meddle with worldly amusements. Suspect the things that the world is enamored with. Do not blind yourselves with creaturelove and creaturebeauty. Do not lull your conscience asleep with an outward religion, a fantastic, pictorial, and sensual worship. It is not religion but Christ that God points you to. Forsake everything for Him. Let Him be your all.

Look to Bethlehem, where Naomi and Ruth were headed to. Jesus was born there. Let your heart rest there. Look a little farther, to Jerusalem and Golgotha. He died there, the Just for the unjust. He finished His work. He shed the reconciling blood there. He gave full testimony to the free love of God there. Let your conscience get its purging and pacification there. Let your whole soul go forth and abide there, with Him who died and rose again, and who has promised, saying, *"I will come again and receive you to Myself"* (John 14:3).

Chapter 25

The Priestly Word of Peace

1 Samuel 1:12-18

Here we have an earthly high priest dealing with a child of sorrow. In his treatment of her we find both a contrast and a comparison with the heavenly High Priest. The contrast comes out strikingly. Eli shows, *first*, a lack of knowledge, for he speaks under a mistake – in ignorance of the person and the condition of her whom he addressed; *second*, a lack of mercy, for he charges her at once with drunkenness; *third*, a lack of patience and caution, for he does not wait to inquire; and *fourth*, a lack of tenderness, for he speaks harshly as well as rashly. How great the contrast in all these respects between the earthly and the heavenly High Priest. Contrast this scene with that of the woman of Sychar, or the woman taken in adultery. What a contrast between Eli and the Lord! How differently does Jesus deal with a sinner from the way in which Eli does! The way in which Eli acts makes it necessary for the woman to *defend herself*. The way in which Jesus acts creates no such necessity; for they to whom He speaks feel that their unworthiness is no barrier to His grace, and that the admission of their unworthiness does not alter that grace in the least. The words and acts of Jesus do not *set them upon selfdefense,* as did Eli's. How great the difference between this holy man of Israel and Him who is *the Holy One of Israel* (Isaiah 30:15).

But there is comparison or likeness as well as contrast. Eli, though imperfectly, does represent the better High Priest; even Him who can *be touched with the feeling of our infirmities* (Hebrews 4:15 KJV), who can have compassion on the ignorant, who is *a merciful and faithful high priest in things pertaining to God* (Hebrews 2:17), and who *always lives to make intercession for [us]* (Hebrews 7:25). This will come out as we consider (1) the application to the high priest, (2) the answer, (3) the confidence, and (4) the consolation.

1. *The application.* Hannah deals directly with Eli. She is in Jehovah's tabernacle; she has access to its altar; she speaks to the high priest face-toface. She makes two special requests: (1) *"Do not consider [me] as a worthless woman"* (verse 16) – do not treat me as a sinner, and (2) *"Let [me] find favor in your sight"* (verse 18). These are our two special petitions in our dealings with the better High Priest: Do not deal with me as a sinner, and let me find favor with You. Forgiveness and favor are what we need, and they are what we come to the High Priest for; for He is the High Priest of the good things to come. Let us deal with Him directly. Let us put our whole case into His hands. We make an appeal to Him as the Son of God, as the High Priest, the Godman who sits on the throne of grace. He waits for us, let us wait on Him. He is our Eli, our Aaron, our Melchizedek; all fullness is with Him. He sets open that fullness to us. Though sinners, let us remember we have to do with one who can manage the worst case and can undertake for the chief of sinners.

2. *The answer.* His answer is, *"Go in peace; and may the God of Israel grant your petition"* (verse 17). He speaks *peace* to her. She was sorely troubled and tempesttossed. She needed peace, and it is with peace that he begins. So is it with peace that *our* Eli begins. God has made peace, and He speaks to us the peace that He has made. *"Go in peace,"* He says to everyone who comes to Him, for *"the one who comes to Me I will certainly not cast out"* (John 6:37). This answer is sure to everyone who comes to Him. He does not stand on ceremony with His petitioners. He gives what is asked. He sends no one away empty. Let us believe that we have what we ask of Him. And then, as if speaking to us about the Father, He says, "May Jehovah hear you, and *fulfill all your petitions*" (Psalm 20:5). We do not hear His voice, but just as surely as Eli speaks to Hannah and grants her petition, so He speaks to us and does for us *exceeding abundantly*

above all that we ask (Ephesians 3:20 KJV). Everyone who goes to our High Priest is certain to receive an answer, a gracious one. He sends no one away unsatisfied. Peace and favor from the God of Israel, these are the things He gives. Hannah went to Eli uninvited, but we go invited. It is our heavenly Priest who says, *"Come to Me"* (John 7:37).

3. *The confidence.* Hannah went her way. She did not trouble, annoy, nor offend Eli with a second or a third solicitation. She took him at his word, like the nobleman who came to Jesus about his son. This is how we are to deal with our Eli. Take Him at His word. Trust Him. Do justice to His faithfulness and honesty. Let us not stand on ceremony, or approach in terror and doubt; but let us believe that He is the rewarder of everyone who seeks Him. Nor let us deceive ourselves and mock Him by saying, "I don't distrust Him, I only distrust myself." This is absurd. You are really distrusting Him and doing so on the ground that you are not fully complying with His conditions (as if He made any conditions!), whereas He bids you to trust Him just as you are. If your faith is not good enough, come with it as it is. If your way of coming is imperfect, add that to the number of your sins, and still trust. Let nothing in yourself produce distrust, so long as it is true that Jesus Christ came into the world to save sinners. *In You they trusted and were not disappointed* (Psalm 22:5) is a truth for us now.

4. *The consolation.* She not only went her way, but she also ate, and her countenance was not sad anymore (literally, no more what it was). Her sorrow had been deep. Now it passed away at the gracious voice of the high priest. Thus we learn what it is that relieves a distressed soul. It is the voice of the Great High Priest: *"Go in peace"* (Mark 5:34). We have a High Priest with whom to communicate in our troubles, a greater than Aaron or Eli. So we know, even more surely than Hannah when she heard Eli's voice, that His words to every soul that comes to Him are, *"Go in peace."* He is not meticulous, nor does He wait to scrutinize the quality or excellence of our manner of approach. The moment that He hears our words, *"God, be merciful to me"* (Luke 18:13), His answer comes down: *"Go in peace."* Let us *be sure of this.* Let us give credit to His promises, even though we do not actually see His face or hear His

voice. Our petition must be successful. He cannot deny Himself. He cannot dishonor His priesthood nor break His promises. We cannot be more certain that we have asked than that He answers. How long are we to wait before believing Him? How many signs are we to ask for before we are sure that He will do as He has said? Why will we persist in *doubts,* which all take for granted that He is not true to His word, and which disguise their wickedness under the name of humility, and under the pretense that if we do not know whether we have asked correctly, we cannot know whether He will answer until He has answered. Let us beware of the Pharisaism that is always asking for a sign before it will trust the Son of God.

Chapter 26

Human Anesthetics

1 Samuel 16:14-23

Of Saul we may say, *You were running well; who hindered you?* (Galatians 5:7). He began well but ended poorly. His first days and works were better than his last. So it was with Demas, the church of Ephesus, and the Jews, whose following Jehovah at first was misrepresented by their last apostasy. So it still is with souls, churches, nations, and ages.

1. *Saul's sin.* The root of everything was *sin*. This sin was simply disobedience to a command of God. He was told to kill Agag and his people. A cruel command, some would say, to which disobedience was better than obedience. But it was a *divine* command, whether the wisdom, justice, or mercy were visible or not. God had His reasons for it and that was enough. Saul's sin was not misrule, oppression, nor wickedness, but simply *disobedience* to a command that some might call arbitrary, if not harsh and stern. God stresses *obedience,* simple obedience, unreasoning obedience. His will must be done, for He is sovereign and He is the only wise God. Saul's sin was the preference of his own will and wisdom to God's. Let our consciences be sensitive to this, and let us beware of acting on our own reasons, our own ideas of fitness, or doing our own will. *"To obey is better than sacrifice"* (1 Samuel 15:22).

2. *The consequences.* The consequences are: (1) his crown is taken from him and he is rejected from being king; and (2) Samuel leaves him (1 Samuel 15:35). But the two special things mentioned here are these:

   a. *The Spirit of the Lord departed from Saul* (verse 14). I do not take up the question as to whether Saul was a true child of God. This passage does not determine the point. He might be so; and these words might be like Paul's: *Whom I have handed over to Satan, so that they will be taught not to blaspheme* (1 Timothy 1:20); and *I have decided to deliver such a one to Satan for the destruction of his flesh* (1 Corinthians 5:5). But certainly the Spirit that departed from Saul was good, not evil. It was the reversal of what is said: *God changed his heart* (1 Samuel 10:9). God gave him a heart for governing, which He now takes away. The good Spirit is grieved and departs. Saul's last act of disobedience has quenched Him. Saul is left without heavenly guidance.

   b. *An evil spirit from the Lord troubles him.* He is not left alone. For as one spirit departs, another enters.

      i. *He is troubled.* His soul is now the abode of darkness and fear. He becomes moody and sad. He is vexed, perplexed, and despondent. This is the fruit of sin!

      ii. *He is troubled by an evil spirit.* The clean spirit goes out, and the unclean spirit comes in – comes in to torment, sadden, and vex.

      iii. *He is troubled by an evil spirit from the Lord.* God lets Satan loose upon him. The unclean spirit returns with others more wicked than himself, and his last state is worse than his first. These words are very awful: *"So I will choose their punishments"* (Isaiah 66:4), and *God will send upon them a deluding influence* (2 Thessalonians 2:11).

   Thus is his chastisement double – negative and positive; a departure of the good and the arrival of the evil. And this affliction is Jehovah's doing. Not chance, disease, nor natural depression of spirits, but a visitation from God; judgment for disobedience, judicial punishment.

3. *Human contrivances.* Here is music, religious music – the music of the harp, the harp of David. This is soothing, but it does not reach the seat of the disease. It is something human, something external, something materialistic and earthly, something that man can originate and apply. It is effective to a certain extent. It drives away the evil spirit and restores temporary tranquility, thus possibly deceiving its victim. In like manner we find the human spirit afflicted in every age, sometimes more and sometimes less. And in all such cases man steps in with his human and external contrivances. I do not refer to the grosser form of dispelling gloom – drunkenness and immorality, in which men seek to drown their sense of need and make up for the absence of God. I refer to the *refined* contrivances – those of art, science, music, and merry-making, by which men try to minister to a diseased mind. What is Romanism and ritualism, but a repetition of Saul's minstrelsy? The soul needs soothing. It is vexed and fretted with the world, its conscience is not at ease, and it is troubled and weary. It takes itself to *forms,* something for the eye and ear; to chants, garments, postures, performances, sweet sounds and fair sights, sentimental and pictorial religion, which is but a refined form of worldliness. By these the natural man is soothed, the spirit tranquilized. The man is brought to believe that a cure has been worked, because his gloom has been alleviated by these religious spectacles, these exhibitions that suit the unregenerate soul so well. They but drug the soul, filling it with a sort of religious delirium. They are human sedatives, not divine medicines.

4. *The results.* A partial and temporary cure resulted. It is said that the evil spirit departed, but not that the good Spirit returned. Saul's trouble was alleviated, but not removed. The disease was still there. The results of David's harp were only superficial and negative. So it still is with the sinner. There are many outward applications that act like spiritual chloroform upon the soul. They soothe, calm, and please, but that is all. They do not reach below the surface, nor touch the deepseated malady within. Men try rites, sacraments, pictures, music, apparel, and the varied

attractions of ecclesiastical ornament, but these leave the spirit unfilled, and its wounds unhealed. They cannot regenerate, enliven, heal, or fill with the Holy Spirit. They may keep up the selfsatisfaction and selfdelusion of the soul, but that is all. They bring no true peace, nor give rest to the weary. They do not *fill*, they merely hide our emptiness.

Our age is full of such contrivances, literary and religious, all used for the purpose of soothing the troubled spirits of man. Excitement, merrymaking, balls, theaters, operas, concerts, ecclesiastical music, dresses, performances – what are all these but man's tools for casting out the evil spirit and healing the soul's hurt without having recourse to God's one remedy? These pleasant sights and sounds may "take the prisoned soul and lap it in Elysium," as John Milton said, but what of that? They do not bring it nearer to God; they do not work repentance, produce faith, or fix the eye on the true cross. They leave the soul still without God and without reconciliation. The religion thus produced is hollow, erratic, superficial, and sentimental. It will not save nor sanctify. It may produce a sort of religious inebriation, but not that which God calls godliness, and not that which the apostles pointed out as a holy life, a walk with God.

Chapter 27

Spiritual and Carnal Weapons

The men of Israel said, "Have you seen this man who is coming up? Surely he is coming up to defy Israel. And it will be that the king will enrich the man who kills him with great riches and will give him his daughter and make his father's house free in Israel." – 1 Samuel 17:25

Here are two men, and in these men are two nations, two religions, two bodies or companies – the seed of the woman, and the seed of the serpent. Israel and Philistia are now brought face-to-face. There must be war, not peace, not even an alliance, and not even a truce. The world's table is not spread for the church, nor the church's table spread for the world. The earth may sometimes help the woman and swallow up the floods that would overwhelm her, but friendship with the earth is not to be cultivated or sought after. *The friendship of the world is enmity with God.*

Here are two men – the one the personification of power, the other the personification of weakness; the one of selfreliance, the other of confidence in God. We see man, nothing but man, in the one; and God, nothing but God, in the other. In the Philistine we see man fighting *against* God; in David we see man fighting *for* God. What the world admires and prizes is to be found in the one, and what it despises in the other.

One thing marks them both: they are full of courage and confidence; both equally sure of success, though the one boasts, and the other does not boast. The sources and grounds of their confidence are very different, but their confidence itself seems very much alike.

The *object* of each is, in one respect, different; in another respect, the same. They meet for battle – each bent on the overthrow of the other. But Israel has not provoked nor challenged the conflict, nor is Israel desirous of seizing Philistia. She has Jerusalem. Why should she seek Gaza? But Philistia would gladly have Israel and her land in her power, and she makes continual inroads for this end. She is not content with Gaza and Ashkelon. She must have Jerusalem and Bethlehem.

But I do not ask you to especially notice the Gentile giant, but rather the Jewish boy, the youth of Bethlehem. In him we have:

1. *The rejection of human weapons.* He was fully aware of (1) the greatness of the issue depending on this combat, (2) the strength of the adversary, (3) his own weakness, and (4) the great things to which he had pledged himself. Yet he declines to avail himself of any of those things that would have helped to make up for his deficiency, and that would have made him, as man would say, adequate for the struggle. He takes only that which is expressive of feebleness – which would make him incur the accusation of being a fool, like the apostle in later years. He had to become weak as well as a fool, so that he might be both wise and strong. His taking *unlikely* and *unsuitable* human weapons was more expressive of his faith than if he had taken none; for through such, God got the opportunity of showing His power – His power, not as directly coming down from heaven, but as coming through the feeble instrumentality of a shepherd, and a shepherd's sling. It was God identifying Himself with David and using the sling as His own twoedged sword. Thus the true beginning of all strength is weakness. The starting point for success is the rejection of selfpower and human contrivances. How often is it true of individuals, churches, and societies, that they are too strong for God to work by or with; too well equipped, or too well organized; too rich, numerous, or great, for God to get glory from! He must have His work done by hands, regarding which there will be no mistake as to who the doer of the whole work is, and the author of all the success. David did not reject these weapons because they were *sinful*. He often used the sword, spear, and shield in fighting the battles of the Lord. He had built a tower for an armory, wherein there hung a thousand shields,

all shields of mighty men. But, in certain cases, that which is lawful is not expedient. Lawful instruments sometimes become, if not unlawful, at least inexpedient and useless, when they give God no room to make bare His arm. We are, generally speaking, far too solicitous about our strength, and we forget that it is always by weakness that God works. We are too solicitous about intellect, learning, numbers, and money, as if we could have no hope of success without these. No one is too weak to work the work of God; many are too strong. We are slow to believe this, slow to act on it. Yet it is one of the great truths on which God has set His seal during the ages past.

2. *The adoption of divine weapons.* David leaves the human weapons to the Philistine; he prefers the divine. The sight of human weapons in his adversary had not made him afraid to do battle with him, nor made him say, "Oh, I want a sword like his!" And as he drew nearer, and saw his whole strength and array, his confidence did not sink, it rose. He sees in the giant an enemy of the living God, and his weapons as, therefore, directed against *Him*. That sword, that spear, that shield are used against Jehovah, God of Israel. David is not dismayed, but goes forward triumphantly, assured of being more than conqueror. He has a weapon – only one – framed by no human hand, brought out of no earthly armory. It is called *the name of the Lord of hosts* (1 Samuel 17:45). With this he can face not only Goliath and the Philistine armies, but also Satan and the hosts of hell. This *name* is still our weapon. It is sword, shield, and spear. Armed with it we can do any work, fight any battle, engage any foe. Only let us be sure that we are on God's side, and that our enemy is against Him; then we can go forward with confidence. *If God is for us, who is against us?* (Romans 8:31) is one side of the maxim. "If we are for God, who can be against us?" is the other. In using this name as a weapon, or as a plea, I come as if God and I were one; as if God, and not I, were on the battlefield. We stand in God's stead, and He in ours. We fight in God's stead, and He in ours. It is not so much that we work, as that He works. Using His name is simply confiding in His revealed character and sure word, and in nothing of ourselves – making use of no arm of flesh, no power of man's arm or man's intellect, but Jehovah's alone, the Lord God of Israel. Have faith in God! Not in man, the flesh, in genius, in science, in numbers, in rank, in influential names, nor in great schemes, but in the living God – David's God and ours.

Chapter 28

Divine Silence and Human Despair

When Saul inquired of the Lord, the Lord did not answer him, either by dreams or by Urim or by prophets. Then Saul said to his servants, "Seek for me a woman who is a medium, that I may go to her and inquire of her." And his servants said to him, "Behold, there is a woman who is a medium at Endor." – 1 Samuel 28:6-7

The scene of this sad, strange narrative is the valley of Jezreel, a place of battlefields. The Philistines are in the north, at Shunem. Israel is in the south, at Gilboa. It is a critical hour for Saul and for his people. The enemy is strong, Samuel is dead, Saul's conscience is not at ease, and he has provoked the Lord. How should he face the enemy? *He was afraid and his heart trembled greatly* (1 Samuel 28:5). He does not know what to do. He does, however, the right thing so far: He consults God. But this inquiry is in vain. *The Lord did not answer him, either by dreams or by Urim or by prophets.* Then in his despair he goes to the woman with the familiar spirit.

Thus heaven, earth, and hell are brought before us. A little part of the veil is drawn aside, and we learn something of the workings of the invisible as well as of the visible. We notice: (1) God's silence, and (2) Saul's despair.

1. *God's silence.* Saul in his terror cries, but there is no answer of any kind. No dream of the night reveals the secrets of the future; no prophet

comes instead of Samuel; no voice comes from the high priest. Everything is silent; silent just when utterance was most desired and needed. Saul knocks at the gate of heaven, but it is barred against him. There is no response. That silence, how dreadful! The roar of thunder, the crash of the earthquake, the rush of the hurricane would have been a relief – though terrible in themselves. But that *silence,* it is absolutely intolerable. It is the silence of heaven. The silence of Him whose voice was so anxiously expected. We read of the silence of the desert, the silence of midnight, the silence of the churchyard and the grave, but this is something more profound and appalling: the silence of God when appealed to by a sinner at his breaking point. There must be a meaning in that silence. It is not the silence of indifference, the inability to hear, nor weakness, nor perplexity. He is alive to the case; He can hear; He is able to deliver; He knows what would suit the case. Yet He is silent. It must then be the silence of refusal, rejection, displeasure, and abandonment. Terrible silence! Anything would be better than this.

Such is the position in which God represents the sinner at certain times: *"Then they will call on me, but I will not answer"* (Proverbs 1:28); *"I will not be inquired of by you"* (Ezekiel 20:31). The foolish virgins going for oil too late; the knocking for admittance too late; the crying, *"Lord, Lord,"* too late; the calling to the rocks and hills in the great day. The only answer is silence! Oh, terrible silence for the sinner! He did not call when he would have been heard, and now it is too late! God called on him during his lifetime, but he would not hear. Now he calls, but God keeps silence. Yet even this awful silence will be broken. God will speak. He will speak from the throne. *"Depart from Me, accursed ones"* (Matthew 25:41) will be the breaking of the silence, and the answer to the rebel's cries!

2. *Saul's despair.* Danger presses; the Philistines are mustering; the crisis has come. Yet there is no answer. What will he do? There were three courses open to him: (1) He might sit down in quiet hopelessness and let the evil come. (2) He might, in faith and repentant submission, commit the whole matter to God, even amid this awful silence. (3) He might go to hell for counsel since heaven was deaf. He chooses the last! In his despair he goes to the enemy of that God who was refusing to answer; he turns to the psychics whom he himself had put away; he

turns from the living to the dead; he consults with hell. It must have been a dreadful day of suspense for Saul; a dreadful night, when having formed the fatal purpose, he sets out across the hill to Endor. We do not know what his thoughts and feelings were in that awful hour. They must have been of the wildest and gloomiest kind. "God has cast me off, I will go to Satan; heaven's door is shut, I will see if hell's is open." And when crossing the hill, and approaching the village of the enchantress, he must have felt, "Now I am going on an errand to Satan. I am going to try to see if he can do for me what God will not." Oh, terrible journey! He is determined to get a glimpse of the future, though his prophet is the evil one himself. The past is dark; the present is gloomy; what is the future to be? God will not tell him. Will Satan? Thus he rushes on in despair. He, the king of Israel, the friend of Samuel, the conqueror of Israel's enemies; the forty years' monarch and warrior, who has never trembled before an enemy; he, the tall, stately Benjamite. Thus, in melancholy madness, he moves in that dark midnight, over the heights that overlooked his own camp and that of his foes. What a picture! Nothing in Milton is half so grand or sad – hardly anything out of hell is half so terrible – as this man of war, and might, and commanding stature, striding on over these hills to the gate of the pit. His despair had blinded him. He had not learned to say with one who was a greater sufferer than himself, *"Though He slay me, I will hope in Him"* (Job 13:15). He despaired because God was silent. Yet the silence was meant to lead him to repentance and acknowledgment of sin. It was God's last appeal to his conscience. Let us learn:

1. *The perils of backsliding.* Here is one who once seemed likely, whom God favored and honored, the friend of Samuel, turning his back on God.

2. *The terribleness of the silence of God.* It means something dreadful: *It is a terrifying thing to fall into the hands of the living God* (Hebrews 10:31); to cry and get no answer; to find no light!

3. *The evils of despair.* No sinner here should despair. His case may be sad, God's silence long and deep, his sins many; yet on no account should he turn his back on God, but rather let him fling himself into His arms. This would be blessed despair.

Chapter 29

Jewish Unbelief and Gentile Blessing

Thus the ark of the Lord remained in the house of Obededom the Gittite three months, and the Lord blessed Obededom and all his household. – 2 Samuel 6:11

It was into the house of a Gentile that the ark was brought – a Philistine, a dweller in Gath, a Gittite; but one who knew the Lord God of Israel.

It was the sin of an Israelite that led to its being brought here. Uzzah offended and was slain. He was afraid to trust the ark to take care of itself. He laid distrustful hands upon it when the oxen stumbled. Perhaps this was not his first offense of this kind. He seems to have been *brazen*, and perhaps proud – proud of his office.

It was David's unbelief that brought it about. He did not rightly interpret God's dealing and was afraid. He was afraid of God because He was holy and ready to vindicate His holiness. He began the work, but broke it off in the midst, through fear – unbelieving fear.

He dreads danger to himself, but strangely, he does not so for Obededom. He was willing that Obededom should run the risk that he would not run. What a strange conflict of feelings in which this was done! There is more unbelief and less faith in David than we should have expected. He thrusts the ark into Obededom's house, so that whatever ill might happen, might fall on him. It was not with love to Obededom, nor with a purpose of honoring him, nor with the wish to confer blessing on him. None of these motives seem to have influenced David except blind fear – a wish to keep himself out of danger. He does not seem to have cared about this Gentile. It would seem as if he were saying, "If there is danger, let it fall on a Gentile." He does not seem to have meant it for good to him, yet good came.

The ark of the God of Israel came to Obededom. It knocked at his door seeking shelter, seeking a home. He received it gladly. He was not forgetful to receive this stranger; and truly he received an angel unawares. He seems to have been a man of faith, one who knew the God of Israel – who knew Him even better than Israel's king did! When David, in terror, would have nothing more to do with the ark, Obededom opened his door and bid the God of Israel welcome. Truly it might be said, *"Truly I say to you, I have not found such great faith with anyone in Israel"* (Matthew 8:10).

In this unexpected way, blessing entered this Gentile house; indeed, God Himself entered, and with Him all blessing. It was but a transient stay of the ark, a three months' sojourn; but God Himself had taken up His abode, and He would not depart. No doubt all kinds of blessing came in, worldly and spiritual, and these did not leave. What a gainer Obededom became by David's failure! Through David's fall, salvation came to this Gentile! God was not unrighteous to forget his work of faith. Truly he had his reward. It was a high one. David was a loser, but Obededom was a gainer. Jerusalem was a loser, but Gibeah was a gainer! Thus, wonderful are the ways and works of God! Now turn to the lessons.

1. *How God punishes irreverence.* It was irreverence in Uzzah to put forth his hand. God had provided for the carrying of the ark by the Levites. He will not allow this to be encroached upon. He will not permit men to do evil that good may come of it, or to be judges of what is right, when He Himself has spoken. Beware of irreverence in the things of God; irreverence in church; in touching holy vessels; irreverence as to the name, book, or day of God. Woe to the irreverent! They are Uzzahs, and will know it at length, though they be long spared.

2. *How God's people misinterpret His dealings.* David did so. He shrunk from the ark, he dreaded it; he shrunk from God, he

dreaded Him. He went back to Jerusalem without the ark that he had specifically gone to get, misconstruing this judgment upon Uzzah and his irreverence. God in striking Uzzah did not mean to repel or terrify David. He merely wished to warn – to check undue familiarity. David in haste and unbelief supposed it to mean that God was frowning upon him, that God was a hard Master – eager to take advantage of every slip or stumble. Thus, David wronged Jehovah.

3. *How much they lose by this misinterpretation.* Professing to shun Uzzah's presumption, they fall into David's unbelief; and like David, they lose the honor and the blessing that might have been theirs. Such is the way in which hundreds lose the blessings of the gospel. They misinterpret God and His dealings. They flee from Him, they doubt Him, they suspect Him. So, peace is lost, fellowship is lost, and God Himself is kept out of the soul.

4. *How much they gain who receive God simply.* While David was the loser, Obededom was the gainer. He was not afraid of God. The ark came knocking at his door asking admittance, and he gladly received it. And God came in with the ark, and with God, all blessing. Everything prospered in his house now that God had come in. See how God can overrule the unbelief and failures of His people.

   a. *Beware of flying from God or shutting out God.* He comes to you and knocks, whether you are a Jew or a Gentile. Do not be alarmed. He is a friend, not an enemy.

   b. *Let God in.* Both into your heart and into your home. Let God dwell in you and in your house. Bid Him welcome. Do not forget to entertain Him. He comes in love. Fury is not in Him. He is seeking entrance for Himself, and shelter for His ark among the sons of men. Don't let Him pass by your door. Go out to meet Him and bid Him welcome. He will bless you.

Chapter 30

The Restoration of the Banished

"For we will surely die and are like water spilled on the ground which cannot be gathered up again. Yet God does not take away life, but plans ways so that the banished one will not be cast out from him." – 2 Samuel 14:14

Such is "the wise woman's" argument, or rather Joab's, addressed to King David, in order to persuade him to be reconciled to Absalom. God does not deal with us as you deal with your son, though we have deserved His anger. He punishes, yet He devises means for the canceling of the punishment and the restoration of His exiles. He is just, yet He is the Savior. Remember the woman's statement.

1. *We must die.* This is the law, the inevitable, inexorable law, not of nature or fate, but of God. *"To dust you shall return"* (Genesis 3:19), and *it is appointed for men to die once* (Hebrews 9:27). This is no probability, but a certainty, a necessity; greater than that the sun will rise and set tomorrow. "He died," is the conclusion of each man's history. Our world's story is one of death. It might be Methuselah's nine hundred years or David's seventy years, but it is death at last. Even when the Son of God took our nature, He had to die. No one has escaped this, except two; no one will, except those who are

alive when Christ comes. You may have health, friends, riches, and honors, but you must die. When, where, and how, you do not know.

2. *We are as water spilled on the ground, which cannot be gathered up again.* Man lies down and does not rise. He is not like some building, which when ruined may be reerected; nor like fallen fruit, which may be gathered up; but he is like water, which mingles with the soil and cannot be picked up. He mixes with the earth, and cannot raise himself, nor be raised by his fellow man. He passes away and does not return. Look at the churchyard; there is the water spilled on the ground. Look at earth's battlefield; there is the water spilled. Look at the depths of the ocean, which have swallowed up tens of thousands; there is the water spilled. Not one drop has yet been gathered up of all that has been spilled since the world began, except *one* drop, one precious drop – even Him who saw no corruption. No grave has given up its dust. Each slumbering atom lies till the great morning. We may walk among them and weep over them, and raise monuments with names and epitaphs, but we cannot gather them up. There they remain until He comes, who is the resurrection and the life, to put forth His hand and take up each forgotten particle.

3. *God does not respect persons.* In His sight everyone is alike, as sinners, as creatures, as sons of Adam, as dying men – young or old, low or high. He cannot be bribed to spare any. He accepts no man's person. The sickbed and the deathbed are spread for everyone. The tomb opens for everyone. It may be simple turf or some rich marble monument, but it is still a tomb, a receptacle for human bones and dust. No ornaments can make it otherwise. *"You must die"* is the recorded sentence, and God makes no exceptions.

4. *He devises means for the restoration of His banished ones.* He is righteous and will not alleviate sin, nor repeal His sentence. Yet He does not leave us without hope. Note here:

    a. *His banished ones.* We are God's banished ones, no longer in our Father's house or the king's palace, no longer cast out like Adam from Paradise, Cain from God's presence, Absalom from Jerusalem, or Israel from Canaan. Sin has done it all. The brand of exile is upon us. It is God Himself who has banished us. Elsewhere we are described as prodigals leaving our Father's house, here as criminals banished from His presence. O man, you are an exile! Perhaps you do not feel your loneliness, and you have become familiarized with the place of exile; nevertheless, you are a banished man, banished from Him who made you and in whose favor is life.

b. *God's love to the banished.* He has expressed His displeasure against their rebellion by banishing them, yet He has not forgotten them. He pities them, yearns over them, and calls them back. Distance has not erased their names from His paternal heart. No one else may pity them, but He does. The Father sees His prodigals in the faroff country. Their misery, loneliness of heart, and weariness call forth His pity. He stretches out His hands, and the words of His lips are, *"Come unto me; return, return."*

c. *God's design to restore them.* He has a purpose of grace. The good pleasure of His goodness shows itself in a gracious design, a plan of mingled sovereignty and goodwill, righteousness and grace. He has resolved that they will not remain far away. His purpose will stand.

d. *His means for this.* These are not stated here, but the Bible is the revelation of these. He does not spare His Son, but sends Him in quest of the exiles. He comes into the land of banishment, lies in an exile's cradle, becomes a banished man for them, lives a banished life, endures an exile's shame, dies an exile's death, and is buried in an exile's tomb. He takes our place of banishment so that we may take His place of honor and glory in the home of His Father and our Father. Such is the exchange between the exile and the exile's divine substitute. Though rich, for our sakes He becomes poor. Though at home, He comes into banishment, so that we may not be expelled forever. And here, in connection with our restoration through a substitute, there are three questions.

i. *Will the Father accept a substitute?* Yes, He will. Indeed, He has. His purpose of grace has been carried out by His providing the Substitute. He has sent His Son! He has sent Solomon to seek Absalom, to bear Absalom's penalty. He has not spared His Son so that He may spare us.

ii. *Is the Son willing to become a substitute?* Will Solomon leave Jerusalem and David's palace, and take the place of the banished Absalom? He will. Indeed, He has done it. He has come down in pursuit of us. He has borne our sins.

iii. *Are you willing to take this Substitute?* He has come. He offers the exchange. Give Me your guilt and take My righteousness. You rebellious son, you banished Absalom, you hater of your heavenly Father and conspirator against His government, will you not return? Your Father's heart yearns over you. He longs to have you back. Return, return! If not, He weeps over you as over Jerusalem; and when you die, He cries out, *"O Absalom, my son, my son!"* (2 Samuel 18:33).

Chapter 31

The Farewell Gift

When they had crossed over, Elijah said to Elisha, "Ask what I shall do for you before I am taken from you." And Elisha said, "Please, let a double portion of your spirit be upon me." He said, "You have asked a hard thing. Nevertheless, if you see me when I am taken from you, it shall be so for you; but if not, it shall not be so." As they were going along and talking, behold, there appeared a chariot of fire and horses of fire which separated the two of them. And Elijah went up by a whirlwind to heaven. – 2 Kings 2:9-11

This is the parting of two friends: the master and the servant, Elijah and Elisha. They journey together, they cross Jordan together, they come up to the gate of heaven together. They must separate; the one to go up to heaven, the other to remain a little longer on earth. They part, not in anger like Paul and Barnabas, but like David and Jonathan – in love. Elijah speaks first, and his love for his faithful companion shows itself in the words, *"Ask what I shall do for you before I am taken from you."* All that he possesses, all that is in his power, he will give.

But Elisha's request goes beyond what Elijah had expected or what he could grant. *"You have asked a hard thing,* a thing beyond my power to give; a thing which only God can give. I must refer you to Him, but I am permitted to give you this sign: *If you see me when I am taken from you.* That is the token that God grants your request; if not, then the request cannot be granted."

The sign was given. Elisha saw his master ascend. Indeed, he was allowed to obtain the mantle of his master, in token of his receiving his spirit. And acknowledging this sign, he tears his own clothes into two parts, as if putting his former self aside and putting on Elijah.

But the request of Elisha is a striking one. It was not what Elijah expected or could grant, but it was in sympathy with his own feelings, and he therefore referred it to God. It was for the Spirit – that Spirit that rested on and dwelt in Elijah – no, a double portion of that Spirit. He admired and loved his master, and his desire was to be like him; no, to get beyond him, to rise higher, to do and say greater things than Elijah said or did.

In this narrative we find in Elisha the indication of such things as the following:

1. *Spiritual sympathy.* He is of one mind and spirit with his master. He has been a witness of his life and doings. He sees the spirit that has pervaded all his words and deeds; not merely the spirit of power and miracles, but also of holiness, zeal, prayerfulness, and boldness. Sympathizing with all these, he longs to have the same mind, to be filled with the same spirit. How well for us if our sympathies were thus with the men in whom the Spirit of God dwells or has dwelled in ages past! Our sympathies should not be with this world, nor with the spirit of the world, but with the world to come, and with the spirit of it. Not with the men of the world's genius, science, or learning; not with earth's poets or philosophers; but with prophets and apostles. Whatever there is of truth and beauty in Homer, Plato, Demosthenes, Shakespeare, Bacon, Milton, Wordsworth, or Tennyson, let us accept, but let our spiritual sympathies ascend far higher. Let us realize our true oneness with Enoch, Elijah, Elisha, Isaiah, and Ezekiel; our fellowship with that Holy Spirit who dwelled in them. The sympathies of this age are confessedly not with prophets and apostles. These are looked on as fragments of obsolete antiquity and oldfashioned narrow-mindedness. Let us, however, go back to these ancient times and men, not concerned with being "abreast of the age" if we be "abreast of the Spirit."

2. *Holy imitativeness.* His desire is to be *like* Elijah. He wishes not merely to have *the* Spirit, but also *your spirit,* the spirit that dwelled in Elijah. He desired to be like him in the divine features of his character; like him in the possession of the Spirit, and in that special form in which he possessed it. That was what he sought. There is certainly only one great model, but there are subordinate ones also. Paul said, *Be imitators of me* (1 Corinthians 4:16); and Hebrews 11 is a collection of models and a book of patterns, in each of which we may find something to copy. While copying Christ, then, let us not overlook the inferior models, either among the inspired men of Bible days, or the uninspired honorable ones of later times. May the spirit of Elijah, Paul, and John rest on us; the spirit also of Wycliffe, Huss, Luther, Calvin, Knox, Welsh, Rutherford, Whitefield, M'Cheyne, and Hewitson.

3. *Divine ambition.* Elisha was not only full of admiration for his master, he not only wished to be like him, but he also desired to go far beyond him. He asked for a *double portion* of his spirit. This is true ambition. This is coveting earnestly the best gifts of which Paul speaks, and in connection with which he points out the more excellent way of love, in which especially Elisha seems to have risen higher than his master, with Elisha's ministry being more one of love than Elijah's. In such things as these let us be ambitious. There is no fear of aiming too high or seeking too much. Let us not give way to the false humility that says, "Oh that we had one hundredth of what Elijah had!" Let us rather at once, with Elisha, seek to have far more. Let us seek a double portion of his spirit. This is true humility. It is desiring to be what God wishes us to be. It is honoring His fullness and His generosity. It is acknowledging the extent of blessing in reserve; reckoning on it as quite limitless, and therefore not confining ourselves to what others have had before us, but going up into the divine fullness for far more than has ever yet been obtained even by the fullest.

4. *Quiet expectation.* He speaks and acts like one who fully expected to get what he asked for. Elijah had referred him to God for the *hard thing* he had asked for. It was in God's hand alone. "It is not mine to give" (as if anticipating the Lord's words (Matthew 20:23)). Elisha owns

the divine sovereignty and is calm, but he realizes the divine love and expects. He believes, and therefore does not make haste, but goes quietly on beside his master to see the end. He believes, and therefore he assures himself that God is not likely to be less gracious than his master, nor to deny him what Elijah would gladly give if he could. Let us *believe!* Have faith in God. Trust Him for much, for He *is able to do [for us] far more abundantly beyond all that we ask or think* (Ephesians 3:20).

5. *Conscious possession.* He accepts the sign: he sees the prophet caught up. He seizes his mantle, and returns by the way he came, conscious of having received the *double portion*. He believes, and therefore he speaks and acts. The sign promised has been given. Can he doubt that the thing promised is also given? He may have nothing new in *feeling* to corroborate it, but that does not matter. He has it in simple faith in the bare word of the true God. The *double portion* is mine, he says to himself; and he goes back to exercise his prophetic calling, in the calm consciousness of possessing more than his master did. What is Jordan to him now? A stroke of the mantle divides it, and henceforth his life is to be one of mighty and gracious miracles. Let us speak and act as men who believe that God fulfills His word to us. Let us *trust* that word when we use it. There is more in it than in Elijah's mantle. It is living and divine. Let us not blunt or deaden it by our lack of confidence in its power.

Chapter 32

God's Dealing with Sin and the Sinner

Er, Judah's firstborn, was wicked in the sight of the Lord, so He put him to death. – 1 Chronicles 2:3

Here we have, in one brief sentence, a statement of the way in which God deals with sin and the sinner. It is the repetition of a verse in Genesis, in a very unlikely place – in the midst of names and genealogies. So, God is letting us know the importance He gives it. It is not for nothing that He repeats it. Such clauses as this, flung in apparently by chance, or by what is called the transcriber's taste, are full of meaning. *This* certainly contains a very distinct and awful utterance.

Looking at it generally, we may say that it brings out, in a very outstanding and unambiguous form, things such as these:

1. *God's estimate of sin.* It differs widely from man's estimate. It is the *Judge's* estimate, not the physician's merely, nor the father's. It is one of condemnation. It is not simply disease, or misfortune, or an accidental deviation from the straight line, but it is *guilt,* which must be reckoned with according to relentless law. Sin, in the divine judgment, is not something vague, loose, and shadowy, but is welldefined and substantial. It is not a thing of sentiment or feeling, but a thing to be determined by the sharp test of unchanging law – law interpreted by an inflexible tribunal,

and applied by an infinitely righteous Judge, without respect of persons; without fear, favor, or partiality; without the remotest risk of mistake, or the possibility of miscarriage of justice.

2. *God's treatment of sin.* He does not merely pronounce a sentence or verdict without intending to carry it out. His deeds correspond with His words. He hates sin. He tells us this. He treats it accordingly. His treatment of it is:

   a. *Prompt.* Though He does bear with the sinner, yet this *patience* is not at variance with the *promptness*. He is both patient and prompt, yet He is not hasty. It does not take Him unawares, nor show Him as if at a loss in how to deal with it. He is always ready to meet it and deal with it, whether in the open or in secret, greater or less.

   b. *Decided.* He does not trifle with it, as if undecided in how to proceed, or hesitating as to what sentence to pronounce. There may be, for wise and gracious reasons, some delay, but the delay does not arise from any lack of decision, changeableness, or instability. He is altogether decided in words and ways. *"He is unique and who can turn Him?"* (Job 23:13).

   c. *Severe. The Lord took his life* (Genesis 38:7); that is, He struck him down, and cut him off by a violent death. He did not die the death of men, but perished like Korah. God made a fearful example of him before the eyes of his brethren, though what it was we do not know. When God arises to strike, He is infinitely terrible in His vengeance. He is in earnest, and He punishes in earnest even when His wrath is kindled just a little.

   d. *Watchful.* His eye is on the wicked, *His eyelids test the sons of men* (Psalm 11:4). Nothing escapes Him. No sin, however small, is overlooked. Though fury is not in Him, yet He is watchful. His eyes are as a flame of fire.

But it is not merely *sin* that God would have us consider here. It is also *the sinner* especially. For this noninformation as to *the sin* (we are not told what the sin was) seems to be for the purpose of making prominent *the sinner.* And then the silence as to the personal history of the sinner fixes our eye on the other circumstances thus brought out in relief.

He is a firstborn son. To him would belong unique honor, and in him would center unique expectation. Yet he is slain – slain by God. How often do we find the natural order broken in upon, and human hope frustrated! It was so in Cain. It was so in Esau. *Sin* breaks up all order and disappoints all hope. Were it not for sin, the river of human order (family and social) would flow on undisturbed.

He is the firstborn of Judah. "*Judah, your brothers shall praise you*" (Genesis 49:8). Judah, in God's purpose, is already the royal tribe; and this sinner, slain by God for his wickedness, is the first of the royal line, the first link in Messiah's royal chain. As Esau and Reuben had been set aside because of their sin, so is Er. Sin breaks the line, and the blow that severs it is dealt by God Himself. *But Er, Judah's firstborn, was evil in the sight of the Lord, so the Lord took his life.* And if anyone says, "*Why does He still find fault? For who resists His will?*" (Romans 9:19), our answer is, "*On the contrary, who are you, O man, who answers back to God?*" (Romans 9:20).

Yes, God is not afraid to break Messiah's line. He can rectify the breakage in His own way, but rather than that sin should go unpunished, He does not hesitate to break that line; to set aside Judah's firstborn. So infinitely does God hate sin!

But there is something yet more remarkable. The broken link was to be refastened by the permission of sin as great as that which had broken it: the triple sin, first of Onan, then of Judah, then of Tamar! How mysterious! *How unsearchable are His judgments and unfathomable His ways!* (Romans 11:33). What a strange fragment of human history is this breaking and this mending of Messiah's royal line! *Oh, the depth of the riches both of the wisdom and knowledge of God!* See how He hates sin, how He strikes the sinner, and how He does not spare even the firstborn of Messiah's tribe! Yet see how His purpose stands! And see how He can make use of sin for remedying the breaches that sin makes! What a God is ours! So righteous, so wise, so powerful, so loving and gracious!

But how terrible the lesson regarding sin! God cannot pass it by. On whomsoever it is found, it must be punished. Even when God's purpose is to remedy it, it must be punished; punished before it can be remedied, lest men should make light of it, or think that God is trifling with it.

Yes, and when sin is at last found (though but by attribution) upon His wellbeloved Son, it must be punished. He must die. Yet He dies only to live, and He lives that we may live also. Judah's royal Son, David's Lord, is our Redeemer from sin.

Jesus, the true firstborn of Judah, He whom His brethren will praise, was *made . . . to be sin on our behalf* (2 Corinthians 5:21); though not *wicked in the sight of the Lord,* but good – His beloved Son, *"in whom [He is] well-pleased"* (Matthew 3:17). He was treated as evil and slain by the Lord; was made *a curse for us* (Galatians 3:13), though He was the blessed One, for *it pleased the* LORD *to bruise him; [and to] put him to grief* (Isaiah 53:10 KJV). Thus, He takes our evil as if it were His own, and we get His good as if it were our own. God dealt with Him on our account as if He were evil, not good. God deals with us on account of Him as if we were good and not evil. God killed Him, that He might not kill us. God condemned Him, that He might pardon us. We listen to God's testimony concerning Him, and, in listening, we drink in the everlasting life.

Not only *life,* but also *glory;* royal glory. For in receiving that testimony we are grafted into Judah's royal line. We become part of the *church of the firstborn* (Hebrews 12:23). We inherit a kingdom. Ours is David's palace, David's city, and David's heritage. Ours is the better Canaan; the new Jerusalem; the throne and crown of the Son of God. We are joint heirs with Him in His royal glory; sharers in His holy reign.

Chapter 33

God Finding a Resting Place

1 Chronicles 21:1-30

There is something very peculiar about this fragment or episode of Israel's history. It is abrupt, and in a way, isolated, though not completely. It also has some very remarkable points about it. It is the introduction to the history of the temple. It shows the way in which David was led to Moriah as the temple site, and to Ornan's threshing floor as the place for the altar of burnt offering. It was through David's sin and punishment that God pointed out the *rest* that He had chosen, and the spot where He had purposed to place His name (2 Chronicles 3:1). Thus, God overrules human sin; indeed, He takes occasion from it to display His grace. It was their king's sin that was the link between Israel and Moriah, between Israel and the temple, between Israel and the place of burnt offering. This is strange, but suitable and striking. It is sin that is, in one sense, the link, or at least the point, of contact between us and Jesus.

There is this peculiarity also about the spot: it was the place of division between death and life, between condemnation and pardon, between pestilence and health. Everything up to this point was judgment, but here the sword stopped. This hill, this threshing floor, stood between the living and the dead. Such is really the character of the temple and the altar. Here life begins and death ends. Everything up to this is death and vengeance; that temple was the shield of the world.

There is also this peculiarity. The spot where the plague stopped was Gentile, not Jewish ground. It was the property of a Jebusite – the last heir of the Jebusite kings (2 Samuel 24:23, Araunah) perhaps of Melchizedek; so that thus Moriah passes from Melchizedek to David. It was on Jebusite or Gentile ground that the angel of judgment sheathed his sword, and Israel's temple was erected. How much of that temple was Gentile, not Jewish? The ground, the cedars, the gold, the silver, the bronze (1 Chronicles 18:7, 11), and the workers were Gentile; everything except the stones, which were Jewish. Israel was thus to learn that the Gentile had an interest in these courts. The Gentile could say, "That rock is mine, that gold is mine, that cedar wood is mine, that workmanship is mine." Yes, in that temple all nations met with one another, and met with God. "One in Christ" was the teaching of the temple, as well as of the cross.

Let us notice further that it was in connection with the *numbering* of Israel that the temple site came to be fixed. God's special promise to Abraham was that his seed should be as the sand of the sea and the stars of heaven. Now, when this promise is abused and made a minister of pride, the judgment comes because of it. Yet, out of the judgment comes the Voice that says, *"This is My resting place"* (Psalm 132:14). The point of the destroying sword (not a voice from glory) marks the temple; its flash reveals the longappointed spot. That temple was to be a seal and pledge of Israel's numbers without number – *the fountain of Israel* (Psalm 68:26).

Let us notice further still that it was in connection with the common occupations of life that this revelation of the temple site was made. Ornan and his sons were threshing wheat at the time when the angel came, and his sword stayed at the threshing floor. They had no share in David's sin and Israel's punishment, and they were not alarmed at the pestilence. They were not clad in sackcloth, like David and the elders. They were not on their knees, but were engaged in the common duties of the day. God finds them at the threshing floor and does not blame them. Indeed, He honors them and their employment. He honors that piece of ground where they were working by turning it from a threshing floor into an altar. Let no one be ashamed of his honest trade or think that God will not meet with him in the midst of it. Ornan's threshing was not a lowly thing in the eyes of God.

Let us notice again that this ground was bought at its price by David for Israel. There are only two spots that have passed by purchase into

Jewish hands: Machpelah and Moriah – the one for a burial place, the other for a temple; the one bought by Abraham, the other by David. Of all the rest of the land Israel took possession, as God's gift, without money and without price. Strange that, for a spot on which to fix the symbols of resurrection and reconciliation, Israel (in the persons of Abraham and David) must pay the full price! It was as if to remind them that, in both cases, it was by ransom that the blessing was reached: *"A ransom for many"* (Matthew 20:28; Mark 10:45); *I [will] ransom them from the power of Sheol* (Hosea 13:14).

One thing more we notice: this fixing of the temple site had nothing to do with the tabernacle, the ark, the priesthood, or the Urim and Thummim. There was a break between them. The ark was on Zion, and the tabernacle (at this time) was at Gibeon, and it was not to the high priest that God made this new revelation, but to David, Gad, and the elders of Israel. There was a lot in the temple that was a repetition or fuller development of the tabernacle, and there was a lot in it that was new. The tabernacle was linked with Levi; the temple, in great measure, with Judah. It is the king, not the priest, who builds the house. God asks the help of David, Solomon, Nehemiah, Zerubbabel, and such civil governors in the maintenance of His worship. Their giving it honors them and does not defile the temple of God. God, in His sovereignty, led the ark around to Gilgal, Shiloh, Kiriathjearim, and Zion. Now that His purpose is served, He sets it aside, and chooses a new site for His place of worship. That place is no longer a tent, but a temple; no longer connected with priesthood only, but with royalty as well; no longer frail and movable, like a pilgrim, but fixed and unchanging – a type of the *house not made with hands, eternal in the heavens* (2 Corinthians 5:1).

Such is the end of the tabernacle age. It began with Moses and ended with David. It began with Sinai and ended with Zion. It began with the thunder of the burning mountain and ended with the pestilence and the devouring sword. A wonderful mixture all throughout of mercy and of judgment!

The temple age ended in more awful judgment – the desolation of temple, city, and people. For man is always treasuring up wrath against himself and ripening for the final stroke. *Evil men and impostors will proceed from bad to worse* (2 Timothy 3:13). *The end of all things is near; therefore, be of sound judgment and sober spirit for the purpose of prayer* (1 Peter 4:7).

Chapter 34

The Moriah Group

1 Chronicles 21:1-30

We have taken up some general aspects of this narrative, chiefly in connection with the temple and Moriah. Let us look at it from another point of view. Let us see the different characters or people in it. Each comes out in a peculiar way.

1. *Satan.* He is very explicitly spoken of here, as in Job and elsewhere, as a true being, not an influence. He is connected with *earth.* Not with its heathen kingdoms only, but also with Judea. He is not only in Babylon, but also in Jerusalem. He has access not only to Nebuchadnezzar, Herod, and Nero, but also to David. He is watchful; he lies in wait for opportunities. He hated man at first in Paradise. He hates David, he hates Israel, and he hates God. *Resist the devil and he will flee from you* (James 4:7). *Be of sober spirit, be on the alert. Your adversary, the devil, prowls around* (1 Peter 5:8). He is powerful, cunning, and subtle. He is that old serpent, the dragon, the devil, Satan. He will go on with his schemes and malice until the Lord comes to bind him.

2. *David.* He is a man of God, yet of comparable passion with others, exposed to Satan. Note: (1) His sin: pride, ambition, selfaggrandizing – like Nebuchadnezzar – *"Is this not Babylon the great?"* (Daniel 4:30). (2) His repentance (verse 8): his conscience is touched; he cries out of his

iniquity and his acting *foolishly,* even before the message of judgment came. (3) His chastisement and humiliation: he is struck at the very point of his pride – Israel's numbers; he clothes himself with sackcloth and falls down before God. (4) His alarm (verse 30): he does not know what to do – the tabernacle is in Gibeon, with the altar of burnt offering; what is he to do? The sword is between him and it; and besides, it is busy at work, and he has no time to go to Gibeon. (5) His forgiveness (verse 26): he cannot go to God, but God comes to him – to the spot where he is. He answers his sacrifice by fire; this is forgiveness and acceptance. All is well. The light of God's countenance has returned; the blood of the burnt offering has done its reconciling work; and on that spot where the blood was shed and the fire came down, Israel's daily propitiation was to be offered up in all days to come.

3. *Joab.* He is a rough warrior, often rude in speech and stern in his actions. But he is a man of faith. He knows the law of the Lord, and he trembles at His word. He knows that, for certain ends, it was a right thing to number Israel, but here he sees this turned into evil and used to cherish pride. He remonstrates. His conscience is sensitive in this matter. He sees the sin and the danger. He is bold also, not fearing the wrath of the king, but he is also obedient. We have here the bright side of Joab's character, and learn to think well of him, not only as one of David's mighty men, but also as a man of faith and conscience.

4. *Gad.* He and Nathan were David's prophets, his divine counselors, two of his statesmen. It does not appear that David consulted Gad about this numbering, or, if he did, he did not heed his advice anymore than that of Joab. But now Gad is sent from God to the king. He was, no doubt, a man in communion with God, and was waiting to know the divine will in secret. God comes to him and gives him His message. It is a twofold one: (1) judgment (verse 10), offering the king his choice of woes; and (2) mercy (verse 18), commanding the altar to be built, a symbol of divine pacification – forgiveness for David and for Israel through the blood.

5. *The elders* (verse 16). They acknowledge the stroke and the sin: *The angel of the Lord.* They clothe themselves in sackcloth and they fall

upon their faces. As far as we know, they had not shared David's sin, yet they at once place themselves by his side in confession and humiliation. David had sinned (verse 8); Israel had sinned (2 Samuel 24:1). They identify themselves with both. It is in this way that we should take up a ruler's sin, a brother's sin, or a nation's sin; not blazoning it abroad in private gossip or in the newspapers, but taking it on ourselves and carrying it to God.

6. *Ornan.* A Gentile, a Jebusite, a king (2 Samuel 24:23), owner of Moriah. He is quietly working with his sons, apparently ignorant of what was going on, until he is alarmed by the angel (verse 20) and astonished by David's visit. He was a believing man, who did not acknowledge the gods of the Jebusites, but the Lord God of Israel; a generous man, handing over to David freely his own ancestral possessions. He is honored by God, and his land is honored. He loses his property in the land, but for a marvelous honor. The history of his threshing floor is interesting. It is probably the great rock, to this day, under the great mosque. In the temple, in the altar, in the rock, Ornan is held in everlasting remembrance.

7. *The angel.* There are specifically three destroying angels mentioned in the Old Testament: (1) The angel who was sent to Egypt to inflict the plagues. (2) The angel who was sent to the Assyrian host to slay its myriads. (3) The angel who was sent to Israel to slay the seventy thousand. He is the messenger of wrath and vengeance, and he comes directly from God. He is like one of those seven spoken of in Revelation that sound the trumpets, who pour out the bowls, or like him who launched the symbolic millstone against Babylon the great. Yet, in the case before us, he utters mercy as well as inflicts judgment. He is terrible in his might; yet he bears the message of forgiveness – the forgiveness of Him who is able to save and to destroy.

8. *Jehovah Himself.* He shows Himself as the hater of sin and its avenger, even in His saints. He has a watchful eye over all His people, to bless and to discipline. He has Satan in control and uses him at pleasure. He has angels in command and sends them on errands of judgment and

mercy. He is holy and righteous, yet compassionate and gracious, not only to Jerusalem, but even to Nineveh. He strikes, yet He spares. He chastises, yet He blesses. His tender mercies are over all His works. He has no pleasure in the death of the sinner. He is not willing that any should perish, but that all should come to repentance.

Chapter 35

Diverse Kinds of Conscience

But I did not do so because of the fear of God. – Nehemiah 5:15

When Joseph was dealing with his brethren, he said in Genesis 42:18, *"Do this and live, for I fear God."* Such was Joseph's motive. When Colonel Gardiner was challenged to fight a duel, he answered, "I fear *sinning; you* know I do not fear *fighting."* Such was his motive. So, when Nehemiah kept aloof from the evil ways of others, he gave his reason: *"But I did not do so because of the fear of God."* Here, then, is Nehemiah's principle of action, both in what he did and in what he did not do. The fear of God. This was the one thing that kept him right and prevented his turning aside to the right or left. Of the unrighteous it is said, "The fear of God is not before his eyes." Of the righteous it is said, "The fear of God is before his eyes." This is the great feature of difference between the two. It was this that operated, and that influenced all his proceedings, that molded his life. He was, as we say, a Godfearing man, and he showed this in what he did and in what he did not do. He was conscientious, not only as to actual duties, but also as to *responsibilities.*

Here then we have true *conscientiousness.* Not merely natural uprightness of character, but also the desire to have a conscience void of offense towards God and man. It is conscientiousness arising from the sense of God's presence, the wish to please Him, the fear of offending Him, the desire to do all that is wellpleasing in His sight. As the love of Christ constrains, so the fear of God makes conscientious.

Are we thoroughly *conscientious*? Is our conscience constantly at work? Not in the spirit of bondage or terror, but in that childlike gentleness and tenderness of conscience that desires to have God's approval in everything we do and every word we speak? What a regulator to our life and conscience this fear of God would be! Let us consider the different spheres and operations of conscience. There is:

1. *The religious conscience.* By this I mean the conscience exercising itself in the things of religion, in religious belief and actions. In our dealings with God, in the service of God, in our testimony for God, let us be thoroughly *conscientious;* not formal, superficial, or indifferent, but conscientious. If I act religiously simply because others do so, or because it involves my good name, or because of habit, I am not acting *conscientiously.* Let our religion mold our conscience, and let our conscience penetrate and pervade our religion. I do not merely mean that a religious man should be a conscientious man, but also that he should carry his conscientiousness into all that concerns religion. He should be alive, not only to duty, but also to *responsibility.*

2. *The secular conscience.* Though not of the world, we are still in the world. We are constantly coming into contact with the world in public and private. Every movement of our daily life comes, more or less, into contact with the world. It may be collision, or it may be interaction and mutual help in common things. Let us in all these be thoroughly conscientious, in what we do or in what we abstain from doing. Never let the world say of us, in reference to either word or deed, "There goes a religious man without a conscience." In all secular and social things let us manifest a conscientious spirit and show to others that the fear of God is before our eyes. Let that fear regulate our daily interaction and walk. Let a sense of *responsibility* toward God and our fellow man be ever on edge.

3. *The commercial conscience.* By this I mean conscience throwing itself into all our business transactions: buying or selling, giving or

receiving, bargains, speculations, whether merchant, lawyer, banker, farmer, tradesman, mechanic, or whatever our worldly calling may be. Let us continually take counsel with conscience. Let the fear of God be before our eyes in the accounting department, the shop, the warehouse, the market, or wherever our calling may place us. Harddriven bargains, advantage taken of men's necessities, grinding of the poor, overcharges, unjust measures, dishonest statements as to goods sold or purchased – these are not things into which conscience can enter. Let every man of business, on whatever scale, be absolutely conscientious, having the fear of God before his eyes.

4. *The family conscience.* Into each circle of life, outer and inner, conscience must enter. The fear of God must reign in the *family*. We must be conscientious in our family dealings, making each member of it feel that we are acting in the fear of God. Let us be conscientious in our family rules, at our family table, in our treatment of our children, and in their education. Be conscientious *with* them and *before* them. Never let them say that we do an unconscientious deed. Conscience says to each father and mother, *Train up [your] child in the way he should go* (Proverbs 22:6). Oh, be conscientious with your children! They know what conscience is, how conscience operates and shows itself. Let the fear of God be stamped on all family arrangements. Servants, be conscientious to your masters, and masters, to your servants.

5. *The private conscience.* I must be conscientious in all my individually private actions. I must be conscientious in all personal things, whether alone, unheard, or unseen. I must be conscientious in my closet as well as in my family. I must be conscientious about my solitary, hidden actions. The fear of God must fill every chamber of my heart. I must be upright before myself and before God.

6. *The local conscience.* I must be conscientious everywhere, at home or abroad. I must carry my conscience with me when I travel, just as when I am at home. I read sometimes of Christian travelers spending their Sabbath in sightseeing. I find that some think it no evil to climb Mount Sinai or Mount Hermon on the Sabbath because these are sacred

scenes. They would not climb Snowdon or Ben Lomond, but they would climb these foreign mountains! What sort of local conscience is this? Should not a Christian carry his conscience into every place, and, when tempted to do abroad on the Sabbath what he would not do at home, be able to say, "I did not do so because of the fear of God"?

Cultivate a tender conscience, an enlightened conscience, a conscience void of offense; not morbid, diseased, crooked, onesided, critical, lofty, or proud, but simple, bold, and sensitive. Beware of a blunted or seared conscience. Shun compromises where principle is concerned. They always leave a stain upon the conscience. Let the fear of God reign in you always and everywhere. Beware of the fear of man. Cultivate the fear of God. The gospel, as well as the law, makes demands on your conscience. Conscience speaks to you in the name of Jesus Christ as well as in that of God.

Chapter 36

The Soul Turning from Man to God

"Behold now, I have prepared my case; I know that I will be vindicated. Who will contend with me? For then I would be silent and die." – Job 13:18-19

This is the utterance of a justified man, and of one who knew that he was justified, and was prepared to defend his position as such against all accusers.

Job's declaration here may primarily be the assertion of his innocence against the accusations of his friends. But we may use it for something beyond this.

We do great injustice to the Old Testament saints and to their privileges, and no less so to the God who made them what they were, when we conceive of them as possessing an imperfect justification, or an imperfect and uncertain knowledge of their justification. Paul's declaration was explicit on this point: *I know whom I have believed* (2 Timothy 1:12), and yet it was not a jot more explicit than that of Job: "*I know that my Redeemer lives*" (Job 19:25). When Paul said, *God is the one who justifies; who is the one who condemns?* (Romans 8:33-34), he was only speaking what Job had spoken ages before: "*I know that I will be vindicated. Who will contend with me?*"

In connection with the words of our text, let us note the following passages: Psalm 32:1, 5; Isaiah 50:7-9; 51:12; Romans 8:31, 34; and

1 John 1:9. In all of these we have the same truth, the same tone, the same confidence, the same assurance, and the same source or channel for the flowing of all these into the soul. The old and the new are alike. We cannot say that the old is better or the new is better; both are good and both are the same. In both we have the utterance of the one creed of the church, and the voice of the one Spirit, the Spirit of adoption, through the one Redeemer.

In our text (along with the context on both sides), we have the expression of an old saint's feelings in reference to man and to God. He has no hope from man, but he has all hope from God. One would have expected the opposite. Imperfect man might be expected to bear with an imperfect fellow man, but can a perfect God be expected to do this? Yet it is God that he falls back on. The infinitely holy, allsearching God is felt to be a surer refuge for a sinner than unholy, sinexcusing man. Such must be the spirit of our dealings with God. His holiness and His omniscience are not only no discouragements, but they are also the opposite. He knows the very worst in us, and He hates it; yet He pities us. We cannot tell Him worse of ourselves than He already knows. And is this not encouragement? Man's narrow heart makes us despair of Him; God's infinite heart gives us hope. Have we not often been comforted with the thought that God knows us fully? Let us then notice the feelings or attitude of a saint towards God.

1. *It is confidence.* "*I know that I will be vindicated.*" It is no mere hope, or possibility; it is a certainty. It is of this that Paul speaks: *For we have become partakers of Christ, if we hold fast the beginning of our assurance firm* (Hebrews 3:14). This was the attitude of Old Testament saints, and much more that of New Testament saints. It is the feeling of the child; it is simple trustfulness, for everything, beginning with pardon.

2. *It is confidence as a sinner.* Job speaks as a sinner, simply as such, not as a better man than others. He goes to God simply as such, and he trusts as such. He realizes this blessed truth that a man's evil is no reason for distrusting God. When Adam fled from God, he did not know this. He thought that his sin was a reason for distrusting and flying from God, until God taught him differently, and showed him what grace was.

3. *It is confidence arising from God's character alone.* He has looked into the face of God and learned there that a sinner may trust Him, just because of what He is; indeed, that a sinner can only glorify Him by trusting Him because of what He is. It is not only because of His grace that he trusts, but also because of His holiness and power. For these are no longer against the sinner, but are on his side. Everything in God's character has, by the cross of Christ, been turned into a reason for trusting Him. The more man knows of Him, the more he trusts. Trust is the natural and inseparable response of the soul to the divine revelation of the character of God. It is not what man sees in himself, his good deeds or good feelings, his graces, his repentance, his regeneration, or his faith, but what he sees in God, that calls out confidence.

4. *It is confidence of personal justification.* "I know that I will be vindicated." It is no vague confidence in some unknown god, some sentimental trust in God's universal fatherhood, or mankind's universal sonship. It is of personal justification that he speaks; thus, he is acknowledging personal condemnation in the first place, and then, as the result of a judicial act, personal justification. It is of this that the whole Bible speaks. It is this that the cross seals to us. This is not a state in which we are born, but into which we come by believing in Him who was delivered for our offenses and was raised again for our justification. Do you *know* this? Is this the beginning of your religion, the starting point of your heavenward course?

5. *It is confidence in spite of all accusers.* From verse 20 to verse 27 Job is pleading with God, confessing sin, and uttering confidence. In verse 28, and in the next chapter, he turns to man as his accuser. Who is he? A man that will die. What do his accusations matter? Let the whole world condemn; what does that matter? Will this shake a confidence resting on the word and name of God? Let Satan and conscience accuse. Will they shake a confidence that comes from above? If their charges are all true, what about this? *Who is the one who condemns?* (Romans 8:34). *Who will bring a charge against God's elect?* (Romans 8:33). We plead guilty to the accusations, but not with less confidence do we claim an acquittal from the Judge, simply on the ground of what our Surety has done.

Chapter 37

Man's Dislike of a Present God

"They say to God, 'Depart from us! We do not even desire the knowledge of Your ways.'" – Job 21:14

The men who speak thus are not atheists. They do not say there is no God. They may be scoffers, blasphemers, and ungodly, but they are not atheists. These people whom Job describes are *worldly* men. The world, with its riches, possessions, pleasures, and friendships, is their all. They have nothing beyond it and they do not wish anything else. They are satisfied. They love the world and are resolved to make the best of it that they can. When anything comes in between it and them, or threatens to prevent their enjoying it, such as pain, sickness, or death, they thrust it away. They do not ask whether the intervention may not, after all, be true and important. It mars their enjoyment of the world and so must not be for a moment entertained.

In our text we have worldliness *versus* God. For it is worldliness that is speaking out here. It is not man contending against man because of injury or encroachment. It is not man protesting against pain, mortality, or life's brevity. It is man protesting against God. God seems to him as a dark shadow overclouding all his joy. Why is this?

1. *Not because God has injured him.* He does not pretend that any wrong has been done or has threatened to be done. He does not speak as an injured man, nor plead against God because of injustice.

2. *Not because God hates him.* He has no reason to conclude such a thing, either from what God has said or what He has done. He cannot point to any mark of hatred.

3. *Not because God has interfered with his prosperity.* He is evidently a prosperous man, mighty in power, and the rod of God is not upon him (verses 7 and 9).

It is not because of these things that he says to God, *"Depart from us!"* Indeed, he does not hide his reason altogether: *"We do not even desire the knowledge of Your ways."* He has no liking for God or His ways, and he looks on Him as an obstruction, an unpleasant visitor, a dark cloud, a spoiler of his pleasure.

But these worldly men in Job's time were but a specimen of the men of many ages – our own as well as others. In these different ages we find a variation in the feeling and in its expression. Sometimes there is more of infidelity in it, or even direct atheism, and sometimes less. But in everything there is a desire to be freed of God, God personally, though perhaps not God abstractly; a desire to thrust Him into a corner of His universe where He will disturb the children of men the least. In the present day we find this state of feeling widely spread and working, not only in the world but also in the church. Men who call themselves Christians lend themselves to cry out, *"Depart from us!"* At the bottom of all this feeling is the *love of the world.* It is this that prompts men to seek to be freed of God.

1. *They try to be freed of Him.* They tolerate Him afar off, but not nearby. They tolerate a religion of uncertainty, but not one of certainty, fellowship, or conscious nearness. They would leave Him alone, if He would leave them alone; but if not, they raise the cry, *"Depart!"* An abstraction, a creed, a system of theology they bear with, because it does not interfere with their worldliness; but God Himself can only be tolerated as a shadowy, impalpable, far-distant being. To anything else they say, *"Depart!"*

2. *They try to be freed of His Christ.* Some superhuman being, such as paganism delighted in, they tolerate; but not the Christ of God, the Word made flesh. They will admire and sing of a Christ that will assist them in their great endeavor to keep God at a distance,

but the Christ that brings God near, that makes His love a reality, and His favor and forgiveness a certainty, they cannot deal with.

3. *They try to be freed of His Spirit.* They dislike the supernatural, and do not wish to hear of a world outside their own, from which influences and operations are continually coming to modify things here, or transform men, or protest against sin. The Holy Spirit, as the special expression and representative of the supernatural and divine, in connection with man's nature and soul, they either refuse to believe in, or treat Him as a mere inspiration, a breath, an influence.

4. *They try to be freed of His book.* The Bible is God's visible representative and commissioner here. It is the silent protest in every house in favor of God. And thus it is set aside by many or only read for its poetry, morality, and antiquity. To believe as little of it as possible is the object of multitudes; to cast doubt upon its authenticity; to reject its inspiration; to treat it as not a book for this advanced age – these are the ways in which men are seeking to get rid of God's book.

5. *They try to be freed of His law.* They say it was not for us but for the Jews; they tell us that the morality of Socrates was higher than that of Moses; they (in a more refined fashion) speak of it as buried in the grave of Christ, so that we have been freed of its exactions and sanctions. No Sabbath for us; the law is dead! No restraint on us; the law is dead!

Thus, the age tries to be freed of God. It does so, because it dreads Him; it has no relish for Him; His presence is a gloomy shadow; His nearness would interfere with all worldly schemes and pleasures. Therefore, men say, *"Depart!"* The old pagans never said to Jupiter, *"Depart!"* They looked on him as in sympathy with their sins, lusts, and pleasures. But to the living and true God men say, *"Depart!"* because they feel that they cannot have both Him and their sins. They cannot clothe Him with the robes of their own worldliness.

Yet He has not departed. In love He lingers, seeking to bless. He knows the void His departure makes, and that nothing can fill it. Therefore, He lingers; yearning over the sons of men, pleading with them to take Him for their portion and all.

Chapter 38

True and False Consolation

"How then will you vainly comfort me, for your answers remain full of falsehood?" – Job 21:34

Man needs consolation – *For man is born for trouble* (Job 5:7) – especially a man in Job's condition, overwhelmed with calamity. Not one day's consolation, but many days; indeed, he needs constant consolation, for between the little cares and the large sorrows of life, its ripples, waves, and breakers, there is no day exempt from trouble. Life has many burdens, heavy or light. But much depends on:

1. *The state of mind in which the calamity finds us or produces in us.* Where irritation, murmuring, rebellion, and unbelief prevail, it is idle to speak of consolation. We are not in a fit state to receive it. We repel the hand and the medicine of the physician.

2. *The persons who administer it.* If they are not thoroughly trusted or respected, if they are suspected of selfishness, insincerity, or unkindness, then their words are useless, and perhaps worse.

3. *The kind of consolation administered.* Sometimes it is hastily and thoughtlessly poured in, or rather flung at us, as water is hastily snatched up and flung over a flame to extinguish it. Sometimes the most indiscriminate statements are made, and commonplace

maxims uttered, as if anything would suit anybody, or everything would suit everybody.

Much depends on these three things, as much on the last one as on any of them. In regard to this, let us note what is not consolation; for man is skillful in administering false consolation.

1. *Sentimental sayings are not consolation.* These are often poured into the ears of sorrow, but they are not medicine. They are only the relief found in the intoxicating glass. Fine figures, poetical rhapsodies about the sorrows of life, these are dangerous things. They soothe for an hour, and that is all.

2. *Appeals to natural selflove will not do.* How commonly do we hear a professed comforter reminding a sufferer of the multitude of his sorrows in order to make him feel like a martyr? Everything that appeals to pride, vanity, and self is worse than vain.

3. *Taking refuge in fatalism will not do.* "We must submit" is the frequent language of the sufferer. This is not faith, but unbelief. It is man feeling himself overpowered by a hand stronger than his own, not falling back on love and wisdom.

4. *Ascribing all to our own deserved punishment.* Though there is truth in this, yet the way in which it is generally done is wrong. "If I had not deserved it, it would not have come." If we begin in this way, where will we end? What we deserve! What is their measure? Hell! Let us be thankful that it is not according to what we deserve that sorrow comes, but on a far higher principle. A sorrow may point to the kind of sin, or the seat of sin, but no sorrow of ours can measure the punishment of sin. That is measured by the cross and sorrow of Christ alone.

5. *Giving oneself to pleasure will not do.* This is the most wretched and perilous of opiates – it is *strong drink* or *mixed wine* that ruins the soul while it makes us forgetful of our sorrow for a few hours. It is not in pleasure that we are to drown our grief; no, nor even in business.

There is a vast difference between real and unreal consolation, between the true and the vain. It is of this that Job speaks. He needed consolation.

Never did someone need it more. He was thirsting for it. His friends came to administer it, but they failed. How and why? Because in their answers there was falsehood. It was not *the truth* that they administered. There can be no real consolation, then, that is not founded upon *the truth*. It is the truth that comforts. There can be no consolation in a falsehood. A lie may heal our hurt slightly, but not effectively. The water of truth from the cup of truth can alone refresh, heal, and console. That cup of truth is always full.

1. *There must be the true interpretation of God's ways.* We must see their meaning and bearing on us, what it is in us that they point to, and what God's purpose is in sending the calamity. We have to deal honestly both with ourselves and with God, asking, What is God condemning in me? What sin is He seeking to eradicate? What truth to communicate? What Scripture to illustrate?

2. *There must be the true understanding and discrimination of our circumstances.* We must know ourselves and then apply well each dealing of the divine hand, tracing out the aim of each blow or each burden. The sinner must not take hold of words that suit only the saint. There are words for everyone. Let us apply wisely, or else the consolation will be vain.

3. *There must be the right knowledge of God's character.* No "consolation" or "answer" can be of any use that is not made to spring out of this. God is wise, God is great, God is holy, and God is love. We must keep these things in mind in every dispensation.

It is the amount of *truth* we speak that is the measure of the consolation imparted. It is not strong language nor soothing words that will do. Therefore, in the day of trouble we should deal much with Scripture and its words. Then we are on sure ground. God's words are mighty for consolation; for He is the God of all consolation. The exhibition of Christ and His fullness is true consolation. The presentation of the Spirit as the Comforter – the Spirit and the Spirit's *love,* holy love – is true consolation. At all times administer only truth, not error, especially in the day of sorrow. Falsehood is not consolation, it is not peace, and it is not medicine. It is poison. *Truth,* the truth of God – that is consolation and strength.

Chapter 39

Gain and Loss for Eternity

"For what is the hope of the godless when he is cut off, when God requires his life?" – Job 27:8

The word *hypocrite* means properly the "ungodly," and corresponds to the "wicked" and "unrighteous" of whom Job was speaking. To this passage, probably, our Lord refers when He asks, *"What will it profit a man if he gains the whole world and forfeits his soul?"* (Matthew 16:26). What becomes of the vain hope of the ungodly when this life is done? Whatever they may have of *gain* here, all is *loss* hereafter. This may be their "time to *get*," but that will be their "time to *lose*." And their loss is not for a day, but forever.

It is not all gain with the *godly* here. Paul says, *For whom I have suffered the loss of all things* (Philippians 3:8). He who casts his lot in with the people of God must prepare for *loss* as well as *gain*. He must count the cost beforehand and be ready to pay it when the day comes for payment. There is the taking up of our cross, the denying self, and forsaking all. He loses: (1) *This world.* Whatever may be in it of pleasure, satisfaction, pomp, or merrymaking, he loses, for he cannot have both worlds. (2) *His name.* Perhaps he stood high in reputation with the men of this world and had a name for many things, but he loses this, for his name is cast out as evil. (3) *His religion.* For the likelihood is that he had a sort of religion or religiousness like Saul of Tarsus; all this past religion of his must be left behind – it will serve him no more. (4) *His goods.* This may not always be demanded to the full extent, as in days of persecution, but still he must be prepared to part with everything, counting it no more his own.

But his hope is never lost. He is saved by hope; his eye is on the *things hoped for* (Hebrews 11:1); he abounds in hope. This well never runs dry. This treasure house is never exhausted. Whatever darkness may rest on his present, his future brightens with hope, and that hope *does not disappoint* (Romans 5:5); it contains the incorruptible and everlasting. And even *now* he has abundant compensation for loss and trial.

Not so for the ungodly. He has indeed a hope; a hope of being saved, or, at least, of not being lost; a hope of going to heaven, or, at least, of not going to hell. But his hope is not the *good hope by grace* (2 Thessalonians 2:16). It is a selforiginated hope; an unscriptural hope; a groundless and unreasonable hope; an invalid hope; a hope that will not be sickness-proof, nor deathbed-proof, or if it is, it perishes at death; it is wrapped up in his shroud and buried in his grave, because for that kind of hope there is no resurrection.

Thus, the one thing that seemed to be gain to him, goes from him at death; and everything is loss – utter, infinite, irreparable, eternal loss! For him there is no morning, but only night; night without a star, or even a meteor gleam. His losses cannot be enumerated or estimated; they are so many and so terrible. He loses such things as the following:

1. *His soul.* I might say his *body* too; for if the man is lost, then soul and body are gone. But it is the *soul* that is the special and supreme loss. The loss of that which disintegrates in the grave is after all subordinate, but the loss of that which cannot die is great beyond measure. He who has lost his *soul* is poor indeed. Yet, in the case of the ungodly man, that fearful loss is incurred. He loses his soul. Not that the soul perishes or is annihilated. That would be some relief to the poor doomed victim of sin. The soul is *lost* but cannot *die.* The loss of the soul consists in eternal condemnation and ruin. Everything is gone for which the soul existed. It exists now only for woe. Life is no longer life, for the soul cannot enjoy it. All that constituted *life,* true life, in time

or eternity, is gone. Life now becomes worse than death, for the soul is lost in darkness, woe, anguish, and an endless hell; lost from God and goodness, blessedness, and from all holy beings forever and ever.

2. *Heaven.* The future state and place of blessedness has many names: a kingdom, an inheritance, a city, a new heaven. All of these are names of joy. *Heaven* is a noble and glorious name, embodying in it all that is excellent, divine, and perfect. Its joy is perfect, its light is perfect, its holiness is perfect. Its songs are perfect, its service is perfect. It is day without night. It is the blessing without the curse. All of this is lost to the ungodly. What a loss must a lost heaven be! To be shut out from such a kingdom, dispossessed of such an inheritance; indeed, made the heir of such sorrow and darkness – how infinitely woeful! Think, O man, amid all your losses, past or expected, what a loss it would be if you lost heaven! A lost kingdom, a lost city, a lost inheritance! Who can measure such a loss?

3. *Christ.* Yes, Christ is lost, and this is the heaviest loss of all. There is none like it, so infinite and so irreparable. This is the loss of losses, the woe of woes. A lost Christ! What can equal that? This is the loss of the ungodly. This loss is great because of: (1) what Christ is in Himself – the glorious Immanuel; (2) what He has done on the cross; (3) His love; (4) His sympathy, and fellowship, and consolation; and (5) His reward. This loss is indeed unutterable. Men do not see this or think of it. Yet it will be felt one day. In hell it will be realized as the loss of losses, that which makes the place of woe so unutterably woeful. "I might have had Christ," the lost sinner will say, "but I did not want Him, and now He is gone forever; I cannot have Him now. Instead of Christ, I have Satan; instead of heaven, hell."

Consider your losses, O you ungodly! They are unspeakable and eternal. Look at them now and prevent them. There is little compensation now for such losses, either in the world's pleasure, lust, or wealth. There will be no compensation then. It will be unmingled woe, a cup of undiluted, unsweetened gall and wormwood.

What a disappointment to you who have been hoping and hoping! To lie down with a false hope and go up to the Judge expecting to be received! How dreadful the agony of such a disappointment!

It is not too late. Your soul is not lost, heaven is not lost, Christ is not lost yet. All may still be won! The gate stands wide open. Go in, go in! God's record still stands true concerning His Son. Believe it and be saved.

Chapter 40

Man's Misconstruction of the Works of God

"By these He judges peoples." – Job 36:31

This verse suggests Acts 14:17: *"And yet He did not leave Himself without witness, in that He did good and gave you rains from heaven and fruitful seasons, satisfying your hearts with food and gladness."* Both passages call on us to listen to the voice of God speaking to us through what are called "natural phenomena." By the word *judging*, we understand more than inflicting judgment, more than sitting as judge, sentencer, or executioner. It means "ruling" as well, wielding the scepter and governing. By people, we especially understand the gentile or idolatrous nations of the earth, or generally the inhabitants of earth. Two things are declared here: first, that God judges the nations; second, that He does so by the changes and occurrences of nature.

1. *He judges the peoples* (or nations). This judging is not merely a thing of the *past* nor of the *future,* but of the *present.* He has been, and He is now judging. *Creation* is past, the *new creation* is future, but governing is *now.* All are equally sure and true, and they who deny the present governing or the future interposition in the great day, might as well deny creation. God's connection with earth is as close and as direct now

as ever; not so obvious or so visible, but quite as real. A thing does not need to be visible, audible, or palpable in order to be direct and real. Many things are the latter that are not the former. The power of the silent and distant moon over the sea, of the atmosphere over all life, of the soul over the body in every movement: these are instances in point. Only God's connection with earth is more real and direct than these; *for in Him we live and move and exist* (Acts 17:28). His purpose comes in contact with the earth and its dwellers; not generally and by means of laws, but directly and minutely. His will, His voice, His hand, and His arm all come into contact with this world as well as with all other worlds, the creation of His power. He has not left them alone. He sustains and rules as truly as He creates. Not for a moment does He let go of His hold. He is the governor among the nations. He rules by His power forever. His eyes behold the nations. He does according to His will in the armies of heaven and among the inhabitants of the earth. It is with no distant, unheeding God that we interact, but with that God who fixes the bounds of our habitation, who counts our hairs, who feeds the ravens, who notes a sparrow's death, and who clothes the lilies of the field. He is nearer to us than the nearest earthly object or being; more closely in contact with us than we are with one another. All other links are as nothing compared with this. They are threads. This is an unbreakable chain.

2. *He judges the people by means of the changes of nature.* We use the word *nature* for lack of a better word: we mean earth and sky with all their motions, alternations, and transformations, great and small, all "natural phenomena" as they are called. These phenomena, or appearances, appear to us as common things; by some they are ascribed to chance, by others to "laws of nature." Here they are ascribed directly to God. They are His voice by which He speaks to us, His finger by which He touches us, His rod by which He corrects us, and His sword by which He strikes us. It seems to be the thought of many that in none of these can we or should we recognize, directly and especially, the interposition of God; that it is fanaticism to interpret them so as to make them special messengers of God to us. But the words before us are very explicit: *By these He judges peoples.* The things by which He

is here said to judge the people are the common things of the day and year – the rain, clouds, lightning, and such. He uses these as His voice in warning, commanding, chastising, or comforting. These common things do not come by chance, at random, or by dead law, but they go out from God as His messengers. Thus everything has a divine meaning and a heavenly voice. Let us listen, interpret, and understand. Summer speaks to us with its green fields and fragrant gardens. Winter speaks to us with its ice, snow, and frost. By these God judges the peoples. Consider the pestilence, famine, earthquake, lightning, storm, shipwreck, and overthrow of kingdoms and kings. Each of these has a special message to the nations – and to each of us. Let us see God drawing near to us in them; showing His care and love; manifesting an unwearied concern for our welfare. Woe to us if we either misinterpret them or refuse to interpret them at all. The common daily changes of personal or family life all speak in the same way. Not only the sweeping calamity that carries off its hundreds, but also the sickness, pain, or the gentle indisposition have a voice to us. He that has an ear, let him hear!

We separate God from *creation,* and so we see nothing in it of divine life and power. We separate God from the changes of creation, and so we find no meaning in these. We separate God from the beautiful or the terrible, and so we realize nothing in them that overawes, attracts, purifies, or comforts. We have learned so well to separate God from His works that we seem to imagine that they contradict each other. The fair sky, clear stream, and green hills all speak of divine goodness and bring to us a gospel that can hardly be mistaken. But we have learned to deny the gracious meaning, and to say that all this beauty means nothing, contains no message from God, and embodies no glad tidings of great joy.

This separation of God from His works is one of the awful features of human unbelief. How much more of Him we would know if we were to interpret His works correctly and hear His voice in each of them, whether in love or discipline. These skies of His are not bent over us in beauty without a meaning. These seas of His do not roll for nothing. These flowers of His are not fragrant and fair for nothing. They do not say to us, "God is your enemy; He hates you"; but rather, "God is your friend; He pities you, yearns over you, and wishes to make you happy." How full a gospel creation preaches to us, according to its kind and measure!

The separation of the works of God from His Word is another sad feature of human unbelief. Creation and inspiration are in harmony. The Bible does not contradict the works of Jehovah. It means what they mean, and they mean what it means. Each little aspect of both speaks out very intelligibly. God wishes to be understood in both. Men would misinterpret both; they try to discover as little of God as they can in both. Yet both preach the same gospel. In both we see the goodness of God leading to repentance; in both we discern the loving-kindness of the Lord. The fact that we sinners are out of hell is one gospel; that we, who should have been in hell, are dwellers on a fair and fruitful earth, is another. God is showing in these ways that He has no pleasure in our death or misery, but in our life and joy.

Chapter 41

The Two Cries and the Two Answers

Many are saying, "Who will show us any good?" Lift up the light of Your countenance upon us, O Lord! – Psalm 4:6

There are two cries here: the cry of the sons of men, and the cry of the sons of God. They are very different. Yet they are both unrelenting. They go up unceasingly. Earth is full of them. Wherever you go, you hear either one or the other. They are the cries of men like us; of men who have souls to fill; who know what sorrow is, and what joy is. The men who utter them are made by the same God; placed in the same world; heirs of a common mortality; moving on to one eternity. We find them often side by side in one city, one village, one family. Not the Hindu using one cry, and the European the other, but intermingled: the two cries constantly going up from the same places.

1. *The cry of the sons of men.* "Who will show us any good?" Let us note what it is, and what it means.

    a. *It is the cry of emptiness.* These sons of men feel that there is something lacking. They were not made for this perpetual hunger and thirst. They are empty and therefore they cry. They are poor and needy, but find no supply.

    b. *It is the cry of weariness.* They who utter it are seeking rest but finding none. They labor and are heavy-laden. They would gladly rest, but they do not know how or where to rest. Unrest! This is their portion. Unrest here; a sad prelude of the eternal unrest, the neverending weariness.

c. *It is the cry of darkness.* Everything is darkness and blindness. They grope about, not knowing which way to look or turn, and they cry, "Show us. Show us something, for our eyes are blind. We have tried in vain to see."

d. *It is the cry of helplessness.* They have tried many expedients. They have tried to create good for themselves or to get it from others, but in vain. They find themselves helpless.

e. *It is the cry of earnestness.* It comes forth often amid bitter tears and groans. Men are bent on being happy. They would do or give anything for happiness. They are mistaken, yet in earnest. They would take any good if they could get it.

f. *It is the cry of despair.* Who, who, who? They have tried everyone, everything. Everything in vain. They are emptier, hungrier, thirstier, and sadder than when they started.

g. *It is a loud and universal cry.* Many. Yes, the whole world. It is Esau's loud and bitter cry reverberating through the earth. It is the cry of the many, not of the few. The world is unhappy. It has no rest. It is thirsty and does not know where to drink. It is hungry and does not know where to find bread. It weeps and does not know how to dry its tears! Every man walks in a vain show, going about asking, "Who will show me any good?"

2. *The cry of the sons of God.* Very different in all respects. They know what is written: *He has told you, O man, what is good* (Micah 6:8).

a. *It is the cry of the few, not of the many.* For the sons of God are a little flock. One here and another there; not like fields of grain, nor gardens full of flowers, but plants in a desert – a few scattered ones here and there.

b. *It is a certain and definite cry.* They know what they want and how to get what they want supplied. They do not grope about everywhere. They go straight to the source.

c. *It is a cry to God.* It is God alone in whom is their hope. They go straight to Him. Whom do I have in heaven but Him? He is their portion and their all.

d. *It is a cry for light.* They have some light already, but they want more. We have a sun, but we need it daily, more and more sunshine!

e. *It is a cry for light from the face of God.* Light! Light from God! Light from the face of God. The light of God's countenance! This means that God was to make them happy with His favor and love, of which the gracious smile of the countenance was the expression. *"Lift up the light of Your countenance upon [me]"* is our lifelong prayer!

f. *It is a cry that will be answered.* The cry of the sons of men goes up in vain. They speak to the rocks and get merely the echo of their own voice. But this cry is heard daily and constantly. Light streams down and into them. God's countenance is their sun. There is health in it – "healing in His beams." What a contrast between the two cries and the two answers!

O you sons of men, how long will you love vanity? How long will you dote upon this vain world and worship it as your idol? How long will you treat its broken cisterns as if they were the fountains of living water? Oh, do not love the world!

What will its good things profit you in the day of the Lord? Will its pleasures cheer a deathbed or brighten the gloom of the grave? What is the ballroom when "its flowers are fled, its garlands dead"? What can the music and measure of the dance do for you when sickness comes or the last trumpet sounds? Will that beautiful dress of yours do for a shroud? Or will it suffice instead of *the fine linen [which] is the righteous acts of the saints* (Revelation 19:8)? How will these revelings and banquetings appear to you in the retrospect of time, even more in the retrospect of eternity? What will you think of your idle words, your foolish talking and jesting, your filthy communication, your riotous mirth, your luxurious feasting, when you stand confronted with the last enemy or before the Judge of everyone? You have gone from scene to scene, from merrymaking to merrymaking, from party to party, from vanity to vanity, from novel to novel, from ball to ball, in the dreary emptiness of your poor aching hearts, crying, *"Who will show us any good?"* When the end comes, what is your gain? Is it heaven, or is it hell? Is it joy, or is it woe?

Chapter 42

The Knowledge of God's Name

Those who know Your name will put their trust in You. – Psalm 9:10

There are three things here that sum up this passage – the name, the knowledge, and the trust.

1. *The name.* A name is that which differentiates one man from another, by which one man addresses another; and, in Eastern lands and early days, that expresses the character or circumstances of the man to whom it belongs. Thus God's name differentiates Him; by it we address Him; it embodies His character. Thus He Himself gives it: "Jehovah, Jehovah Elohim, merciful and gracious," etc. It is this name that is written all over the Bible, but especially exhibited in Christ Jesus, who came to declare to us the Father's name. It is a name of:

1. *Greatness.* Jehovah, God, Creator, El Shaddai; all expressive of majesty, power, and glory. The Lord God omnipotent.
2. *Grace.* It is the declaration of free love. *Merciful and gracious* (Psalm 86:15). He to whom it belongs must be the fountainhead of love. *God is love* (1 John 4:8). In Him are infinity of compassion and long-suffering.

3. *Forgiveness.* He pardons iniquity, transgression, and sin; all sin, great and small. There is forgiveness with Him, that He may be feared. There is forgiveness to the uttermost.

4. *Righteousness and holiness.* It is holy love that is to be found in Him; righteous grace to the unrighteous, and righteous pardon to the guilty. God's pity on the sinner is holy pity. It is as the Holy One that He loves, pities, and blesses. It is a name revealing everything that a sinner needs. It unfolds the mind and heart of God, gathering into one glorious sun the light scattered over the universe, diffused throughout the Bible. It is the name of names. In it is music, light, medicine, peace, and assurance forever. The great and gracious character of God, thus embodied in a name, brought to a point, is made much more accessible, placed more within our reach and comprehension; pledged to us by the very fact that it has been deposited in a name. No man likes to sully his good name, to act inconsistently with his own name or the family name. And will God not act consistently with His name? Should He treat us in a way that will misrepresent the name that He has taken to Himself? When we plead that name and appeal to it, will He not immediately and cordially respond?

2. *The knowledge.* For a thing like this to be of any use to us, we must know it. So long as it remains unknown, it is useless; it is as good as nonexistent. The sun is of no use to me if I am shut out from its light. Food is of no use to me if I do not know of its existence. So, all the love of God is useless to the sinner unless he knows it. The knowledge of it is that which introduces its blessings to the needy soul. Nothing more is needed; nothing less will do. This knowledge is not a price that we pay, a qualification by which we are fitted for blessing, nor a recommendation that invites God to bless us. It is simply the natural way of letting in the blessing, as opening our window blinds is the natural way of letting in the light. The child's knowledge that his father loves him makes him happy. The father's knowledge that his child has recovered from a deadly sickness brings immediate relief. The criminal's knowledge that his sovereign has pardoned him removes his burden. In all these cases and similar ones,

it is the simple knowledge of what is good and pleasing that does the work, and we never think of puzzling ourselves with asking, "But is my knowledge the right kind? Is it the quality and quantity that will secure blessing for me?" As if our getting the benefit of good news depended upon a certain peculiar way of knowing it, on which peculiarity turned the whole virtue of the thing known. Ah, it is not thus that we deal with earthly love! It is not thus that we conjure up difficulties and distinctions, and metaphysical questions that can never be properly adjusted, and which, if they were adjusted, would leave us just where we were. Say what we want, knowledge is just knowledge, and not something else. Knowing the love of a person is just knowing it. It is not some mysterious act or feeling or combination of emotions that the poor man cannot fathom, and about which philosophers have wrangled for ages.

3. *The trust.* Such is God's name that it cannot be known without evoking trust. The trust arising from this simple knowledge is the truest and most blessed of all. God's character is of such a kind as to call up confidence as soon as it is known by a sinner; and he who has no confidence in God does not yet know Him or His name. If he did know it, he could not help trusting Him. When we come into contact with a lovable object, we cannot help loving. When we come into contact with a trustworthy object, we cannot help trusting, unless we are persuaded that it is a false report that we have heard concerning this lovableness or this trustworthiness. The knowledge of the name of God is that which leads to trust. Therefore, we preach that name – that name of grace and love, of mercy and truth! We bring true tidings concerning it; and we give evidence, in the death and resurrection of the Son of God, that these tidings are quite as true and as good as they profess to be. It is on the basis of "infallible proofs" that we rest our gospel. Our tidings are as sure as they are blessed.

Chapter 43

Deliverance from Deep Waters

He sent from on high, He took me; He drew me out of many waters. – Psalm 18:16

We take these words as the expression of (1) David's experience, (2) Christ's experience, and (3) every Christian's experience. In all of these we learn much about God; David's God; the God and Father of our Lord Jesus Christ; our own God. For it is *His* character that is thus unfolded to us. He is the God of all grace. Indeed, God is love. In Him there is help, and with Him is abundant redemption. It is He who redeems Israel out of all of his troubles. It is *He* who is *above*. It is *He* who *sends* from above. It is He who *takes* (lays hold of). It is He who *draws* – and that out of many waters. Such is the God with whom we have to do! He is infinite in power and grace. To know Him is life eternal. To rest upon His love and power is the true strength and solace of the soul! The knowledge of ourselves *troubles* and *casts down*; the knowledge of this God relieves and lifts up. The great use of knowing ourselves is not that we may be *qualified* for receiving and being received by Him, but that we may become more and more dissatisfied with self, and more and more drawn to Him who is altogether unlike self, more and more emptied of everything, so that as empty vessels we may be in a state for containing Him and His fullness. For it is our emptiness that attracts and makes us suitable for His fullness; and it is in knowing self that we are emptied of self. We decrease, He increases.

1. *David's experience.* This whole psalm refers to this subject, and his whole life is an exemplification of the text. He was constantly in the deep and many waters, from the day that Samuel anointed him king. First Saul, then the Philistines, and then Absalom threatened to overwhelm him. They surrounded him, they raged against him, they poured their billows over him until he seemed to be sinking in the waters; not once nor twice, but many times. In each successive peril God drew near to save; He sent from above, He laid hold of him, He drew him out of many waters. Jehovah's love and power never failed. As low as David went down, they went lower still. Whether as the young shepherd of Bethlehem he was exposed to any danger except that of the lion and the bear, we do not know. But no sooner is he named king than enemies arise, the floods attack him. That which we should have expected to be the termination of trouble and danger stirred these up, introduced him to conflict, raised the storm, and drew the rage of enemies around him. What could David have done, had it not been for Jehovah his God? *His* arm, *His* shield, *His* sword – they were his protection and deliverance.

2. *Christ's experience.* These psalms of David are the psalms of the Son of David. This psalm is His resurrection psalm. All His life He was exposed to foes. He was made to feel the wrath of God, as the bearer of our sins. *Your wrath has rested upon me, and You have afflicted me with all Your waves* (Psalm 88:7). *All Your breakers and Your waves have rolled over me* (Psalm 42:7). It was so during His life, as when He said, *"Now My soul has become troubled"* (John 12:27); it was so in Gethsemane, when He said, *"My soul is deeply grieved, to the point of death"* (Matthew 26:38); it was so on the cross, when He cried, *"My God"* (Matthew 27:46); it was so when He lay under the power of death. But *He sent from on high, He took me; He drew me out of many waters. He rescued me, because He delighted in me* (Psalm 18:16, 19). As our SinBearer, our cursebearer, and our deathbearer, He had Jehovah's wrath

poured upon Him. This was the depth out of which He was plucked by the Father's hand, and His deliverance is ours. It was as our Surety, our Substitute, that He was drawn out of many waters.

3. *Every Christian's experience.* By nature, he is in these many waters, though at first, he does not know it. "Under wrath" is the description of his condition; *"the wrath of God abides on him"* (John 3:36). He is not alive to this. His eyes and ears are closed. He does not see, does not hear the roaring waves of wrath. Like Jonah, he is asleep in the storm. When the Holy Spirit shows him where he is and what he is, terrors seize him. He is overwhelmed and does not know how to help himself. All help is vain. He looks upward and sees Him who was drawn out of many waters, and Him who drew Him. He remembers the words, *"Everyone who calls on the name of the Lord will be saved"* (Acts 2:21). He appeals to that name, and immediately the help comes down, and he is delivered, and henceforth his song of grateful joy is, *He sent from on high, He took me; He drew me out of many waters.* So it is in conflicts, daily troubles, times of sorrow, on his bed of death, and in the day when his body will be delivered from death and the grave.

Thus, he ascribes everything to God, from first to last; the sending, the taking, the drawing – all are of God. Salvation is of the Lord. Of Him, to Him, and through Him are all things. Yes, Jehovah saves! He does not help us save ourselves. He saves! However far down we may be, however deep the waters, however near the perishing – He can rescue! His arm is not shortened that it cannot save, nor grown feeble that it should fail to grasp us or to draw us up. His is salvation to the uttermost; deliverance from the lowest hell.

All true religion must begin with salvation. God's hand must lay hold on us and lift us up. Untrue religion may begin in any way and can go on without salvation, pardon, reconciliation, or any putting forth of the mighty power of God. But the true, real, and divine must begin with this conscious rescue, this plucking from the waves of wrath; and it must, though perhaps with feeble voice, sing Messiah's song: *He sent from on high, He took me; He drew me out of many waters.*

Chapter 44

The Excellency of the Divine Lovingkindness

How precious is Your lovingkindness, O God! And the children of men take refuge in the shadow of Your wings. – Psalm 36:7

There are two special things, fitting the one to the other: (1) divine lovingkindness, and (2) human trust.

1. *Divine lovingkindness. How precious is Your lovingkindness, O God!* David speaks as one who had known it, who had tasted that the Lord is gracious. Here he is telling his experience to God Himself, but in the hearing of man, so that he may know it too. He speaks because he believed and felt. His whole history had been an exhibition of the lovingkindness of the Lord, as indeed is the history of each of us. And this lovingkindness is genuine, true, and deep. There is no pretense about it. It is as true as God Himself. *God is love* (1 John 4:16); *God, being rich in mercy* (Ephesians 2:4); *God so loved the world* (John 3:16). There is nothing more *real* than the love of God. But it is not of its *reality* that David speaks here. He takes that for granted. No one who knows Jehovah could doubt it. But it is of its *excellence* that he speaks. God's love is such an excellent and glorious thing! It is *precious* beyond all gems or

gold, for that is the meaning of the word. It is the most costly and rare of all things. It is beyond all price and all excellence of earth. What can equal in costliness the love of God? Its preciousness is measured by the gift it gave, and by the innumerable gifts contained in that one gift – life, pardon, salvation, peace, and the glory to be revealed. In this love there are unsearchable riches – exceeding riches of grace. There are no riches to be compared to this great love of God. Having it we are rich indeed. Without it we are poor, life is blank, and eternity is dark.

2. *Human trust.* It is of Adam's sons that David speaks. *The children of men take refuge in the shadow of Your wings;* that is, they take themselves to You as their refuge. God's character is then the basis of human confidence. That character is the attraction to the sinner, for it is just such a character as suits him – irrespective of his being anything but a man and a sinner.

This love that so suits the sinner and calls forth his confidence is that which is exhibited in the cross of Christ. That cross is the revelation of God's love as a righteous thing, and thus appeals both to man's heart and his conscience. The love furnishes the ground for trust, and the cross removes every reason for distrust.

Let us here note the following:

1. *Man's ignorance of God.* With the Bible in his hand, he still does not know God. He worships an unknown God. *"They do not know Me"* (Jeremiah 9:3) is God's testimony against man. Ignorance of God is a sin of no common heinousness.

2. *Man's mistakes as to God.* He imagines Him to be such a one as himself. He entertains a bad opinion of Him. He thinks of Him as a God still to be appeased by work, prayer, or sacrifice. He mistakes His character, His words, and His gospel.

3. *Man's distance from God.* Departure from God is the sinner's own act. He has fled from God, and he prefers this state of distance. He does not like the idea of nearness. To get as far from God as possible is his goal. And not only does he depart from God, but he also says to God, "Depart from me."

4. *Man's distrust of God.* He does not merely mistake God, but he also thoroughly distrusts Him. He cannot imagine God to be anything but his enemy. He has no confidence in Him. He cannot feel himself safe in the hands of God. To be simply at the mercy of God, without claim, merit, or recommendation, is a hateful as well as a dreadful thought.

Let us note God's remedy for all of these. It is a double one – subjective and objective.

1. *Subjective.* The subjective is the moral or spiritual rectification of nature and character by the power of the Holy Spirit. *"You must be born again"* (John 3:7). It is the recreating, the transforming of the whole man, enabling him to love what he hated, and to hate what he loved. It is the renewal of every part of the man's soul and being, creating him in Christ unto good works, for we are His workmanship; we are the clay and He is the potter.

2. *Objective.* This is the representation given of Himself in His revelation. He shows Himself to the sinner in an aspect at once gracious and glorious. He makes Himself to be seen as the sinner's friend and not his enemy. He unveils and unfolds His whole character as the God of all grace, the merciful and gracious Lord God pardoning iniquity, transgression, and sin.

It is to the overshadowing, protecting wings of God that David points us to, those wings of which the Lord spoke as stretched out to shelter Jerusalem, those wings under which Israel encamped or marched through the desert. He stretches out His wings and calls. He tells us of a sure and sufficient shelter, and bids us at once to take refuge there. These wings are broad, large, and strong, fitted to shelter all the sons of Adam. And thus, stretched out they themselves invite us. They contain their own invitation. They say, "Come and be safe, come and be blessed, come and be sheltered from present wrath and from the wrath to come. Come, for all things are ready; the love is ready, the deliverance is ready, the protection is ready." Oh, well with those who have taken shelter beneath the shadow of the everlasting wing.

To those who see no danger and desire no security, these expanded wings may be nothing. For what is a Savior to a sinner that does not know his peril? But to those who know what wrath is and what sin is, what condemnation is and what the judgment to come is, who know that *God is a consuming fire* (Hebrews 12:29), that the day of vengeance is coming, and that an unpardoned, unreconciled sinner must then have to face an angry God – that wing, that hiding place, that shelter, that Savior, are of infinite preciousness. And seeing in that outstretched wing the loving-kindness of the Lord, they take themselves eagerly to its shelter, and as *the children of men*, the sons of Adam, the sinners of humanity, they put their trust beneath its shadow.

Chapter 45

The Sickness, the Healer, and the Healing

As for me, I said, "O Lord, be gracious to me; heal my soul, for I have sinned against You." – Psalm 41:4

This is the cry of the needy; of him who has no helper; of him who in the time of trouble finds that there is no refuge but in God. It is the cry from the soul's sickbed – more terrible than the sickbed of the body – to the divine Physician, for the application of His heavenly skill and medicine. It tells us:

1. *Sin is the soul's sickness.* It is an infinite evil, the evil of evils, in comparison with which mere pain is nothing. The end of all bodily sickness, if allowed to run its course, would be earthly death. So the end of all sin, if unchecked, would be eternal death. It is infinitely *varied* in its nature, though comprehended under some general descriptions, and capable of being classified under certain topics. All the diseases, or shades of disease, of the body are but types of the awful varieties of sin. Paralysis, leprosy, fever, blindness, and the like are symbols of sin. The whole head is sick, and the whole heart is faint. There is the disease of unbelief, unrepentance, lust, hostility to God, pride, worldliness, etc. All of these have penetrated our spiritual system and destroyed our spiritual health. Not that sin is mere disease or misfortune, to be rid of gradually by a healthy regimen, diet, or medicine; to be driven out

of the constitution by human skill and effort. It is *guilt* as well as *sickness,* to be dealt with by the *Judge* as much as by the *physician.* Indeed, it is to be dealt with by the Judge first, before the physician can touch it – for as the order of the evil was first, the guilt and then the disease following thereon, so the order of the remedy is first the pardon and then the health.

2. *God is the soul's Healer.* Whether we look at sin as disease or as guilt, or as both together, we find that regarding it we must deal with God alone. The medicine, skill, pardon, and the deliverance are in His hands. We must transact with no other in the matter of sin's removal; not with self, man, the flesh, the church, a creed, or a priest, but with God Himself; and that directly, face-to-face, alone, without any medium or intervention. All others are physicians of no value. They do not heal at all, or they heal slightly, or increase and irritate the disease. Health is with God alone. He heals effectively and eternally. He who is the soul's life is also the soul's health. Whatever the sickness is, deep or slight, long or brief, connected with the eye, ear, hand, feet, head, or the whole spiritual being, the counsel that must be given to the sick soul is, "Go straight to God. Deal with Him and let Him deal with you."

3. *God is most willing that the soul should be healed.* He has no pleasure in our sickness or death. His desire is that we should live and be healthy. Our sickness is not of Him, but of ourselves, just as truly as our health is not of ourselves, but of Him. Yet He does not love the evil of His creatures. He desires their good, not their evil. Why, then, does He allow sickness and death? For infinitely wise reasons, of which you and I know little, but which will be fully known sooner or later. Yet our present ignorance should not lead us to deny the sincerity of God's desire for our welfare. The two things will be found perfectly reconcilable, and both equally true. Let us not take up with onesided truth, but let us receive both sides, according to the divine revelation, whatever our perplexed minds may argue.

4. *God has made provision for the soul's healing.* The disease was so thoroughly beyond human skill that only God could undertake the

cure. He has undertaken it; He has provided the means; He has sent the physician. The medicine is the cross. There is forgiveness that is indispensable as the commencement of the cure, righteous forgiveness through the death of the Surety. At and with the cross the cure begins, and it begins by the pardon of the sinner. But pardon is not the whole. There is fear, trouble, anxiety, weariness, darkness, and the like. The cross also provides for these. And with the medicine there is the Great Physician Himself, Christ Jesus; or rather, there is Christ and the Holy Spirit. Christ dispensing the Spirit and the Spirit revealing Christ. The power and the skill are in their hands. They apply the divine provision, so that everything pertaining to the healing of the soul is truly divine. Hear the Lord's own declaration regarding this: *"As Moses lifted up the serpent in the wilderness, even so must the Son of Man be lifted up"* (John 3:14). We ask then:

1. *Have you been healed?* If so, give God the glory. Assuredly the health came not from man, but from the love and power of God, from the cross of Christ, from the hand of the Holy Spirit.

2. *Will you be made whole?* Perhaps you are still unhealed? So be it. The cross is here for healing. Look and be cured; look and be saved; look and be forgiven. It is not working, buying, or deserving, but simply looking. The sight of the cross is pardon, health, and life. *The leaves of [this] tree [are] for the healing of the nations* (Revelation 22:2).

3. *Can you do without healing?* Is your wound so slight, your disease so trivial, that you can do without the cross, and that you can heal yourself? Or though unhealed, do you think you can go on as you are, well enough, without health? Suppose you could in this world; what of the world to come? Tossed upon an eternal sickbed, think of that! Eternal disease pervading body and soul, think of that! Oh, look and be healed! Apply at once our text: *"Heal my soul, for I have sinned against You."*

Chapter 46

The Consecration of Earth's Gold and Silver

The daughter of Tyre will come with a gift; the rich among the people will seek your favor. – Psalm 45:12

This is a latterday scene, for the whole psalm is resplendent with latterday glory: the glory of Christ the King; the glory of the church the bride; the glory of the palace, the throne, the entourage, and the kingdom. Everything here is glory, gladness, and righteousness. It is the time of the restitution of all things. We ask:

1. *Who is this daughter of Tyre?* She is the old Phoenician city, lying on the seacoast at the foot of Lebanon; the representative of the old world's commerce.

   a. *What she was.* The great merchant city of the old world, the representative of ancient commerce, splendor, and wealth; the center of magnificent villas, extending for miles north and south – down to the water's edge and up the slopes of Lebanon.

   b. *What she is.* Desolate, the old city swept away; the new one, a small seaport; hardly more than a fishing village.

   c. *What she is to be.* More than one prophecy foretells the resuscitation of Tyre in the latter day (for example, Isaiah 23:18). Though the old city will not be found, yet there will be a representative of it – the same great merchant city, only holy.

2. *To whom does she come?* It is to Christ and His church that she comes. She seeks them out and bows before them. For the position of all things and parties is reversed in that day. The church is on the throne. The world seeks her out and pays homage. What a contrast to the condition of things during these ages past! The church is no longer dishonored, trodden on, persecuted, and despised, but is honored and set on high; is sought after by all the earth, even its greatest; *the kings of the earth will bring their glory into it* (Revelation 21:24). The saints, along with their Lord, receive the tribute of earthly homage. The bride of Christ shares His dignity and glory.

3. *What does she bring?* It is simply called *a gift,* but in that, how much is comprehended. As the wise men from the East brought their peculiar gifts, so it is with the daughter of Tyre. She comes and lays her merchandise, her wealth, her splendor at Immanuel's feet. In Ezekiel we have the full enumeration of her articles of value and beauty. All luxuries, necessities, precious metals, gems, apparel – everything that the world admires, gathered from every region. What a gift! Unsought by the church. Tyre brings her gift, hastening to do homage to the glorious King, and adorning her with all that is beautiful, and precious, and perfect.

4. *What does she teach us?* To lay our all at Christ's feet – nationally and individually. That will be the day of full consecration to God, the acknowledgment of Christ's right to the ownership of everything. As yet we have no true idea of consecration – the consecration of ourselves, all that we have, things common or precious, to God and His Christ. But we will know it then and see it as it has never been seen before. And what a consecration there will be in the latter day, even if it were only of Tyre. How much more when it is of far greater cities and kingdoms than Tyre, our own for instance, to which Tyre is a mere village, or a merchant depot. As Tyre was the great commercial metropolis

of the old world, so is Great Britain, with its mighty London, the great commercial metropolis of the modern earth. Everything that made Tyre great and glorious is to be found ten times magnified and multiplied in her.

All things that God has made are precious and meant to glorify Him. Every creature of God is good. We are not to conclude that because gold, silver, and gems have been abused for pride, and luxury, and vanity, that they should be despised by the Christian – even while we don't pursue obtaining this earth's wealth as followers of Christ. Yet they are all capable of consecration to God, ultimately intended to glorify Him. It is not easy to consecrate the splendid and the beautiful things of earth to His glory just now. There are so many evil influences at work, perverting them, degrading them, defiling them. They are, and have been for so long, the ministers of creature pride: idols, vanities, and follies. But still, they are all capable of good and noble uses, and will one day take their proper place in creation, like the stars above and the flowers below.

Meanwhile let us use everything we have for God. The widowed church just now does not need the gems of earth to adorn her. Indeed, they would be incompatible with her widow's weeds. We can dispense with ornament and show that God does not need these at the present time, though He will one day bring to light all the treasures hidden in His storehouse of the beautiful and glorious, and they will adorn the new Jerusalem, and the new earth, where righteousness dwells. Let us consecrate to God our substance and our money, and lay out our gains for Him. He calls on our commercial nation thus to honor Him – to use their gains not for themselves, but for Him. He asks for honor and service from our commerce. Men of business, consecrate your gain to Him. Jesus is worthy to receive everything you have. Give it to Him and do not grudge. He will repay you a thousand times over.

Chapter 47

The Gifts of the Ascended One

> *You have ascended on high, You have led captive Your captives; You have received gifts among men, even among the rebellious also, that the Lord God may dwell there.* – Psalm 68:18

This psalm is *of* and *for* Messiah. It is He whose name is Jah – the Lord God of Israel; He is addressed throughout this psalm as God. It is this psalm that the apostle quotes in Ephesians 4:8, and interprets it to be of Christ and His ascension. It is Christ whom David here addresses: *You have ascended on high.*

1. *The ascension.* This is the last point of Messiah's earthly history, and it sums up the whole. But according to the interpretation of Paul, it includes everything that went before: *What does it mean except that He also had descended?* (Ephesians 4:9, emphasis added). The *ascent* reminds us of a *descent.* He descended to Bethlehem and then He descended to Joseph's tomb. After that, everything was ascension, and the expression of our text includes, or rather expresses, resurrection. He went down into the lower parts of the earth, He came up again, and then He went on high. This ascending was the completion of His work; the carrying out of His love; the Father's testimony of personal acceptance and delight; and His seal to the absolute perfection of the work for which He descended. It was a *real*

ascension, a *glorious* one, a very exalted one, far above all principalities and powers to the Father's throne. *We do see Him . . . crowned with glory and honor* (Hebrews 2:9). All heaven is His, and He has entered into possession of His heavenly inheritance. All power is given to Him in heaven and in earth. He fills all things. The universe is now His.

2. *The triumph. You have led captive.* Whether this refers to His leading forth His redeemed out of their captivity, or leading into captivity those who held them bound, the triumph is the same, and the words point to the same event – the same enemies, the same battle, the same victory. It is Messiah's triumph over His enemies: the Father's and ours. The warfare is that predicted in Paradise, between the seed of the woman and the seed of the serpent. That warfare concerns us; it is *for* us. He who fights is the Captain of our salvation. The battle went on during the ages before He came. It came to a head on the cross; it is not yet finished; and the full consummation of the triumph is reserved for His second coming, when He binds Satan and casts him into the bottomless pit. Then will He complete His triumph and show that He is more than conqueror. Meanwhile His victory upon the cross is ours. He has fought our battle and won our victory. *"Take courage; I have overcome the world"* (John 16:33). What enemy can prevail? No weakness of ours can dismay us. We glory in our infirmities, that the power of Christ may rest upon us. Let us then fight the good fight. The foe is already bruised by our Captain. It is only with his broken and scattered troops that we have to fight.

3. *The recompense. You have received gifts among men, even among the rebellious also.* Thus, the Father rewards His faithful service. Not only does He receive the Spirit without measure for Himself, but also the gifts of the Spirit for others. This is the apt recompense of His selfemptying. He *emptied* Himself, therefore the Father has *filled* Him – filled Him with the Spirit; filled Him with the Spirit's mighty and manifold gifts. Much of the Spirit was given before He came. We read of the Spirit filling holy men, but much was reserved for His glorification, so that the connection between Him and the gift of the Spirit might be manifested. When He was glorified, the Pentecostal shower came down and the residue of the Spirit was given. This fullness of the Spirit was:

1. *For men.* Not for angels, but for men; not for heaven, but for earth. It was as the ascended Godman that He received the Spirit, for those whose nature He took. *"I will pour out My Spirit on all **mankind**"* (Joel 2:28, emphasis added); not on the unfallen but the fallen sons of Adam.

2. *For the rebellious.* For those who stand farthest off, full of hostility and resistance. Not for the good, but for the evil. As of the Son of Man on earth, so of Him in heaven we may say, *"[He came] to seek and to save that which was lost"* (Luke 19:10); *"not . . . to call the righteous, but sinners"* (Matthew 9:13).

Thus, Christ has received the Spirit for sinners, as Egypt's corn was entrusted to Joseph for the hungry. Go to Him who has the seven Spirits of God. Deal with Him who freely dispenses this Spirit. Come to the waters. *"If anyone is thirsty, let him come to Me and drink"* (John 7:37).

4. *The final result. That the Lord God may dwell there.* God had been driven from earth, from among men. His object is to return. Everything that He has done in and through Christ is to secure that return. He does this:

1. *By incarnation.* The Word became flesh, and dwelt among us (John 1:14). God thus lived with men.

2. *By the cross.* It is the propitiation that makes it a righteous thing for God thus to dwell. It is the blood that brings it about. No blood, no indwelling.

3. *By the Holy Spirit.* It is this that is referred to in our text. The Spirit purchased by the blood comes down and comes in.

He has been doing this in individual souls. They are the habitation of the Spirit, temples of the Holy Spirit. He is yet to do so more conspicuously when Jesus comes the second time. Then this prophecy will be fulfilled. The tabernacle of God will be with men. God will be with them, their God. Earth will be full of the Holy Spirit, and glorious with His gifts.

Chapter 48

The Speaker, the Listener, the Peace

> *I will hear what God the Lord will say; for He will speak peace to His people, to His godly ones; but let them not turn back to folly.* – Psalm 85:8

Let us meditate on this verse under the following topics: (1) the listener, (2) the Speaker, (3) the message, (4) the confidence, and (5) the issue.

1. *The listener. I will hear,* says the writer of this psalm. He speaks as a *listener,* as one whose ears are open. *"He who has ears to hear, let him hear"* (Mark 4:9). This is our true attitude into which we came at conversion. God said, *"Listen, that you may live"* (Isaiah 55:3). *He awaken[ed] My ear to listen as a disciple* (Isaiah 50:4), that is, as one who is under teaching. So, we began to listen, and *in listening* we found life. Such is to be our life; a life of listening, not to man, nor self, nor the world, but to God. As creatures, listening is our proper attitude, much more so as sinners. Let the willing ear be ours. How much we lose by the closed ear!

2. *The Speaker.* God, the Lord; God, even Jehovah. Other speakers may win the ear of the multitude, but it is to God the Lord whom the saint listens. His voice is powerful. Its tones are penetrating, its words attractive. God speaks as one entitled to be heard,

expecting to be heard. He speaks with authority, waiting for our obedience to the heavenly voice. To less than such a speaker we do not feel constrained to listen, but to Him we must. He speaks, and we cannot help but hear.

3. *The message.* He will speak peace to His people. It is peace that Jehovah speaks, for He is the God of peace; *"Him who establishes peace in His heights"* (Job 25:2). Peace is the substance of the message that has all along been carried to us; peace, peace to him that is far away and to him that is close; peace in heaven and peace on earth; peace between man and God; the peace of pardon and the peace of reconciliation; the peace that passes all understanding – peace through the blood of the cross, through Him who is our peace. It might have been wrath; indeed, it *should* have been wrath, but it is not wrath, only *peace;* for He is longsuffering and slow to wrath. Indeed, God is love.

4. *The confidence.* The psalmist knows what he is to expect from such a God. Before the peace comes, he knows that it is coming because he knows the God whom he is called upon to listen to. This is the confidence that he has in Him. He does not listen uncertainly, as if not knowing what will come forth. He has heard of this God before – what He does and speaks – and he opens his ear in happy confidence. He is sure that no wrath will come, only love, only peace. This God is the God of salvation – the God who gave His Son. Will He not then speak peace?

5. *The issue. Let them not turn back to folly,* or, "they will not return to folly." He does not say, "Let them not turn to folly" and *then* He will speak peace to them; but He will speak peace first, and then they will not return to folly. This is God's order, the true and divine order, the reverse of man's. It is not first holiness and then peace, but first peace and then holiness. The root of all holiness is peace with God. Until the clouds are rolled away and the sun shines out, we cannot be warmed and enlightened. Until the frost is gone and the ice dissolved, the river cannot flow on and water the fields. Christ did not say, "Go, and sin no more, and I

will not condemn you," but, *"I do not condemn you, either. Go. From now on sin no more"* (John 8:11).

We are in rebellion. Our chief controversy with God is as to the gospel of peace. Our unbelief of this is our sin of sins, our master sin, to which all others are subordinate. How can we abstain from the lesser sins so long as the master sin remains; so long as there is no peace between us and God, but only rebellion and controversy? The first step to a holy life is being at peace with God.

In order to live a holy life, God must come in and dwell in us. He cannot do this until He has brought us into peace with Himself – until we have listened to and believed the tidings of peace that He has spoken. Reconciliation must be the beginning of all indwelling, and this reconciliation is the result of our believing His message of peace.

Nor indeed has the soul freedom to do good works or grow in holiness until the question of peace has been settled. That question must always be foremost, engrossing us absolutely, and leaving no time nor inclination for anything else. It is too momentous to be left in uncertainty; too vast to be taken up along with others. Once this great point between us and God is settled, we are free to devote our undivided energies to the work of progress, but not until then.

A saint, then, is one who has listened to God, who has heard the words of peace from His lips, who has believed them, who has been reconciled, and who knows that he is so. Therefore, he seeks to be holy. He hates his former folly. He does not return to it. He does not make his free pardon a reason for returning to it.

Brethren, be consistent! Beware of sin, folly, and unholiness of every kind. Be Christians out and out. Show that the peace you have received is a holy peace.

Chapter 49

The Believing Man's Confident Appeal

Preserve my soul, for I am a godly man. – Psalm 86:2

Some mountain heights, whether of the Alps or the Grampians, look very formidable and inaccessible, so that a traveler turns away from them in despair, perhaps in fear. But at length he learns that on one side there is a slope and a pathway that make the ascent quite pleasant. So it is with this text, from which many turn away as being terrible and repulsive until they learn what it really means. It was the same with Luther and the texts relating to "the righteousness of God." Let me show that our text really has no terror in it; that it is just such as any believing man when coming to God should use – not only David, or only the son of David, but also all who acknowledge Him.

It is the word *holy* that makes many shrink. They say, "I am not holy, I cannot use it." How then, I ask, could David use it, when he had to say, *Behold, I was brought forth in iniquity* (Psalm 51:5), and in this psalm once and again he casts himself on the God of mercy as a sinner? But this word has no reference to spiritual perfection or even any approach to it. It does not mean "free from sin." It means one on whom God's favor rests, or, as in the margin, "one whom You favor." The question then is, Who are they on whom God's favor rests, and how do we enter into this favor?

There are some who have never been out of favor: the angels above. There are some who once were in favor but have lost it and will never regain it nor taste it again: Satan and his angels. There is only one on whom that favor rests in infinite measure: the Son of God – *"This is My beloved Son"* (Matthew 3:17). But there are some who, though they have lost it, may regain it, and such are we. God has provided a way for this – for complete restoration to His favor, and that forevermore.

This restoration is not for the least depraved, but for the chief; not for those who have some strength left, but for those who have none. Nor is it on account of or in proportion to our freedom from sin. It is entirely through another, and on account of Him in whom God is well pleased, and in proportion to His good pleasure or satisfaction in Him and in His work. God's infinite favor towards Him and delight in Him is the foundation of His favor towards us and His delight in us. Our belief of God's testimony to His wellpleasingness in His Son brings us into the state of being well pleasing to Him.

Respecting this wellbeloved Son, God has recorded a testimony. In connection with it He has given a promise that whosoever receives the testimony is immediately brought into favor with Himself. It is not a testimony without a promise, nor a promise without a testimony. It is a promise based upon a testimony, and so connected with it that we are to consider ourselves assured of the favor as soon as we receive the testimony. The moment, then, that we believe, we enter into favor, and may use the cry of our text: *Preserve my soul, for I am a godly man*. We may use this without hesitation and without presumption. So long as I do not acknowledge the divine testimony and confide in the divine promise, I am not in God's favor. Indeed, the wrath of God abides upon me. But as soon as I acknowledge and confide, I am in His favor, and I should know and rejoice in this.

There are thus, properly speaking, just two states in which a man can be before God: wrath or favor, according as he rejects or receives the testimony; and in one of these two he must come to God. Such is the alternative. He must either come saying, "Preserve my soul, for I am under wrath," or say with David, *Preserve my soul, for I am a godly man*.

Men have framed for themselves other states, less decided than these. There is:

1. *Wrath.* This is when there is an open and decided rejection of God's testimony. Then it is acknowledged that there is wrath.

2. *Semiwrath.* This is when the open rejection has ceased, and there is what is called a wish to believe or a trying to believe. Then men hold that there is a modification of the wrath – only halfwrath, and with this they pacify their consciences.

3. *Semifavor.* This is supposed to be when the sinner has taken some good steps in the right direction, made some advances toward God, though he has not fully believed the testimony, or believed it in the right way, with the necessary quantity of feeling. He is reckoned as making progress in the way to favor.

4. *Favor.* This is supposed to be when the sinner has summed up his evidence and ascertained the excellent quality of his faith. Then looking to that quality of his faith he can count on God's favor, not because he has ascertained that *it is a trustworthy statement* (1 Timothy 1:15), but because his faith is of sufficient substance and excellence.

5. *Uncertainty.* This is the general state of things. Men, professing to believe the gospel, do not know what they are, who they are, nor where they are. They are uncertain as to wrath. They speak as if there were such a thing as semiwrath, or semifavor. Indeed, they rather glory in this uncertainty as being true humility and genuine Christianity, whereas it is certainty that makes us humble and holy.

But all this is in contradiction to the Bible. In all this there is no right comprehension of either the law or the gospel. There is no approach to David's posture or David's cry, *Preserve my soul, for I am a godly man.*

Ah, surely a believed gospel was meant to do more for this. It brings us at once out of wrath and into favor. As such, we live, speak, feel, and pray. We find that in His favor is life.

Chapter 50

The Love and the Deliverance

"Because he has loved Me, therefore I will deliver him." – Psalm 91:14

This is one of the psalms of Messiah, and Satan's quotation of the eleventh verse shows that it was accepted as such by the Jews and by Jesus Himself (Matthew 4:6). Yet it is not (except for one verse) spoken *by* Messiah but *to* Messiah. It contains the Father's proclamation to Him, and to men regarding Him; and still more, it contains the Father's assurance to Him of fellowship and protection while dwelling in the land of strangers and enemies. It contains some of the words poured into His ear morning by morning when He wakened His ear to hear as one that is taught (Isaiah 50:4). For as man, He was counseled, comforted, strengthened, cheered, and taught of God.

The first and second verses are the introduction or key to the whole. In the first verse, the Father – as the Son is about to enter into His mission on earth amid all the diseases, troubles, hatreds, strifes, and conspiracies of this fallen state of danger and sorrow – proclaims, *He who dwells in the shelter of the Most High will abide in the shadow of the Almighty* (Psalm 91:1). In other words, he that *enter[s] into [his room]* (Isaiah 26:20), or takes up his abode with God *in His tabernacle* (Psalm 27:5), will be under the protection of the Almighty. Or rather we may say that the Father pours these words of cheer into the ears of the Son, making known the secret, the one secret of *the security of creaturehood*. In the second verse, the Son, in words of happy confidence, replies, *I will say to the Lord,* **"My refuge and my fortress, My God, in whom I trust!"** (Psalm 91:2, emphasis added). Then the Father, from the third to the fourteenth verse, pours into the filial ear words of blessed assurance. Deliverance, security, protection, victory over enemies and dangers, power over evil, angelic ministry – these are the assurances given by the Father to the Son in entering into His awful work in this fallen world. "Be of good cheer, for I am with you" is the substance of the assurance thus so fully given. And if ever such assurance was needed, it was then, when the thirtythree-year battle was to be fought with sin and hell.

Then in the fourteenth verse, the Father proclaims to the whole world – to men and angels – the grand principle of His dealings with His Son: what He did for Him, and why He did it, so that we may know why and what He does for us. *Deliverance* and *exaltation* are the two special blessings promised. The reasons for these are: (1) He set His love upon me, and (2) He knew my name.

Let us inquire, first, into the deliverance, and second, into the love.

1. *The rescue.* Messiah was always *in danger,* and always crying for deliverance: *Rescue me, O my God* (Psalm 71:4). How often that word was on His lips! See Psalm 22, 40, and 69. Enemies surrounded Him, as Saul surrounded David, and sought His life. Death took hold on Him. *Our* iniquities (He calls them *mine!*) took hold on Him. The snares of hell took hold on Him. The grave took hold on Him. Innumerable evils surrounded Him. But when He was sinking in deep waters, God sent and drew Him out. When uncomfortably pressed on every side, God fought for Him, and put His enemies to flight. He, the poor and needy one, was *rescued!*

2. *The reason for it.* "Because he has loved Me." God would not permit one who loved Him so much to be overpowered. Love like His must be honored! Love like His must not go down before His enemies. God's desire is to be loved, for He is infinitely lovable! He never found one before that loved Him as Christ did and could. For Christ loved Him with a *divine* strength! Oh, how gloriously was the commandment fulfilled in Christ, when He loved Him with the whole of the divine strength, that infinite capacity for

loving that belonged to Him. God honors Christ's love by granting Him continual deliverance. He loved, and He was delivered for His love! Learn this:

a. *That God wants to be loved.* He desires the love of creaturehood. He made us to love Him, and He cannot be satisfied without our love. *"You shall love the Lord your God with all your heart"* (Matthew 22:37) is not merely a command, but also a thing of earnest desire. God is not indifferent as to our love, nor heedless of our coldness. He asks for love, and He feels the refusal of it. "Love me" is His message to us; "Give me your heart." He gave us His heart when He gave His Son, and now He asks for ours in return.

b. *He is infinitely worthy of it.* He is the infinitely lovable and glorious one; just such a being as to command our entire affection and fill our souls. The only question would seem to be, "Are we permitted to love such a glorious being?" For if so, then let us pour out the whole fullness of our hearts upon Him. Who are we that we should be allowed to love Him; indeed, commanded to love Him; indeed, punished for *not* loving Him?

c. *He blesses and rewards those who love Him.* The crown of life hereafter is for those who love Him; and the present blessings of deliverance, support, defense, and comfort are to those who set their love on Him. No good thing will He withhold from those who love and fear Him. He is their light, joy, staff, shield, tower, arm, and strength. He surrounds them *with songs of deliverance* (Psalm 32:7).

Let us learn to love Him for what He is in Himself, and for what He has done and has promised to do for us. Let us love Him for His love and for His lovableness. *We love [Him], because He first loved us* (1 John 4:19). He has set His love on us; let us set our love on Him. God's love to us and our love to Him – is not this the essence of true religion? What poor, empty, shriveled things are these hearts of ours unless filled with the love of God? What a poor thing life is if it is not consecrated, gladdened, and brightened with this glorious love!

Chapter 51

The Sin and Folly of Being Unhappy

Serve the Lord with gladness. – Psalm 100:2

I once had the question put to me, "Do you think a sinner has any right to be happy here?" Without entering into the truths or errors that the question suggested, I simply answered, "Is there any religion in being miserable?" and I added at another time to a similar question, "I do not think that gloom is a bit better or more acceptable to God than the most frivolous silliness." *"Do not put on a gloomy face as the hypocrites do"* (Matthew 6:16), said the Lord. Let us consider the *sin and folly of being unhappy,* especially of rendering unhappy service to God. His yoke is easy, and His burden light.

1. *God is happy.* He is the blessed God, in whom are the fountains of all gladness. Thus that expression, "the joy of God," is one denoting the joy that is *in God,* even more than the joy He gives. Christ was a Man of Sorrows during His earthly life because He was bearing our sins. But He sorrowed so that we might not sorrow but rejoice. He served the Father in sorrow so that we might serve Him with gladness.

2. *The angels are happy.* They are the blessed angels. They only know what sorrow is by seeing it in us when they come to minister to us. Their heaven is a happy heaven, all around them is happiness;

their wells never run dry, their sky never clouds, and their sun never sets. They do not sigh, weep, wring their hands, nor sprinkle ashes on their fair heads. They always drink from the rivers of pleasure, which are at the right hand of God. Sometimes their joy rises higher, as when they shouted for joy over the newly made world, or as when they are called on to join in the joy of God over one sinner that repents. They serve the Lord with gladness.

3. *Forgiven men are happy.* This is David's testimony: *How blessed is he whose transgression is forgiven* (Psalm 32:1). These are a twofold class: (1) those who have departed and are with Christ, and (2) those who are still here. Of the latter section of redeemed men, we say they are happy though imperfect, because they are forgiven. They are in an evil world and have much evil within them – many trials, sore warfare, great feebleness – yet they are happy. Why? Because they are forgiven. The favor of God rests on them. They know it and find that in His favor is life. Being forgiven, and knowing this, they serve the Lord with gladness.

It would appear, then, not only that there is happiness in heaven with God and the holy angels, but that there is happiness also here on earth, and that we may be partakers of it. The basis and the beginning of that happiness must be the forgiveness of sins and the favor of God. These are attainable. They are presented to us as free gifts; we are implored to accept them, and we cannot reject them without sinning. We see then that it is both sinful and foolish to be unhappy; that is, where there is unhappiness, it must be the result of our own sin and folly in refusing to be happy. Let me notice then:

1. *We can only be unhappy by refusing pardon.* The pardon is provided, and it is preached to the sons of men. It is: (1) a *free* pardon, (2) a *righteous* pardon, (3) a *present* pardon, (4) a *comprehensive* pardon, covering all sin, and (5) a pardon to be had in *simply believing* what God has told us about the propitiation of His Son. God is not refusing pardon, bargaining about it, affixing unreasonable conditions or indeed conditions of any kind, nor making it an uncertainty or the reward of a good life. On the contrary, He is making it known in the clearest terms. He is

laying it down at our feet. He is taking it up and putting it into our hands, pressing us with exceeding and infinite urgency to receive it at once, absolutely, unconditionally, and unchangeably as His free gift. If so, then must not the absence of this pardon be the fruit of our own rejection of it, and not God's sovereignty or unwillingness? We are unhappy not simply because we are sinful and foolish, but also because we are resolutely indulging in the sin and folly of rejecting God's gift, and so of refusing to be happy. A sinner's unhappiness is the result of his sin and folly. O sinful, foolish man you are, to refuse the happiness provided by God; to prefer the "sad countenance" of the hypocrite to the face shining with pardon.

2. *We can only be unhappy by refusing Christ.* It is not Christ's refusing us (He never did so), but it is our refusing Christ that keeps us unhappy. He is the free gift of God to us; He, the living, the dying, the buried, the risen Christ; He, the Word made flesh; He, the great vessel of divine fullness; He, the depository of eternal life; He is God's free gift to us, a gift that we are not merely at liberty to accept, but that we also refuse at our peril. We can only be unhappy by refusing Christ! Oh, the folly and sin of remaining unhappy! Persistence in the rejection of Christ is the true cause of all the unhappiness of earth. You shut your eyes and ears against Him. How can you be happy?

3. *We can only be unhappy by determining not to turn.* God says, "*Turn back, turn back from your evil ways! Why then will you die?*" (Ezekiel 33:11). Turn and live. It is vain for us to throw the blame off ourselves and say, "I want to turn, but I cannot, and God will not help me." This is not true. "I am most willing to be converted, but God will not convert me" is just as if the drunkard were to say, "I am most willing to give up drinking, but God will not help me to be sober"; or if the swearer were to say, "I am most anxious to cease swearing, but I cannot, and God will not give me the power." Whatever, then, the solemn truth of God's sovereignty may be (and He would not be God were He not sovereign), it is not that sovereignty that is hindering you from turning, but your

own determination not to do so. Your not turning is the cause of your unhappiness. You cannot be happy until you turn. Your being unhappy is, then, your own sin and folly. O foolish sinner, to refuse to be happy! O folly, without parallel! But in that unhappy state you cannot serve the Lord.

In like manner it is with all of us. We might be always happy if we were always receiving the gifts that Christ presents to us; crediting the divine testimony as to the sufficiency of the great sacrifice, and the freeness of the great love.

Unhappiness thus is willful. "You *will* not come to me." It profits nothing. It does not liberate, strengthen, sanctify, nor comfort. To be unhappy is our folly and our sin. When happy, we can work so much more vigorously and successfully. No toil is irksome; no trouble or annoyance is felt. When unhappy, everything is reversed. Be happy then in God (this is one great part of our testimony), taste His love, live in His smile. Then you will see what a wise and holy thing happiness is, and when Jesus comes the second time you will enter into His joy.

Chapter 52

The Book of Books

Proverbs 2:1-5

The words *my son* are not spoken at random or inserted without a meaning. In them God speaks to us as unto children (Hebrews 12). It is a father's voice that speaks to us in the book of Proverbs. Solomon's counsels to Rehoboam are God's messages to us.

The subject here is the divine Word, its nature and use, with the way in which we are to receive it. It is assumed to be:

1. *True.* Not partially so, but absolutely and perfectly.

2. *Infallible.* Not domineering or dictatorial, yet infallible.

3. *Precious.* Containing infinite treasures.

4. *Profound.* It will bear searching, digging, and meditation. It has much on the surface, and far more beneath. Go as deep as you like; the vein is not exhausted.

5. *Intelligible.* Though spoken by God, it is quite as intelligible as that spoken by man. A father's words to his child are meant to be understood.

This Word is called here by many names: *my words, my commandments, wisdom, understanding, knowledge.* The way in which we are to deal with it is spoken of under various figures of speech: "receiving," "treasuring," "making the ear attentive," "inclining the heart," "crying for," "lifting up the voice for," "seeking," and "searching." Each of these implies honesty, earnestness, perseverance, and faith – each successive word embodies some more meaning, some deeper truth than its predecessor.

Let us note then:

1. *Solomon's object in the Proverbs.* It is good to go back to the original speaker or writer in order to remember the instrument through which the Holy Spirit spoke, whether it was Moses, David, Solomon, or Isaiah. This not only brings out better the human side of the book or passage, not only enables us to realize the words as thoroughly human words, but it also gives a point, interest, and meaning to them that otherwise is lost. Paul's words are not Peter's words nor John's, yet they all are the words of the Holy Spirit. So the words of Solomon the king and Amos the Tekoan sheepherder are both the words of God, yet there are differences, and these differences have a meaning. The Proverbs of Solomon would have been equally true if Amos had uttered them, yet they would not have had the unique point that they possess when coming from the lips of the greatest, richest, and wisest of kings. The royal lessons of this royal teacher and father are summed up in *the fear of the Lord* and *the knowledge of God* (verse 5). This is his object, even in that book that seems filled with common life, and its maxims and scenes. Fear God and know the Lord. This is the sum of everything that He has to say to us.

2. *God's object in the Bible.* It is to teach us to know and fear Him. There are many subordinate things, but this is the main thing; this is the result of all its precepts, warnings, facts, and histories. The Bible ends with God just as it begins with Him. It comes from God and goes back to Him, leading us along with it. The Bible especially has to do with the world to come, even in those books that are occupied with the duties and concerns of this. Let your Bible lead you straight to God. Let every perusal teach you more of Him. As was God's object in writing the Bible, so let yours be in reading it. Be sure to find Him everywhere.

3. *The way in which He would have us treat the Bible.*

a. *Receive it.* Take it as true, divine, and infallible. Listen to it as His voice and His message. Let its words flow into your ears and heart.

b. *Prize it.* It is not a common possession. It is treasure, riches, and gold – all divine. As such it must be used lovingly, reverently, devoutly, and believingly.

c. *Study it.* It must be *hidden* (verse 4), laid up, sought out, searched, and weighed. No surface work, no holiday work. Day and night it must be studied with the whole vigor of our souls.

d. *It must be prayed over.* In the study of it we must deal with God. He has the key for unlocking its chambers, and the light for showing us all its recesses. We must go to Him to be taught: *If any of you lacks wisdom, let him ask of God* (James 1:5). Like old Bradford, we must study it on our knees.

Let us notice in conclusion the connection of all of this with Christ. He is *the Word of God,* and the Bible is "the Word of God." He connects the two together when He says, *"If you abide in Me, and My words abide in you"* (John 15:7). The testimony of all Scripture is to Christ. He is its Alpha and Omega. It is through Him that we have the knowledge and the fear of God. To know Him is to know the Father, and we find Him in the Word. The more we dig into the Word, the more we find of Him. They are those that testify of Him. Search the Scriptures! They contain life, and they contain *the life* (John 14:6). Let us go to them for both. How little of them do we know. How much we should know and might know if we would only search! Would you be wise? Study the Word and find *the wisdom of God* there (1 Corinthians 1:24). Would you be holy? Study the Word. It sanctifies its readers. Would you be happy? Study the Word. In its words is blessedness – the peace and joy of God.

Chapter 53

The Secret of Deliverance from Evil

By the fear of the Lord one keeps away from evil. – Proverbs 16:6

There is evil in the world. The world is now the opposite of what God made it – it was good, *very good* (Genesis 1:31). It now lies in wickedness. There is evil within and without, evil morally and physically. Every creature of God was made good, but each one has become evil. There is evil in the sense of disorder, pain, disease, sorrow, and death. There also is evil in the sense of *sin*. It is this last thing that our text points to. For evil in the sense of disease, death, or sorrow is not to be cured just now by the remedy our text suggests, or by any remedy whatever. We wait for these cures until the resurrection of the just.

What then is this evil that God calls *sin*? To know this, we must go to the Bible, and the Bible points us to the fall, the flood, Sodom and Gomorrah, Sinai, and Calvary, so that we may learn what it is and what God thinks of it. Especially the last two are important: Sinai and Calvary; not Sinai without Calvary, nor Calvary without Sinai. The law must be read in the light of the cross. There is another revelation or declaration of sin, but it has not come yet: the second death, an eternal hell. And yet when it does come, it will not tell us more than the cross has.

Men make light of sin; fools make a mockery of sin. At the worst they treat it simply as a calamity, an unavoidable misfortune, a hereditary evil for which they are not wholly responsible. God's estimate of sin is unspeakably awful. "It is the abominable thing that I hate; it is an evil that I cannot bear; it cast the angels out of heaven; it rained on the world; it brought the flood; it drew down the fire and brimstone; it slew my Son; it will yet set the world on fire; it will kindle hell." God does not look on sin as man looks on it.

We wonder at all this and say, "Why then does God allow it to remain? Why did He let it enter? Why does He not sweep it off?"

We answer that God allowed it to enter just so that it might spread and unfold itself; and yet also that it might at length be utterly rooted out. He did not destroy it at once, because He wished to show its awful nature, its power to propagate, its manifold aspects, the utter impotency of mere creaturehood, and yet also to crush it forever. God at this moment is carrying on these two processes – letting sin spread and develop itself, and getting rid of it. One great object in redemption is to destroy it from man's heart and from man's earth. The Bible is a revelation of God's means for thus eradicating sin. The Son of Man came to deliver us from it, and He does so by bringing us back to the fear of God.

How am I to get rid of this evil? This is the great question.

1. *Not by time.* Time cures many things, but not this. It wears down the rock, but it does not cure sin. Sin only grows more ingrained when left to itself.

2. *Not by effort.* The strength of human will is no more against sin than the helm of the little skiff in the day of the raging tempest. Human resolution will not do. The Enemy is too subtle and too strong.

3. *Not by human wisdom.* Science and philosophy can do nothing. Human skill, human devices, and physical implements – laws social, sanitary, or political can do nothing. It is too terrible a disease for man to heal.

4. *Not by law.* By the law is the knowledge of sin, not the cure of it. The law is powerless in such a case. It is but a torch held up at midnight to show the ruin, havoc, and woe.

5. *Not by terror.* By terror evil may be pent up – compelled to hide itself, not be driven out. No terror nor force can make a man holy.

If not by these, then by what is evil expelled from us? By *the fear of the*

Lord, our text replies. It is only this that goes to the root of the matter. This is the true medicine, the true corrective, the true deterrent, the true expulsive energy, acting both from without and from within: from without, because He whom we fear is without; from within, because this fear of the Lord is implanted within us.

By the fear of God, we do not mean the dread of God or the terror of the Lord. Dread may restrain evil, but it cannot eradicate it. It may make a man a plausible hypocrite, but not a saint. The true fear of the Lord, the moment that it begins to act upon the soul, does lead men to depart from evil.

This fear of God has its root in *pardon*. *There is forgiveness with You, that You may be feared* (Psalm 130:4). Forgiveness, ascertained forgiveness, conscious forgiveness – this is the beginning of all true fear. The lack of pardon, a doubtful pardon, a pardon to be worked for all the days of our life may produce *dread,* but not *fear.*

This fear resting on an ascertained forgiveness expels a world of evil from the human heart and keeps it from reentrance. It loosens the hold that sin has on us. It liberates us so that we may be free to be holy. The evil things that God hates – bondage, gloom, moroseness, doubt, hard thoughts, as well as love of the world and love of sin – are all detached from us, and we from them. Like sunshine falling on a frozen river, the fear of God dissolves our frozen faculties, and sets aflow the waters of the soul. It works itself out, and unfolds itself in such things as:

1. *Obedience.* We obey because we fear. This is the true obedience, the result of familial, happy fear. We are constrained to obey, yet we obey freely and joyfully.

2. *Fellowship.* Without the fear that springs from pardon, there could be no fellowship. Dread keeps the soul from God; true fear brings it close. Dread shuts up the soul against interaction with God; true fear leads it to reveal itself without reserve, yet with reverence.

3. *Love.* Fear produces love, and love produces fear. They minister to each other. God's forgiving love kindles love in us; and yet it is reverential love, for He who has forgiven and loved us is so infinitely great and glorious.

4. *Zeal.* Work for this God becomes our second nature. We cannot help

but work. The effect of this blessed fear upon us is to set all our faculties in motion, to make us zealous men. Slothfulness, selfishness, and indifference, when touched by this fear, flee like unclean spirits.

Thus, we say to ourselves:

1. *I fear God; therefore I must listen to Him.* I am not terrified into listening, I am attracted to it. The voice of that infinite Jehovah who has freely forgiven me is to me the sweetest as well as the most solemn of all voices. I love to hear Him speak, and I am always saying, *"Speak, for Your servant is listening"* (1 Samuel 3:10).

2. *I fear God; therefore I must try to please Him.* I must not merely seek to avoid offending or displeasing Him, but I must also try to *please* Him; and I must live, like Enoch, a life of Godpleasing, not manpleasing, nor selfpleasing.

3. *I fear God; therefore I must give up sin.* This new fear of God has turned my love of sin into hatred of it. I hate sin because I fear God. He hates it; therefore I hate it and give it up. The more I think of Him, the more I am disposed to part with all sin.

4. *I fear God; therefore I must do His will.* The will of Him whom I fear must always be my rule of duty. The more that I fear Him, the more His will becomes my rule. Not my will, but Yours be done, is what we say to the God whom we fear.

5. *I fear God; therefore I must seek to be like Him.* Mere dread would never lead us to desire conformity to His image, but fear does. It is because of God's glory that we stand in awe of it, and in beholding it, we are changed into the same image from glory to glory.

Thus, it is that by the fear of the Lord men depart from evil. Yes, this is the divine cure for sin. This is our strength against temptation; our refuge against the fear of man; our help against every adversary. What a glorifying thing it is to God when we say that His fear would deliver you from all sin.

What a solemn thing it is to tell the sinner that it is the lack of this fear that is making you what you are. *Transgression speaks to the ungodly within his heart; there is no fear of God before his eyes* (Psalm 36:1). Yes, the lack of this fear is the cause of all the evil, and the presence of this fear would be the introducer of all good.

Chapter 54

The Voice of the Heavenly Bridegroom

"Arise, my darling, my beautiful one, and come along." – Song of Solomon 2:10, 13

The speaker is the heavenly Bridegroom, the Lord Jesus Christ. It is His voice we hear; the voice that is as the sound of many waters; that spoke the *gracious words* (Zechariah 1:13), the like of which were never uttered on earth. It is to His bride that He speaks; the bride, the Lamb's wife; His chosen, redeemed, called, and sanctified one; given Him of the Father before the world began; His one spouse, His love, His dove, His undefiled, of whom it is written, *Christ also loved the church and gave Himself up for her* (Ephesians 5:25). This bride, this body, is composed of the saints of all ages; all of them washed in the same blood and clothed with the same righteousness.

1. *It is the voice of love. My love* (KJV) is His name for His church. He has other names of endearment for her, but this is the chief name. Everything in Him promises love. Everything that He is, says, and does indicates love; a love that passes knowledge; a love that is stronger than death and the grave; a love that many waters cannot quench, nor the floods drown. It is in this tender love that the Bridegroom addresses the bride.

2. *It is the voice of admiration. My fair one* (KJV) is His name for her. *You are all fair, my love; there is no spot in you.* The *fairest among women* (Song of Solomon 6:1 KJV) is His name for her, even as her name for Him is the *"outstanding among ten thousand"* (Song of Solomon 5:10). The heart of the Bridegroom is full of *admiration* for the beauty and perfection of His bride. She is *"perfect because of My splendor which I bestowed on [her]"* (Ezekiel 16:14). He has ravished our heart, and we have ravished *His.*

3. *It is the voice of authority. The husband is the head of the wife* (Ephesians 5:23); so is Christ the head of the church; and though it is love that speaks, it is authoritative love. *"Arise, . . . and come along."* Obedience is our true position, and no amount of love in Him can ever alter this. It is not bondage, but it is obedience. It is not sternness on His part, yet it is *authority.* Our Bridegroom is Jehovah, Immanuel, King of Kings, and Lord of Lords. Should we treat His voice as that of an inferior or an equal, or as the voice of Him whom no amount of condescension and endearment and admiration can ever make less truly the head of the church, the head of principalities and powers, the head of the universe, of whom it is said to the church, *He is your Lord, bow down to Him* (Psalm 45:11)?

But *when* and *in what circumstances* does He speak these words to His church? Doubtless at His second coming, when calling her to the honor and glory prepared for her.

1. *When He calls her up into the clouds to meet Him in the air.* He comes *for her,* and He finds her in the grave. He speaks to her as once before to Lazarus: *"Come forth"* (John 11:43). *"You will call, and I will answer You"* (Job 14:15); *You who lie in the dust, awake and shout for joy* (Isaiah 26:19). He summons her from the tomb. He summons her up into the clouds, into His pavilion, where the marriage is celebrated: "Come up here." He speaks, she hears, and goes up to meet Him for whom she had waited so long. *Arise, my love* (verse 13 KJV).

2. *When He calls her into the marriage chamber.* The marriage follows the ascension. She goes in with Him to the marriage; blessed are

they that are called to the marriage supper; she goes in and sits down beside Him as His bride, His queen, in gold of Ophir. *Arise, my love.*

3. *When He calls her into the new Jerusalem.* Out of the marriage chamber they come. They rise up from the feast. They enter the city. He calls her into the city that He has prepared – the place that He had gone to prepare for her – the *many mansions* (John 14:2 KJV). *Arise, my love.*

4. *When He calls her up to His throne.* This is the final act of blessing. Come sit with Me on My throne; come reign with Me over a redeemed creation. Now the crown is put upon her head, and the royal robes adorn her. The everlasting kingdom is now hers. She is an heir of God, and a joint heir with Christ Jesus. *Arise, my love.*

Thus He will speak to His church in the day of His coming glory, for then will the song of songs be realized to the full.

Meanwhile, He speaks thus to us individually. As He said to Abraham in Ur, *"Go forth from your country"* (Genesis 12:1), so does He speak to each of His Abrahams, His chosen ones, "Come out and be separate; arise, shine, for your light is come; arise, leave the world; become a pilgrim; arise, leave your sins, become holy; arise, take up your cross and follow Me." He spoke this way to each of us at first. He speaks this way to each of us still every day, for every day is a repetition of the first message on His part, and the first obedience on ours. Arise – come away – follow Me. He speaks as the Savior, and as the Bridegroom. Let us hear, let us follow. Upward, still upward; onward, still onward, is His beckoning. This is no place of tarrying; no congenial air or climate or company for the bride, the Lamb's wife. This is not our rest. This is not the resurrection land, the marriage hall, the new Jerusalem, nor the kingdom. We must not tarry here. We have foretastes here, but that is all. The Lord's Supper reminds us of the marriage supper. It is well to sit for an hour at the earthly table, but it is better to sit down forever at the eternal table. With such a summons and such a hope, let us not sleep as others do. Let us awake and arise, and come away – away from sin, death, and sorrow; away to the everlasting hills, the everlasting city, the everlasting glory. We are joint heirs with Him, partakers of His throne and crown.

Chapter 55

The Love That Passes Knowledge

"Many waters cannot quench love, nor will rivers overflow it; if a man were to give all the riches of his house for love, it would be utterly despised." – Song of Solomon 8:7

Let us take this verse as descriptive of the love of Christ, *the love ... which surpasses knowledge* (Ephesians 3:19). It is He who speaks in the fifth verse, *"Beneath the apple tree I awakened you."* His words here remind us of similar ones elsewhere: *"I have loved you with an everlasting love; therefore I have drawn you with lovingkindness"* (Jeremiah 31:3); *I led them with cords of a man, with bonds of love* (Hosea 11:4); *"He found him in a desert land, and in the howling waste of a wilderness"* (Deuteronomy 32:10). Only these three passages refer to Israel, whereas our text refers to the whole church from the beginning, of which it is said, *Christ also loved the church and gave Himself up for her* (Ephesians 5:25).

We might say that the passage carries us back to Eve, *the mother of all the living* (Genesis 3:20), under the fatal tree. The Redeemer comes and raises up her offspring under that tree, for she is *the mother of all the living;* and there this mother of the living brought her children forth in sorrow, according to the original sentence on the woman: *"In pain you will bring forth children"* (Genesis 3:16).

Jesus thus declares His love to His church, and she replies, *"Put me like a seal"* (Song of Solomon 8:6), not only *over your heart,* but also *on your arm,* your inner and your outer part – your place of love, your place of strength, your place of energy and action. *Who will separate us from the love of Christ?* (Romans 8:35). His love is as invincible and irresistible as death. It is a jealous love, as unyielding and relentless as the grave. Its true figure is that of fire – coals of fire – the very flame of Jehovah. Here, then, is the love of Christ! Its breadth, length, height, and depth are absolutely immeasurable. But our text singles out two things especially concerning this love: (1) It is *unquenchable,* and (2) it is *unpurchasable.*

1. *It is unquenchable.* It is not *all* love that is unquenchable, but this love is. It is love forevermore. As the great old poet wrote:

> Love is not love,
> Which alters when it alteration finds,
> Or bends, with the remover to remove;
> Oh no, it is an everfixed mark,
> That looks on tempests, and is never shaken.
> It is the star to every wandering bark,
> Whose worth's unknown, although his height be taken.

This great love of Christ's is beyond a father's, mother's, brother's, sister's, or a lover's love. It is the one and only love that passes knowledge; the one love that nothing in heaven, earth, or hell is able to extinguish or cool; the one love whose dimensions are beyond all measure. It is here spoken of as a thing of *fire;* and as such it is affirmed that *waters, deep waters* (Psalm 69:1-2) cannot quench it; and as a thing of life that the floods cannot drown (Psalm 69:15; 93:3).

1. *The waters of shame and suffering sought to quench and drown it.* They would have hindered its outflowing and would have come (like Peter) between the Savior and the cross, but this love refused to be restrained on its way to Calvary. It would not be either quenched or drowned. Herein was love! It leaped over all the barriers in its way. It refused to be extinguished or drowned. Its fire would not be quenched; its life would not be drowned.

2. *The waters of death sought to quench it.* Their waves and billows went over Him. The grave sought to cool or quench it, but it proved itself stronger than death. Neither death nor the grave could alter or weaken it. It came out of both as strong as before. Love defied death and overcame it.

3. *The waters of our unworthiness could not quench nor drown love.* In general, we find love drawing to the lovable, and when anything unbecoming occurs, we find it withdrawing from its object. Not so here. All our unfitness and unlovableness could not quench nor drown His love. It clung to the unlovely and refused to be torn away.

4. *The waters of our long rejection sought to quench it.* After the gospel had shown us that personal unworthiness could not restrain the love of Christ, we continued to reject Him and His love. Yet His love surmounted this unbelief and survived this rejection. In spite of everything, it remained unquenched.

5. *The waters of our daily inconsistency sought to quench it.* Even after we have believed, we are constantly coming up short. Ah, what inconsistencies, coldness, backslidings, lukewarmness, doubtings, worldliness, and the like, are flowing over this love daily to quench its fire and drown its life! Yet it survives everything; it remains unquenched and unquenchable.

All these infinite evils in us are like *waters, deep waters;* like *floods;* like torrents of sin, waves, and billows of evil – all constantly laboring to quench and drown the love of Christ! And truly they would have annihilated any other love, any love less than divine. But this is unchangeable and everlasting.

2. *It is unpurchasable.* "*If a man were to give all the riches of his house for love, it would be utterly despised.*" The full meaning of this will come out under the following topics. All that a man has can do nothing in such a case. Love is not merchandise. It is not a marketable commodity. It has nothing to do with gold and silver. A man's whole substance is unprofitable and useless:

1. *As a gift to persuade Him to love.* Love does not come by gifts; least of all does divine love come by human gifts. Christ's favor cannot be purchased by money. He loves without gifts and before all gifts. Let us do justice to His free love!

2. *As payment for having been loved.* Neither before nor after does gold have anything to do with love. Pay a man for loving? How revolting the thought! Pay Christ for loving? What a wickedness and what an impossibility in the thought! Love is altogether free.

3. *As a bribe to tempt Him **not** to love.* Should the whole universe be offered to Christ on condition of His ceasing to love us, it would be utterly despised. *Who [or what] will separate us from the love of Christ?* All earth and heaven together would be ineffective to cool or quench this mighty love. He cannot but love, whatever may be the gifts offered to sustain His love.

4. *As a substitute for love.* As if a man should say to another – a father to a son, or a brother to a sister – "I cannot love you, but here is money to make up for my lack of love." Would not such a proposal be utterly despised? As if Christ were to say to us, "I cannot love you, but I give you heaven, will that suffice?" Would we not answer, "What are all these gifts without love? Though we give our body to be burned, what would this be without love?" Or what can Christ say to us for bringing Him gifts, offerings, prayers, tears, and money – everything but love? Without love, what are the riches of the universe? It is love He asks for; it is love we need. Love we must have. What will be given in exchange for love?

The love of Christ truly passes knowledge. It is infinite like Himself. It emerges out of every storm or flood. It survives all unworthiness, and unbelief, and rejection. It is this that fills the soul, that liberates us from bondage, and that gladdens us in the most sorrowful hour. Love is the true sunshine of life, and with this love Christ is to fill not heaven only, but also earth, when He comes again in His glory.

Chapter 56

The Vision of the Glory

Isaiah 6:1-13

Whether this vision records Isaiah's *first* call to the prophetic ministry does not matter. It is either the introduction to his whole ministry, or to a new section of it, and probably the latter, with the first five chapters describing Israel as ripening for judgment, and the sixth as receiving the sentence. Let us take up the chapter under the following topics:

1. *The vision* (verse 1). It was a temple vision, a vision of glory, the glory of Jehovah of hosts. As such, it was the glory of the King and the High Priest, of the throne and the temple; and all this when Uzziah the king lay dying or was dead – the earthly king passing away, the heavenly King showing Himself. It was truly a royal and glorious vision – Jehovah Himself the center of it – King of Kings and Lord of Lords, true King of Israel and of the earth, true Melchizedek, the High Priest upon His throne. In connection with this King are the seraphim. Probably these are the same as cherubim, as they are almost identical with those described in Ezekiel and Revelation. In Genesis and in the historical books they appear as cherubim, or "figures"; in Isaiah as seraphim, or "burners"; in Ezekiel as *living beings;* in Revelation as *living creatures.* Here they stand upon the train of the royal robe that filled the temple. They have six wings. Two wings cover the face – as if the glory were overwhelming to them

(as when *Moses hid his face* (Exodus 3:6)); two wings cover their feet – to hide their whole person, body (*their bodies* (Ezekiel 1:23 KJV)), and feet from the brightness; and two wings that they fly with, as if ready to go forth on the errands of this mighty King. Is not this the true posture of every saint of God? Solemn awe in the presence of the divine majesty, as unfit to look upon the glorious One; profound selfabasement, as unfit to be looked upon by One so holy; readiness to do the work of God, to go forth in His service on the wings of faith and love.

2. *The voice* (verse 3). It was the voice of the seraphim, a responsive song, *one called out to another.* Their song was: (1) of Jehovah of hosts, and of His threefold holiness; and (2) of earth – the whole earth – earth filled with His glory. Thus, the voice interprets the vision. It is a vision of latterday glory – when the Lord alone will be exalted, when holiness to the Lord will be seen and heard everywhere, and when the glory of the Lord will fill the world. What a contrast the state of things thus revealed to that in the day of the prophet! This holy glory was to Him exceedingly marvelous – a holy glory in connection with Jehovah of hosts as King of all the earth. It is the times of restitution of all things when the Lord alone will be exalted.

3. *The shaking* (verse 4). The posts of the door, or *the foundations of the thresholds,* moved or shook or *trembled* at the voice of the seraphim, and the temple was filled with smoke. The foundations of God's own house are moved at the voice of the marvelous song, and the house is filled with that which symbolizes Jehovah's holy anger against sin (Psalm 18:9). The vision seems to be that of God coming down in His holiness to shake the earth, and to express His hatred against sin, and especially against Israel's sin in His own sanctuary (Isaiah 65:5). He is spoken of here as arising to *shake* terribly the earth – beginning at His own temple, but not ceasing until He has shaken everything that can be shaken, *so that those things which cannot be shaken may remain* (Hebrews 12:27). When God's anger becomes hot against sin, then all the earth will be as Sinai – when the mountain *shook* and was covered with smoke from the presence of the Holy Lord God. The "battles of *shaking*" for our world are yet to come (Isaiah 30:32).

4. *The prophet's alarm* (verse 5). His cry is, *"Woe is me"*; indeed, *"I am ruined!"* The reason for his alarm is a new and deeper view of his own sinfulness, from a new view of Jehovah's holiness. *"I am a man of unclean lips"*; indeed, *"I live among a people of unclean lips."* He gives the reason – *"For my eyes have seen the King, the Lord of hosts."* Thus, the nearer God comes to us, the more are we made aware of our uncleanness (even that of our lips) and feel the uncleanness of a world of unclean lips in which we dwell. The vision of earth filled with holy glory, and with the presence of its glorious King, has overwhelmed him, as in the case of Daniel (Daniel 10:8) and John (Revelation 1:17). The more we realize a present God, and an earth filled with His glory, the more we should feel our own unholiness and cry out in fear, even though we are saints. We feel the awful contrast between our unholy lips and the holy lips of those who are singing, *"Holy, Holy, Holy, is the Lord of hosts"* (verse 3). It was Israel's *unclean lips* that cried, *"Crucify Him!"*; and for the words of their unclean lips, they are now suffering the woes of God.

5. *God's cure for this alarm* (verse 7). A live coal from the altar applied to his lips – that special part that he felt was impure, and in which purity was especially needed by him as a prophet. A prophet is a man like us, yet God must purify his lips so that he may speak. He does this by fire and blood, for the live coal was from the altar of burnt offering. Thus, the blood makes clean, and the fire purifies – *the spirit of burning* (Isaiah 4:4). This application of fire and blood to his lips removes his fears, his personal uncleanness, and national uncleanness; for the fire and blood were meant to apply to the *people of unclean lips* as well as to himself. Thus, the sense of uncleanness is removed. Thus, the terror that the nearer presence of God produces is removed by that which assures the sinner of pardon and cleansing. The man's terrors are dispelled. He feels that he can now act and speak for God.

6. *God's inquiry for a messenger.* Jehovah's voice is heard. Its utterance is twofold: (1) *"Whom shall I send?"* and (2) *"Who will go for Us?"* (verse 8). It is an errand of hardship, painfulness, danger, and shame, from which flesh and blood would shrink, as did Moses, Jeremiah, and Ezekiel. Still, God in every age is looking around and asking for a messenger – for

evangelists, for missionaries, for ministers – Spiritcalled, Spiritfilled, Spiritsent messengers. The work is great, the field is large, the message is judgment as well as mercy. *"Whom shall I send, and who will go?"*

7. *The prophet's answer.* *"Here am I. Send me!"* (verse 8). He answers the second question first, but he answers *both* explicitly. He does not shrink. He is ready for shame, for prison, for death – as indeed he found at last. The spirit is willing, and the flesh has overcome its weakness. The fire and blood have removed the terror and made him bold. Thus it was with Whitefield.

8. *The message* (verses 9-11). It is one of judgment: (1) *for the people,* the worst of judgments; hear on and understand not, look on but do not see; a hard heart, an insensible and impenetrable soul, a seared conscience, given over to a reprobate mind; and (2) *for the land,* to lie waste and desolate, its fields untilled, its cities forsaken. This is the message of double judgment – complete and terrible ruin. This is the end of the people of *unclean lips.*

9. *The promise* (verse 13). All of Israel's judgments have a promise mixed in with them – a hope appended to them. They are not forever. Their unbelief is not forever. Their land's desolation is not forever. There is a *holy seed* or root, in which the blessing lies hidden, even in the midst of the curse; and out of this seed, or root, or *stump,* the future tree is to arise, more glorious than the first. Israel will blossom, bud, and fill the face of the world with fruit. Here is the gleam of hope in the midst of despair and darkness. But how terrible the history through which Israel passes to get to this! How fearfully God avenges unbelief and rejection of His grace! Yet the day dawns at last! The King comes in His glory.

Chapter 57

Man's Extremity and Satan's Opportunity

When they say to you, "Consult the mediums and the spiritists who whisper and mutter," should not a people consult their God? Should they consult the dead on behalf of the living? To the law and to the testimony! If they do not speak according to this word, it is because they have no dawn. They will pass through the land hard-pressed and famished, and it will turn out that when they are hungry, they will be enraged and curse their king and their God as they face upward. Then they will look to the earth, and behold, distress and darkness, the gloom of anguish; and they will be driven away into darkness. – Isaiah 8:19-22

"Man's extremity," says the good proverb, "is God's opportunity." However, we may coin another proverb and say, "Man's extremity is the devil's opportunity." It was so in the case of Saul at En-dor, and of Jehoram at Ekron, when, in the hour of despair, they threw themselves into the arms of the devil. It will be so, as long as there is a devil to waylay and ensnare us. He is always ready with his temptations, but especially in the day of human darkness and depression. He has special work to do at such a time, and he knows how to do it. God and Satan stand with arms outstretched to receive the poor overwhelmed and sorrowful one, but how often does he prefer the embrace and the counsel of hell to those of heaven? He preferred it even in Paradise!

The picture drawn here is that of Israel – Israel especially in the last days, when their unbelief and darkness increase, when the most appalling calamities are overflowing them and their land. It is then that God's Spirit leaves them utterly, when judgments are showering down, when despair takes possession of them, that Satan suggests, "Try my wisdom, my wizards, my familiar spirits." They try these, but it only makes the evil worse. Hardly helped and hungry, they fret and curse both king and God. They look above, but it is all darkness. They look beneath, but it is all trouble and *the gloom of anguish*. All around them is darkness that may be felt. They are passing through great tribulation, their last sorrow; it is the time of Jacob's trouble. Let us learn God's lessons here.

1. *There are critical seasons in the history of a soul.* It has been tossed fearfully; *conflicts without, fears within* (2 Corinthians 7:5). Unbelief, skepticism, atheism, and uncertainty of every kind – these, like the four winds of heaven, rush at once over and through the soul. It feels itself drifting on the rocks. It turns around and in desperation tries to face the storm. Like the stag at bay, it wheels around upon its merciless pursuers. Will it battle them, or give itself up to be torn in pieces without a struggle? These are fearful moments for the soul. It is an unearthly struggle. It seems to be hurrying the sinner to despair. In such a condition, how profound should be our pity! Should we be angry? Should we rage at these troubled ones? Should we call them hard names? No, let us be compassionate with them. They are just upon the rocks; the breakers are whitening over them. If ever there was a case for Christian love, it is here. "Let those rage against you," says Augustine, "who know not with what labor truth is found; with what groans and sighs we get to understand the very least of God."

2. *Of these critical seasons Satan avails himself.* He comes offering help; holding out his hand; offering his own wisdom and strength, or man's wisdom and strength; endeavoring in every way to prevent the soul from taking itself to God, His Spirit, and the Bible. Anything rather than the cross, the blood, or the righteousness! All doubts and difficulties in reference to these are started. It is whispered that the Bible is not true, not wholly

inspired; that there is no hell, or that none will go there; *"you surely will not die"* (Genesis 3:4); that science is more noble than revelation, that reason is a higher thing than faith; that the creeds of other days are obsolete; that there must be progress and development. All these suggestions are pleasing to the pride of man, and eagerly seized upon. In how many cases like these and on how many points has he triumphed. Man's extremity has been his opportunity. He has stepped in with his lies and flatteries, and he has prevailed. The soul has turned away from God and Christ and the Bible, and has turned to *familiar spirits* (Isaiah 8:19 KJV), to *doctrines of devils* (1 Timothy 4:1 KJV), to *strong delusion* (2 Thessalonians 2:11 KJV).

3. *These tools of Satan only make matters worse.* They remove no doubts; they only increase them; deepening the darkness; leading on from depth to depth, from error to error, from unbelief to unbelief, from blasphemy to blasphemy. No man ever gained by yielding to Satan or ever lost by yielding to God. Dark as the soul may be, it only becomes darker by believing Satan's lies. It becomes more wretched and more hopeless the more that it deserts the divine teaching and listens either to that of earth or hell, however plausible it may be.

4. *At such seasons God comes especially near to offer His aid.* He never deserts a man on this side of hell. He follows him into the thick darkness, offering light; into the lowest depth, offering help. He is at hand in the day of evil, even to the evilest sons of men. No man can say, "God has abandoned me to the devil, to myself, to error, and to sin." Christ's tears over Jerusalem are the proof of this.

5. *At such seasons Christians ought specially to pity and to help.* These distractions and doubts that we see around us are the signals of distress, unconsciously held up by a wretched world. These errors and disbeliefs are the rockets sent up from wrecked ships. This is a day of fearful disbelief and change. Men rushing from one opinion to another to soothe their restlessness. Surely it is a day for pity, not for anger; a day for prayer more than for argument. Now the world is in crisis, so let the church's pity and prayers go forth day and night. Now is the time for tears and intercessions. To your knees, O church of God!

Chapter 58

The Day of Clear Vision to the Dim Eyes

Then the eyes of those who see will not be blinded. – Isaiah 32:3

These blessed words tell us four things: (1) There are eyes that do not see. (2) There are eyes that do see. (3) Some of the eyes that see are dim. (4) The time is at hand when they should not be dim.

1. *There are eyes that do not see.* Of the dead idols this is said: *They have eyes, but they cannot see* (Psalm 115:5); and this is not wonderful. But that the same should be said of living men is awful. It is not true of angels; it is not true of devils. They have eyes and see. It is true of men – of millions – of the greater part of our race. They have eyes but do not see. They shut them; they turn them away from their proper objects; they allow scales to grow over them; they deliberately veil them. O fearful calamity! O bitter curse! And yet for all this, they themselves are responsible. It is not God that blinds them, veils them, or darkens them. They are their own undoers. They did not wish to see. They were resolved not to see. *Selfblinded,* not *Godblinded*! They allow this world to blind or dazzle them so that their eyes are useless. They let Satan, the god of this world, put his hand over their eyes or bewilder them with his snares and enticements. Thus, having eyes they do not see.

2. *There are eyes that do see.* These are they whom God has enlightened; whose eyes the Son of God has opened; for it is His work to open the eyes of the blind. They did not open their own eyes. Their eyes did not open by chance. Once they were blind – quite as blind as others, but now they see. There are not many of whom this can be said, yet there are some. And what do they see? They see: (1) God, (2) Christ, (3) themselves, (4) the Word of God, and (5) the things within the veil. They are not like the men of this world, with eyes that see outward things – sun, moon, and stars, earth and sea, woods, hills, and fields. They see beyond all these – that which is spiritual and divine; that which is true and glorious. Yes, they see! In a blinded generation they see! How great a thing and how blessed to be able to say this of them – they see! They have eyes that are not useless; eyes that do not mislead; eyes that present things in their proper light, proportions, and distances! Their eyes have been anointed with the heavenly eye salve, and they see! They no longer stumble nor grope in the dark, nor go after false objects. They *see,* and they *know* that they see!

3. *Some of the eyes that see are dim.* They see, but they do not see afar off (2 Peter 1:9). They see, but it is dimly. Their vision is defective. They see men as trees walking. They are nearsighted and shortsighted. Their eyes require further purging. They *ought* to see fully and truly, but they do not. They were not meant to be dim. God has no pleasure in their being dim. The objects are vivid and distinct, yet they are seen dimly. In what respects is this the case? What they see is: (1) only part or parts of the truth, and (2) imperfectly realized. The gospel is but half a gospel. The cross is not so full of peace and light as it should be. The way of life is only partially known. The coming glory has only a feeble radiance. The advent of Christ has only a little value to them. Christ Himself has only a little of the excellence that He should possess to them and is poorly appreciated. There is no doubt something in the atmosphere of this present evil world that hinders vision and clouds the eye; but still, after all, it is the dimness of the eye that is the evil. How many are afflicted their whole lifetime with this imperfect vision. How much they lose by this! Their faith is not the substance of things hoped for, it is but the shadow of that substance. Hope is to them a vague expectation, with little certainty or brightness in it. Their life has more of the cloud than of the sunshine about it.

4. *The time is at hand when these eyes will not be dim.* There are many partial removals of this dimness even now. Times when we see farther and more clearly. At Pentecost this was the case. At the Reformation also. In times of revival, it has been so. In individual cases this has been known. Paul was a man that saw clearly. Augustine, Wycliffe, Luther, Calvin, Knox, Rutherford, and Edwards were all clearsighted men from whom the Holy Spirit had purged the scales and the dimness. But the reference here is prophetical. The prophet points to a coming era of perfection, when we will see Him as He is, see as we are seen, and know as we are known. No dimness then, no defective vision, no cloudy atmosphere, and no diseased organ of sight. All brightness and distinctness. The cross clear and bright. The light and love unclouded. Christ seen face-to-face, no longer in a glass darkly. Every ray of glory coming freshly from His revealed countenance; every feature fair and perfect; Himself the chief among ten thousand; His kingdom infinitely glorious. No doubting either as to the things of Christ, or our interest in them. No unbelief, error, nor mist. All the perfection of vision, and the perfection of light. O day of brightness and true vision, dawn! O morning star, arise! O prince of light, Light of the World, make haste, end the long darkness of humanity, and cover earth with celestial sunshine!

Chapter 59

The Unfainting Creator and the Fainting Creature

Do you not know? Have you not heard? The Everlasting God, the Lord, the Creator of the ends of the earth does not become weary or tired. His understanding is inscrutable. He gives strength to the weary, and to him who lacks might He increases power. Though youths grow weary and tired, and vigorous young men stumble badly, yet those who wait for the Lord will gain new strength; they will mount up with wings like eagles, they will run and not get tired, they will walk and not become weary. – Isaiah 40:28-31

This was God's answer to Israel of old in their day of trouble. It is still His answer to a desponding spirit that thinks its case hopeless and itself forsaken of God. God Himself thus speaks in His love to such. Instead of taking each clause separately, let us thus classify the various points here brought before us: (1) an unfainting God, (2) a fainting sinner, and (3) an unfainting saint.

1. *An unfainting God*. It is to *Himself* that He draws our eye in our anxiety: "Turn to me"; "trust in the Lord." He wonders that we should not have known nor heard of Him and His greatness; or that having heard

of Him, we should ever give way to despondency. With such a God to go to, how can we be cautious or troubled?

1. *His name.* It is threefold, and each of its three parts is most full and suitable: *The Everlasting God, the Lord, the Creator of the ends of the earth.* What a name, what a declaration of Himself is this! Excellency, duration, life, and power are all here! Ah, surely they who know such a name will put their trust in Him.

2. *His character.* He *does not become weary or tired;* He is unsearchable in wisdom. Here is the unfainting God – the only wise God. Past ages have proved Him such; the experience of those who have known Him has borne testimony to Him. Time, work, and difficulty cannot make Him faint or weary. Nothing in earth or heaven or hell can affect Him. He has been working up to this time, and is still working (John 5:17), but He is not weary.

3. *His ways.* They are not as our ways. They are the ways of bountifulness and love. He is the giving one; He is always giving; giving more and more; never weary of giving; giving power, strength, and all that is needed. Yes, *He who did not spare His own Son, but delivered Him over for us all, how will He not also with Him freely give us all things?* (Romans 8:32).

This is the God with whom we have to do! Such is His name, His character, and His ways! Have we not known Him, nor heard? To know Him is life; to listen to Him is peace forevermore.

2. *A fainting sinner.* The object toward which the power of this mighty God is turned is a *sinner;* one who is *faint, who lacks might.* It is the utter helplessness of the object that attracts Him. It is not "like drawing to like," but the unlike. It is the unlikeness that constitutes the attraction and the fitness. *For while we were still helpless, at the right time Christ died for the ungodly* (Romans 5:6). Thus, the two extremes meet: the weakness of the creature, and the power of the Creator; each so exactly suiting the other, and each requiring the other. It is this state of things that shows the folly of those who despair of being saved because they are so weak. The truth is, they are not yet *weak enough* for God to save

them. They must come down to a lower degree of helplessness before God can interfere. Yes, it is our strength, not our weakness, that is our hindrance and stumbling block. It is the *weak* that God is in pursuit of, not the strong; the weaker the better, for the display of His strength. *To him who lacks might He increases power.* "Only in the Lord are righteousness and strength" (Isaiah 45:24). *When I am weak, then I am strong* (2 Corinthians 12:10). It is our infirmities that God uses as His opportunity for the magnifying of His grace and power. Are you willing to take the place of weakness that God assigns to you, and in which He alone can interfere to save?

3. *An unfainting saint.* The saint is here described as one *who wait[s] for the Lord.* He has come to give up his waiting on all else, and to wait on this living and mighty God alone. It is thus that out of weakness he becomes strong. His weakness is not less than it was, but he gets a substitute for it, in the strength of Jehovah. Everybody else, even the young and vigorous, will fail, but he will not. When everyone gives way, he will stand; he will lift up his head. This is described under four figures of speech.

1. *Those who wait for the Lord will gain new strength.* Our strength weakens by daily use, theirs increases and is renewed. That which would fatigue and exhaust others will invigorate them. They will become stronger and stronger. The greater their former weakness, the greater their present power.

2. *They will mount up with wings like eagles.* They will ascend many lofty heights and look down on the world beneath them, soaring higher and higher, gazing from Lebanon, Hermon, Amana (Song of Solomon 4:8), the mountains of myrrh, and the hills of frankincense. As God bore Israel through the desert on eagles' wings, so will they be borne. They who once did not have strength to creep or move, now have strength to fly aloft as eagles. Such is the way in which strength comes out of weakness.

3. *They will run and not get tired.* They are not always flying or soaring, but when running – running their race here – they will not

be weary. They will run with patience, perseverance, success, and triumph. Theirs will be a blessed and untiring race.

4. *They will walk and not become weary.* The greater part of their life is to be walking. Occasionally they may fly or run. More generally they walk; ever moving onward without ceasing. In this walk they will *not become weary*. It may be long, but they will *not become weary*. It may be rough and dark, but they will not *become weary*. Here then is the unfainting saint, made out of a fainting sinner, by the power of an unfainting God. Wait then, O saint, on God, and you will know His power. You will know how He can uphold and strengthen you even to the end, that you may be presented faultless before Him at His coming. *"He keeps the feet of His godly ones"* (1 Samuel 2:9).

Chapter 60

The Knowledge That Justifies

By His knowledge the Righteous One, my Servant, will justify the many. – Isaiah 53:11

"*Of whom does the prophet say this? Of himself or of someone else?*" said the Ethiopian ruler (Acts 8:34). Of some other man doubtless; of one greater than himself; higher, and yet lower than any of the sons of men. For only of *one*, in all earth's histories from the beginning, could these things be said. Is not His name "Wonderful"? Here we have:

1. *The Father's righteous servant*. *The Righteous One, my Servant*, says God, as if He had never had another. My servant! My righteous servant! *Servant* is a name of subjection and obedience, yet also of honor, according to the rank of Him whom He serves. As servant He is the doer of the Father's will, the Father's servant for us, and in this sense our servant: "*I am among you as the one who serves*" (Luke 22:27); "*The Son of Man did not come to be served, but to serve*" (Matthew 20:28; Mark 10:45). As servant He is the fulfiller of the law; the obedient One in all things; not pleasing Himself, nor doing His own will. *The Righteous One, my Servant*, says God, as delighting in Him; for never before had He gotten such service and such righteousness; divine, yet human service; divine, yet human righteousness. It is of this righteous servant that the whole chapter speaks. It is He who grows up before Him

as a tender plant, as a root out of a dry ground. It is He in whom men saw no beauty; whom they despised and rejected. It is He who was the Man of Sorrows and acquainted with grief. It is He from whom men hid their faces; who was brought as a lamb to the slaughter; who was taken from prison and from judgment; who was cut off out of the land of the living. O wondrous servant! O gracious service! What or where would we be without such a servant and such a service? All we need is ministered to us by You, freely, liberally, lovingly! Why should we be so slow to acknowledge You as the servant, and to accept Your service in our behalf? Your life on earth was one of service for us, and Your life in heaven is still the same. For is not Your intercession and Your advocacy service of the best and truest kind?

2. *This righteous servant justifies.* He is no common servant. He is the great Judge of all; the Justifier of the sinner; He who acquits and pardons the guilty. He acted as such on earth when He said, *"I do not condemn you, either"* (John 8:11); *"Your sins are forgiven"* (Matthew 9:2). He acts as such in heaven. Our justification is in His hands. We go to Him to be justified. In one aspect it is the Father that justifies; in another, it is the Son. He justifies many. All power is given to Him: judicial power, royal power, and priestly power. We get acquittal and acceptance from His priestly royal hands. *Therefore let us draw near with confidence to the throne of grace, so that we may receive mercy* (Hebrews 4:16). He sits there to receive sinners. He takes up the case of the condemned – as such He justifies them, He recognizes all their sin and guilt, and then He delivers them. They come to Him as condemned. He acknowledges the sentence as just, but cancels it – cancels it forevermore. His justifying sentence reverses the law's condemning sentence. It is with the condemned that He deals; it is them whom He pardons. There was justice in the condemnation; there is no less justice in the pardon. The Justifier is the Father's servant; the Word made flesh; the Son of God, who came in the name of the Lord to save us. Grace and righteousness in all their fullness are to be found in Him.

3. *This righteous servant justifies by His knowledge.* Knowledge is the link between the many and justification. He justifies them by giving

them the knowledge of Himself as the Justifier, and of His work as the justifying thing. Knowledge is not here used in the sense of wisdom or understanding; it means that which He teaches them to know. We are justified by *knowing* the righteous servant. It is not by working, or praying, or suffering, but by *knowing,* that we enter into the state of acceptance: *This is eternal life, that they may know You, the only true God, and Jesus Christ whom You have sent* (John 17:3). This is one of the simplest aspects in which the gospel is presented to us. There is no mystery or darkness here. To know Jesus is to be justified! The justified man can say nothing in his own behalf; nothing good has he found in himself, in his works, or his feelings, or his character. All is evil, only evil. He is utterly unfit for pardon, according as men judge fitness. All that he can say for himself is that he knows Jehovah's righteous servant, and in that knowledge he has found deliverance from the wrath and the curse. That knowledge has brought him into the state of *no condemnation* (Romans 8:1). Satisfied with that knowledge (though satisfied with nothing about himself) he can say with certainty and gladness, *Who is the one who condemns?* (Romans 8:34).

4. *This righteous servant justifies by bearing the iniquities of those whom He justifies.* He justifies as a judge; as a judge giving righteous judgment; righteous judgment in acquitting the unrighteous. The ground on which He justifies is not mere grace, it is also righteousness.

Not that sin is trivial, but that He has borne iniquity in place of the unrighteous. This bearing of iniquity was His great work on earth, from His cradle to His cross. It was laid on Him. He took it willingly. He was able to bear it. He has borne it. The SinBearer has triumphed. The sinbearing work is done. *He was pierced through for our transgressions, He was crushed for our iniquities* (Isaiah 53:5). The work is done! Iniquity is borne. That which pacifies has been completed. To all this God Himself has borne witness.

It is on divine testimony that we rest our belief, and from the promise annexed to this divine testimony we draw the blessed conclusion that, in believing, we will enter into that peace that has been made. God has given us a testimony to the work of His Son; and He has added the promise, that whosoever believes that testimony is immediately justified.

We believe and are justified. We know that we are justified because of the sure word of promise to him who receives the testimony. This is what is called *appropriation*. It is the simple conclusion we draw from our believing the testimony. He that believes has everlasting life. We believe, and we know, therefore, that all this life is ours: *"God is not a man, that He should lie"* (Numbers 23:19).

We will know when He comes again how much we lost by not crediting this *true testimony;* how much more peaceful, holy, and successful our life would have been had we believed that testimony in its simplicity and fullness.

Chapter 61

The Heritage and Its Title Deeds

"This is the heritage of the servants of the Lord." – Isaiah 54:17

It is of *servants* that God is speaking here – this is the name He gives them: *servants,* yet heirs, for it is in connection with the *heritage* that He calls them *servants.* The apostle Paul joins together *children* and *heirs* (Romans 8:17). Here the prophet joins *servants* and heirs. Israel gets this name: *servants of the Lord;* the church gets it; apostles get it; each saint gets it. The dwellers in the old Jerusalem had it and the citizens of the new Jerusalem have it too. *His bondservants will serve Him* (Revelation 22:3). We are to serve as angels do; indeed, as Jesus did, for He was the Father's servant. We are to serve the Father, serve the Son – *the Lord Christ* (Colossians 3:24) – serve the church, and we are to serve the world, all in love. For it is to loving familial service that we are called.

But it is especially of these two things that the passage speaks: (1) the heritage, and (2) our title to it.

1. *The heritage.* It is fully described in the previous part of the chapter. In reading it we may say, *The lines have fallen to me in pleasant places; indeed, my heritage is beautiful to me* (Psalm 16:6). It contains:

   1. *Deliverance from sorrow and tempest* (verse 11). The time of these

has been long, but the day of deliverance longer. It is everlasting deliverance.

2. *Glory and beauty* (verse 11 and 12). All that the eye of man or the eye of God delights in, and pronounces good, in earth or heaven, will be ours.

3. *Knowledge* (verse 13). We will be *"taught of the Lord,"* all of us. No ignorance then, nor unbelief; only wisdom. Not the wisdom of *this* world, but of the world to come.

4. *Peace* (verse 13 KJV). Great peace; peace like a river; peace that passes all understanding; God's own peace, within and without, and with the certainty that no future anxiety will ever arise. Eternal peace; in the land of peace, under the reign of the Prince of Peace.

5. *Stability* (verse 14). We are to be steadfast and immovable here. We will be still more so hereafter, for our heritage is the kingdom that cannot be moved.

6. *Security* (verse 14). No possibility of evil from any quarter; nothing but good. Security from: (1) oppression, (2) alarm, (3) enemies, (4) war, and (5) accusations and evil reports.

All these things, negative and positive, go to make up the inheritance of Israel in the latter days; still more the inheritance of the saints in light, the kingdom that cannot be moved, the inheritance that is incorruptible and undefiled. It is the very heaven of heavens – glorious, and marvelous, and perfect beyond conception. Ah, surely this is what eye has not seen nor ear heard. Because of it, *God is not ashamed to be called [our] God* (Hebrews 11:16).

2. *Our title to it.* "*Their vindication is from Me,*" declares the Lord (verse 17). This righteousness avails not merely for personal acceptance, but also for giving us the inheritance. This is the tenure by which we hold it and will hold it forever. Thus, it is secured to us – secured by God Himself; not simply made ours once, but secured to us forever. Our title, then, or tenure, is:

1. *Divine.* It *"is from Me," declares the Lord.* He gives the heritage, and

He also gives the title by which it is secured to us. Indeed, He gives us a *divine* title, such as our Father had not given to Paradise; a title not of self, of man, nor of earth, but of God. A title so truly divine that we may say that God Himself is my title to the heritage that God has given me. For the righteousness by which it is secured to me is the righteousness of God. My title deeds are truly divine; the purchase money is divine; the conveyance is divine; the security is divine. One with Him who bought the heritage for us, we have the same title to it that He has, for we get it through means of His righteousness. As the righteous One, He was the purchaser of the kingdom that He gives to us. His righteousness bought it.

2. *Righteous.* This is implied in the expression, *their righteousness is of me* (verse 17 KJV), indicating that it is by *righteousness* that the heritage is secured to us. This heritage is more than the mere gift of love. It is also the gift of righteousness. We get it in a *righteous* way. We hold it in virtue of a *righteous* price paid for it. Our security for it is more than the grace of God; it is the righteousness of God. Our pardon is a *righteous* pardon, so is our title a *righteous* title – divinely righteous – a title that the *law* recognizes, and that the law will make good to us against all opposers or counter-claimants, if there are such. *If God is for us, who is against us?* In our title deeds there is no flaw nor ambiguity, for they are drawn up by a righteous God, subscribed by a righteous God, and presented to us by a righteous God. Everything connected with our entrance into, and possession of, the heritage is in righteousness.

3. *Free.* Our heritage is a "purchased possession." Purchased for us by another; fully paid for by a divine equivalent. So fully paid for that there is nothing for us to pay. Everything is free. Canaan was God's free gift to Israel, so the inheritance is God's free gift to us. We *could not* pay, were it needed, and we do not need to. All payment is refused. It is so precious that no one except God could pay a price for it, and He has paid the price. As life is free, and salvation is free, so is the heritage absolutely and unconditionally free. Free in the sense of unbought; free in the sense of undeserved; free in the sense of its being the gift of God.

4. *Eternal.* Our title, being thus divine and righteous, must be indefeasible. It must stand forever. An eternal title to an eternal inheritance – this is what we rejoice in. Thus the inheritance itself, and everything connected with it, are described in language that indicates perpetuity absolutely unending and unlimited. No second fall; no second loss of Paradise. No future tempter nor temptation. We enter to go out no more. For the church is "the blessed of the Lord," to whom it will be said, *"Come, you who are blessed of My Father"* (Matthew 25:34). Being one with the Son of God, *partakers of Christ* (Hebrews 3:14), and *joint-heirs with Christ* (Romans 8:17 KJV), our tenure of the inheritance must be as sure and as everlasting as His own.

It is this heritage that God in His gospel is presenting to us. He points to it, as He pointed Israel to Canaan, and says, "Yonder is the glory, trust me for it, and you will enter in." Israel could not enter in because of unbelief; and so it is only this that shuts the sinner out of the kingdom. We preach the kingdom, and we announce that he who receives God's testimony concerning His only begotten Son will obtain it freely. But the Word preached does not profit if it is not mixed with faith in them who hear it. God's testimony is true. It is a testimony intended especially for sinners. Should we disregard it? Should we treat it as worthless? Should we make Him a liar? Should we shut the open gate against ourselves? Should we refuse to enter in? We who have believed do enter into rest. How free, how simple, how ready the entrance! It is God Himself who stands at the open door and bids us to come, beckons us in. Should such a heritage be lost to us? Should such a glory be despised?

Chapter 62

The Meeting between the Sinner and God

> *You meet him who rejoices in doing righteousness, who remembers You in Your ways. Behold, You were angry, for we sinned, we continued in them a long time; and shall we be saved?* – Isaiah 64:5

The verse preceding Isaiah 64:4 is quoted by Paul (1 Corinthians 2:9) in reference to *the hidden wisdom which God predestined before the ages to our glory* (1 Corinthians 2:7), so that we may take it, and our text, as indicating God's thoughts of wisdom as coming out in His dealings with us in Christ; His dealings with Israel; His dealings with the church as seen both at the first and the second coming of Christ; and His dealings with man in grace, that is, according to His own free love. *"My thoughts are not your thoughts, nor are your ways My ways"* (Isaiah 55:8). In our text we have a specimen of God's thoughts and ways.

1. *God meets man. You meet him.* Distance is our natural condition; sin produced it, Adam showed it, and man loves it. We are as far from God as possible. *"Depart from us!"* (Job 21:14; 22:17), men say. So, the Prodigal Son went into the far country. Man wants no meeting with God. He would rather that the distance was preserved forever. The thought of meeting God is unpleasant, thus the irksomeness of religion, and the weariness of Sabbaths, even

though the meeting is of the vaguest and most formal shadowy kind. He must meet Him on the judgment day, but he tries not to think of this, and hopes that he will be ready when it comes. But though of himself man may not draw near to God, yet God calls men unto Himself (John 6:44). *He* does not love the distance and separation. He comes near. He did so in the person of the prophets and similar messengers. He did so especially in the angel of the covenant, and in the Word made flesh. But His object is not merely to visit earth, but also to come up to, and to draw near to, each of His creatures. He is desirous of a meeting, a loving and friendly meeting, not of judgment, or reproof, or vengeance, but of grace. Isaiah speaks as one who knew this. *You meet him,* he says; that is, You are in the habit of doing so. It is Your practice, Your custom to meet the sinner. This is our message in the gospel, that God wants to meet you – to meet each of you. He proposes a meeting. He tells you that there is no coldness nor unwillingness on His part, that all things are ready. Come, meet with Me, I wish to meet with you.

2. *How does He meet man?* In love, as the Lord God merciful and gracious. He meets him as Jesus met the Galilean fishermen, and said, *"Follow me"* (Matthew 4:19; Mark 1:17); as Jesus met the woman of Sychar; and as He met Zacchaeus and Mary Magdalene. He meets him with pardon and reconciliation. He meets him as Melchizedek met Abraham, to bless him. Man dislikes the meeting, either for blessing or cursing. God desires it, so that He may bless.

3. *Where does He meet man?* At the cross. That is the meeting place. There is no other. It is a safe one and a blessed one. There is no wrath there, no condemnation, no darkness. God stands at the cross and cries aloud, "Meet me here. Not on a spot of your own choosing, but here on the spot that I have chosen; here where the blood was shed, and Christ's sacrifice was offered up." This is the meeting place. *Two* meeting places: one the cross, now; the other the judgment seat, hereafter. Which do you choose? You must choose one.

4. *What men are they whom He meets?* Now in what follows we are not to understand that the class is narrowed or restricted; that He shuts out the worst and will have none of them. The description given refers simply to *the footing* on which He receives them – on that footing He is willing to receive anyone and everyone. On that footing everybody may place themselves, and so be sure of a welcome. Our text, however, evidently does not refer exclusively to the *first* meeting, but to the whole subsequent interaction, and describes the footing on which that fellowship is to go on and be maintained. There are three things declared as to those with whom God meets. These three things follow each other in a certain order.

   a. *The rejoicing man.* He is one who has found in the gospel glad tidings of great joy; one of those described by David in the thirty-second psalm, a man of blessedness. He has found the rejoicing of the hope, and he holds it to the end. He has accepted the good news, and as such he is accepted of God. God meets him.

   b. *The man that works righteousness.* He: (1) works – he is not slothful; (2) works righteousness – good works; and (3) works righteousness, because he rejoices. He does not rejoice because he works, but he works because he rejoices. His joy makes him a worker – a doer of the will of God, able for suffering or laboring. His life is a doing of righteousness.

   c. *Those who remember You in Your ways.* This corresponds with the apostolic *fixing our eyes on Jesus* (Hebrews 12:2). We remember God – we remember Him in His ways, His footsteps, and His doings, as recorded in Scripture. When we remember Him, we do so in connection with some of His many ways recorded there.

This meeting is a lifelong one. Not yesterday, today, nor tomorrow, but continual; begun at conversion, carried on through life, and consummated in the kingdom. It is a meeting for pardon; a meeting for fellowship; a meeting for the bestowal of all love and blessing; a prelude to the more glorious meeting when Jesus comes the second time to begin His endless reign.

Chapter 63

God's Love and God's Way of Blessing

"Go and proclaim these words toward the north and say, 'Return, faithless Israel,' declares the Lord; 'I will not look upon you in anger. For I am gracious,' declares the Lord; 'I will not be angry forever. Only acknowledge your iniquity, that you have transgressed against the Lord your God and have scattered your favors to the strangers under every green tree, and you have not obeyed My voice,' declares the Lord." – Jeremiah 3:12-13

Let us note here two things: (1) God's message of love, and (2) His way of blessing.

1. *God's message of love.* He is evidently in earnest about this. There is nothing of coldness, delay, or insincerity. He calls a messenger, a special messenger, for the occasion. He sends him out with, *"Go,"* as did our Lord; *"Go* into all nations," like an arrow from a bow. *"Proclaim,"* speak, lift up your voice like a herald, that everyone may hear, and that there may be no mistake. *"Toward the north,"* where *"faithless Israel"* (Jeremiah 3:11) dwelt, and where her idolatries were practiced, as in Bethel and Samaria. It is like, "Begin at Jerusalem," and go to the worst, to the very center of the sin and the evil; go to Bethel, go to Samaria, go to the chief of sinners; go to the backslider, the apostate, the idolater.

GOD'S LOVE AND GOD'S WAY OF BLESSING

And with what message? The message of love and reconciliation! The chief point of the message is the word *Return*. Like the Prodigal Son they had departed, and the Father's voice calls to them, "Come back, come back to *Me*." God speaks as one in earnest as a father, as a father who has lost a child and yearns over his lost son. *"How can I give you up?"* (Hosea 11:8) is His feeling; how can I part with you? God is not indifferent to our departure nor our absence. Though He has all heaven, with all its angels, He feels the blank made by one sinner's departure. The sea does not feel the loss of a drop, nor the sun of a ray. The monarch of a mighty empire does not feel the departure of one subject, but God feels and mourns over the revolt and alienation of one sinner. While urging home this word, *Return,* God enforces it with encouragements and arguments.

1. *"I will not look upon you in anger."* This is more exactly, "I will not cause my countenance to fall on you." That is, "I will not frown upon you." The words are the same as in describing Cain: *His countenance fell* (Genesis 4:5). Instead of the frown, the smile will come upon My countenance: "I will lift up my countenance upon you." This is grace and tender love. The sinner is thus told what he is to expect from God in returning. *But while he was still a long way off, his father saw him* (Luke 15:20).

2. *I am merciful* (KJV). With Jehovah there is mercy, for His name is the Lord God, merciful and gracious. Israel had tested His mercy to the uttermost, but it was not exhausted. Its fullness was undiminished. Where sin had abounded, grace had abounded much more. The announcement here of His mercy is to tell Israel that all their backslidings, apostasies, and idolatries had not altered or lessened that mercy. It was mercy to the uttermost, mercy to the last.

3. *"I will not be angry forever."* Indirectly this tells the terrible truth that there had been, and still was, anger against them. In wrath He had struck them and scattered them. It had laid heavy and sore upon them. But it was not to be perpetual anger. *His anger is but for a moment* (Psalm 30:5); it passes away, and He teaches Israel to sing, *"For although You were angry with me, Your anger is turned away"* (Isaiah 12:1).

Such is God's message of love; sent in truth and earnestness to Israel, and sent with no less truth and earnestness to us! Return and be forgiven! Return and be blessed! Return and let Me pour out on you the fullness of My forgiving love!

2. *His way of blessing.* There is only one way to this, and it is not by merit, goodness, labor, or earnestness, but is simply by the acknowledgment of sin. In this acknowledgment there is nothing meritorious, nothing *in itself* fitted to attract or secure blessing. But it is the way of God's appointment. It is the channel through which the forgiveness flows, and it places us on that footing in which alone God can bless the sinner. So long as there is on the part of the sinner the slightest thought that he deserves to be blessed, that God ought to bless him, that he has done or felt anything that makes him more fit or qualified for blessing, he is not in a position in which God can be glorified in blessing him. Indeed, he is retaining that selfrighteous position that renders it impossible for God to honorably and righteously bless him. But the moment that he forgoes all claims and takes the sinner's place before God, as one deserving nothing, in that moment he is in the position in which God can and will bless.

"Only acknowledge." These are His words to us, announcing the way of blessing. "Only acknowledge." Thus He still speaks to us (1 John 1:9).

The particulars of the acknowledgment follow: (1) iniquity, (2) transgression against the Lord our God, (3) going after idols, and (4) not obeying the voice of Jehovah. Those are the sins in particular that Israel had committed. It is this particular enumeration of sin that He asks of us. Name the particular sins when you come before the Lord. Beware of *general* confessions. Most times they do not touch the conscience and as such they do not reach God. Be very special and minute in everything that you tell God concerning your sins, with the full confidence of receiving pardon. *If we confess our sins, He is faithful and righteous to forgive us our sins* (1 John 1:9).

"Only acknowledge." This is the one thing that God asks; it is the one thing that the sinner shrinks from, for it brings him down so far. It absolutely strips him of all goodness. Yet on no other footing will God deal with any sinner. So it was in the case of the Pharisee and the publican. This was Laodicea's special sin – refusal to acknowledge poverty. It was to this that the Lord urged her. So He urges us. It is our pride that stands between us and blessing. Take the sinner's place and everything is ours. Let us deal with Him now as sinners, and when He comes again He will acknowledge us as sons and heirs.

Chapter 64

Divine Jealousy for the Truth

"O Lord, do not Your eyes look for truth?" – Jeremiah 5:3

The first clause of the third verse should be connected with the two previous verses in which the Lord complains that truth was gone from His city and His people; that even when swearing by His name men disregarded it. Jerusalem had become a city of falsehood, Israel a nation of false men.

They said, "God does not observe it." He allows the speaker of falsehood to go on unpunished. His eyes are not on such men or such things. They are of no significance to Him. The prophet breaks in here with his question, his appeal: *"O Lord, do not Your eyes look for truth?"* Whatever men may say, "Do You not see it?" "Do You not abhor the untrue?" "Do You not cut off the liar?" "Do You not condemn him who utters error?"

The word *truth* in Scripture refers both to doctrine and practice. It points both to the "error" and the "lie." It classes both together. It condemns both. *False speaking*, whether in reference to teaching or witnessbearing, is declared to be abominable to God. His eyes are upon the truth. They watch over it, to guard it and to maintain it. The eyes of Jehovah are upon the truth, whatever men may say; and that which is *untrue*, whatever form it takes, He observes and will avenge. The untrue thing, whatever its nature or object, the untrue word, the untrue look, the untrue private or public act, is not tolerated by Him, though tolerated by man, and though God Himself bears long with it.

The theory of many is that God's eyes are *not* upon the truth, and that therefore a man may believe what he pleases, and say what he likes, without fearing God's displeasure. It is only when the untrue thing that he thinks and says interferes with human rights, or social privileges, that he is to be visited with punishment. Jehovah's eyes, then, are upon the truth – the truth as found on earth among the sons of men.

1. *They are watchful eyes.* They do not close. He, whose eyes they are, neither slumbers nor sleeps. There is not a sound, thought, or a word from pen or lip, but that He notices it. He who sees the sparrows, numbers the hairs, and feeds the ravens, has His eye on all human utterances, all writings of man – books or tracts, all openings of man's lips in private or public.

2. *They are discerning eyes.* They are like flames of fire. They search and test everything. There is no indifference about their gaze. They are keen to discriminate between truth and error. They are the eyes of a judge who loves the true and hates the false. Man thinks whatever is earnestly spoken is good; not so with God. He discerns, He judges, He sifts, and He tests every word, every phrase, every thought, and every plan. There is such a thing as divine censorship, minute but unerring criticism.

3. *They are just eyes.* They do not make a man an offender for a word, yet they weigh everything in equal balances. There is no overvaluing nor undervaluing of what is spoken or written. Each thing is judged without favor or partiality, and it is approved or condemned according as it is true or false. The standard of measurement is divine and perfect. No bribery here, no acceptance of man's person whether poor or rich. It is "just judgment," a just verdict that is pronounced. The righteous Lord loves righteousness. In every sense, He will be satisfied with nothing less than *truth:* truth from man; truth between Himself and man; truth between man and man; the true word, true thought, true look, true voice, and true tone.

In this watchfulness, discernment, and justice, there are some things especially to be observed.

1. *There is but one standard of truth.* God fixes the standard and acts on it, without whim, partiality, or compromise. Error is a thousandfold – pliable, movable, uncertain – truth is *one*. On this God calls on us to act; on this He acts Himself, so that man cannot excuse his error or his falsehood on the ground that there were more standards than one.

2. *This one standard is definite.* It is not vague or shadowy. It does not merely settle certain great principles, but smaller ones as well. It is so very definite and precise as to leave man without excuse. It lets man know explicitly God's present estimate of truth and falsehood, as well as His future judgment on these. It is so distinct that no one with an open ear and eye can hesitate about it. In our day men call this narrowness, bigotry, and littleness. But if we only insist on being of one mind with God, he that condemns us condemns God Himself. Let us be as broad as He is, but no broader; that is enough, whatever the age may say.

3. *That one standard is universal.* It is for every age and country. It never becomes obsolete. It is like God Himself – unchangeable; like the Christ of God – the same yesterday, today, and forever. It was given to our fathers; it is given to us. It suited the East; it suits the West. It suited the Jew; it suits the Gentile also – barbarian, Scythian, bond, or free. It suited the Asian; it suits the European. It suits the Briton; it suits the Indian and the African. It suits the unlearned; it suits the learned. One standard for all! One universal test or measurement of truth.

4. *That one standard is the Bible.* It is no *secret* standard that He judges us by, or by which He tests truth and error. The test that He gives to us He acts upon Himself. The Bible is *His* book of truth as well as *ours*. That book contains what God calls truth – truth definite, fixed, certain, not movable, nor growing obsolete, nor falling behind the age. The Bible is the one book of the age, indeed, of the ages – of all ages and all countries. Man's present

unbelief seeks to loosen its authority, to dilute its statements, and to render indefinite its doctrines. But the word of the Lord endures forever. *"God is not a man, that He should lie"* (Numbers 23:19). His word is sure, His truth is everlasting, His book is like the sun in the firmament; a light for all ages and lands.

Thus God's eyes are on *the truth*. It is truth that He delights in, it is error that He abhors. It is truth that He is seeking for among the sons of men. What a condemnation to the laxity of thought in the present day! As if man were at liberty to think as he pleases, irrespective of God and His book! God watches over the truth. He notes each error, each deviation from His one standard.

O man, have you received the very truth, and the whole truth of God? He has given man a book for a standard, not so that he may speculate, but so that he may not speculate and believe. What God, in and by that book, demands of men is not criticism, opinion, or speculation, but *belief*. God's eyes are on the truth, to see if men *believe it.*

The day is at hand, the great day of the Lord, when *truth* only will be set on high, and error put to shame. O man, God's eyes are on the truth; let your eyes be on it too. Be true to truth; be true to yourself; be true to God.

Chapter 65

Divine Love and Human Rejection of It

"I have listened and heard, they have spoken what is not right; no man repented of his wickedness, saying, 'What have I done?' Everyone turned to his course, like a horse charging into the battle. Even the stork in the sky knows her seasons; and the turtledove and the swift and the thrush observe the time of their migration; but My people do not know the ordinance of the Lord." – Jeremiah 8:6-7

The prophet is predicting judgment upon rebellious Israel. He is depicting the woes that were suspended over Jerusalem, like the sword of the destroying angel, sorrow upon sorrow, terror upon terror, death upon death.

Through this infinite gloom there shoot rays of light, as once again God makes mention of His love. How brightly these words of love gleam through the terrible darkness! But Israel quenches all these beams. He will have none of them. He loves the darkness rather than the light. He says, "Darkness, you be my light; evil, you be my good; night, you be my day." And at last God leaves him to his doom – *"The Lord has rejected and forsaken the generation of His wrath"* (Jeremiah 7:29).

Let us now look at the two sides of the picture – the divine and the human; the heart of God and the heart of man; God's attitude towards man and man's attitude towards God. For what is written here for Israel is written for us. God's love and man's rejection of it are the two points.

1. *God's love.* "*I have listened and heard, they have spoken what is not right.*" He speaks as one on the watch for good, not for evil; like the Prodigal Son's father looking eagerly for his son's return. The scene reminds us of Christ's "*If you had known*" (Matthew 12:7; Luke 19:42). It reminds us of, *How can I give you up, O Ephraim?* (Hosea 11:8); and of, "*As often as I have spoken against him, I certainly still remember him*" (Jeremiah 31:20). It tells us of God's eager desire to hear the faintest sigh of the returning sinner, His longing to get one word of remembrance from His alienated sons and daughters. It tells us also of God's disappointment at hearing nothing from us – at man's silence, distance, and refusal to return.

God is not indifferent to man's position, danger, or wretchedness. He does not say as we do, "It is his loss, not mine," or, "He has no one but himself to blame for it – let him take it." He never loses sight of us, He pities us, yearns over us, and longs to hear the inquiring voice, and the sound of the returning footstep. When He does not hear it, it grieves Him at the heart. His heart is turned within Him – His repentings are kindled together.

He is hearing and listening at our doors, to catch the lowest word or sigh. Each day He listens – He listened this morning when you rose, He listens now! Oh, the joy it would give Him to hear from any of you who say, "*I will get up and go to my father*" (Luke 15:18). Will you not give Him this joy? Will you grieve Him by your silence? Will His long-suffering not melt you?

2. *Man's rejection of it.* This is very strongly put in our text in several ways and forms.

1. *The wrong words.* He did hear words from them, but not those He wanted. Perhaps they were the words of pride, selfrighteousness, blasphemy, worldliness, and lust. They were not the Prodigal Son's words, "*I will get up,*" which alone are sweet to Him. Perhaps they were the words of the selfsufficiency of the Pharisee: "*I thank*

You that I am not like other people" (Luke 18:11); or, *We are lords* (Jeremiah 2:31 KJV); or, "We are the temple of the Lord," and not, *"God, be merciful to me, the sinner!"* (Luke 18:13). *"They have spoken what is not right"* (Jeremiah 8:6).

2. *The unrepentance.* "No man repented of his wickedness, saying, 'What have I done?'" Their hearts were hardened. Goodness and severity had both failed. There was no sense of sin, no shame because of evil, no dread of danger. Israel's was the unrepentant heart. And such is the heart of multitudes among us; the heart of our nation, we may say, indeed, the heart of our world. Would to God that we could not say the heart of the churches. Unrepentance! How dreadful the condition of one to whom this description belongs! Do you repent of your way, O man? Do you say in bitterness of soul, "Oh what, what have I done?"

3. *The recklessness.* "Everyone turned to his course, like a horse charging into the battle." He is blind, madly blind, both to danger and to sin. Furiously he plunges on in evil, from sin to sin, from lust to lust, daring every hazard, defying God, braving His anger, setting at nothing His threats, scoffing at His judgments, rushing against His armor, mocking at His hell. How much is there of recklessness among us! Recklessness in sin, crime, selfindulgence, pleasure, and lust. Utter defiance of God; bold, unblushing audacity, which nothing will daunt; which mocks at judgments, sorrows, trials, sermons, and ministers, and plunges on in evil, treasuring up wrath against the day of wrath.

4. *The stupidity. "Even the stork in the sky knows her seasons."* We were going to say *brutish* stupidity, but God means to tell us that it is something worse than that. Beast and bird obey the ordained laws and keep to their appointed seasons. They return when the season calls them. But man discerns nothing, heeds nothing; times, laws, seasons, and instincts are all disregarded by him. He is void of understanding, he has closed his eye and ear; his whole intellect has lost its power of perception, not only of duty but also of danger. *"My people do not know the ordinance of the*

Lord." Their hearts have become impure. They go down lower than the beasts that perish.

Yet God does not leave us. He does not say, "Leave him alone," in the sense of "leave him to perish." He stretches out His hands to us, He bends over us, He is long-suffering, *not wishing for any to perish* (2 Peter 3:9). He listens and listens. As He does at the door of the saint (Malachi 3:16), so of the sinner. What will He hear? Ephraim bemoaning himself? Or the words of unbelief, and unrepentance, and sin?

Chapter 66

God's Desire to Bless the Sinner

"Woe to you, O Jerusalem! How long will you remain unclean?" – Jeremiah 13:27

Without dwelling on Jerusalem and her apostasy, which this verse specially brings before us, we pass at once to the application of the words to man in general.

1. *Man's uncleanness.* The uncleanness here spoken of is spiritual and refers especially to unfaithfulness to God – the soul's lust and lewdness, its preference for another husband, and its desire for another love than that of God. It was with this spiritual adultery that God so often charged Israel and Jerusalem; it is with this that He charges the church; and with this the whole race. We are unfaithful to God!

   1. *In heart.* It was meant that He should have the first place there, but He has the last place, if any place at all. He is shut out from our love. We love others, but not God; the world, but not God; friends, but not God; money, but not God. O man, your heart is false to God, unfaithful in all its movements.

   2. *In life.* As is the heart, so is the life; as is the inner man, so is the outer man. God is not in our life. He is excluded from every part, and thrust into a corner. Life is devoted to other objects. It is false

to Him. Word, deed, plan, behavior, business, and education; life in all its movements, life in all its enjoyments, is false to God.

3. *In religion.* A man's religion is often the most untrue and hollow part of his life. In it he is more false to God than in any other of his actions. In religion he professedly comes nearest to God, yet in it he is often farthest away. In it he is like Jerusalem committing spiritual adultery – worshipping false gods, while pretending to worship the true God.

Such is man in relation to God! All falsehood, unfaithfulness, and lewdness. There is no clean part.

2. *God's desire that we should be clean.* He desires truth in the inward parts. He is faithful to us, and He wishes us to be faithful to Him. God is not indifferent to our unfaithfulness, as if it did not matter to Him. Nor does He treat it as a mere affront, or only as a sin, with which He is angry and which He condemns and will avenge. He wants our heart, our whole undivided heart. He wants it all for Himself. He wants to fill it. He is a jealous God. Moreover, He pities us because of the misery that our unfaithfulness brings on us. He sees us gaining nothing, but losing everything by it; He pities us, and He yearns over us. For our own sakes He desires to see us faithful to Himself. Such is the God with whom we have to do. He is one who takes a deep and loving interest in our welfare, and who pities us even when He judges us.

3. *His challenges to us.* Will you not be made clean? When will it be? These are earnest words, words of solemn and urgent appeal to us. His pity is not idle. He comes down to us. He speaks to us. He stretches out His hands to us. Will you? Will you not? When will it be? Will it not be now? Can words be more energetic, more personal, more explicit and direct? Every man must feel that he is being spoken to; spoken to most urgently; entreated, implored, and challenged. He wants us to be cleansed – to turn, to seek His face, to give Him our loyal love; He wants this *immediately.* Not a day to be lost. The time past has been enough; indeed, too long. He presses us with His solemn, urgent, loving plea, *Now!* No delay, no lingering, no hesitation. Give up your unbelief and

give it up *now*. Give up your idolatry and give it up *now*. Turn to Me and turn *now*. Love Me and love Me *now*.

4. *Our refusal.* The passage takes for granted our refusal. Man rejects God, refuses to give Him his heart – deliberately persists in hypocrisy, insincerity, and unfaithfulness. As much externalism as can be asked, he will give, but nothing beyond this. Words he will give, but nothing more. Sacrifices, ceremonies, incense, music, the bended knee, the religious voice and tone – all these he will give, but not the heart. *That* he deliberately refuses. He refuses to love God, trust God, obey God, give God anything except the service of the outer man – of the lip, the knee, and the body.

5. *God's condemnation.* "Woe to you, O Jerusalem!" It was this word that our Lord took up, when He uttered woes against the cities of Galilee. How much is involved in that woe! It is the woe of God! He means what He says. His threats are not empty. He will execute His vengeance in the day of vengeance.

Woe to everyone who does not love God; who loves the creature better than the Creator; who has given his heart to the world in preference to God.

Woe to him who is unfaithful to God, who worships Him with the outer man but withholds the inner man.

Woe to him whose religion is all unfaithfulness, who exhibits his dislike of God in those very acts in which he deals with God.

Yet He who utters, *"Woe,"* also utters, *"Come"* (Matthew 11:21, 28). And between these two are the sons of men. These are the two words that He sounds aloud to us, making us feel His profound sincerity and His unutterable love.

Chapter 67

The Resting Place Forgotten

"They . . . have forgotten their resting place." – Jeremiah 50:6

It was of Israel's apostasy that the prophet spoke. As Moses said, *"You neglected the Rock who begot you, and forgot the God who gave you birth"* (Deuteronomy 32:18), so here Jeremiah says, *"They . . . have forgotten their resting place."* Thus it is with *man*! He has forgotten his resting place! He has left God! *Take care, brethren, that there not be in any one of you an evil, unbelieving heart that falls away from the living God* (Hebrews 3:12).

1. *The resting place.* Israel *had* a resting place. She is compared to a sheep that had a fold, a shepherd, and a pasture. That fold, or resting place, was Jehovah's temple in the Holy City, or, you may say, Jehovah Himself. They forsook Him and His temple to serve other gods. Yet still He was *their* resting place, a place for *their* rest if they would have only taken it. So it is with man, the sinner. There is a resting place for him. He needs it, and God has provided it. It is *His* resting place. It is God Himself – Christ Jesus, in whom there is *rest; "I will give you rest"* (Matthew 11:28). As He is our *hiding place* (Psalm 32:7), so He is our *resting place*. In Him there is divine provision made for giving rest to the weary. He is the Godman, and that is rest; He is the propitiation for our sins, and that is rest; so that, as the Sin-Bearer, and the burden-bearer,

He is our rest. In Him is contained, and presented to us, the great love of God. As the protection from wrath, as the shadow from the heat, as the security from danger, as the divine fullness of all needed blessing, He is our resting place. The Father, knowing what we needed, has made provision in Him for us. Everything that can give a sinner rest is contained in Him; for Christ is all and in all. There is but one resting place, not many. He who gains it has enough; he who misses it misses everything; for there is no other resting place for Israel or for us. One rock, one refuge, one foundation, one salvation, one resting place!

2. *Man's forgetfulness of it.* The simple charge here against Israel is that of *forgetting* the resting place. No strong words are used, such as *despising, dishonoring,* or *rejecting.* All these may be true, but God confines Himself to the mildest and simplest word, so that no man may evade the charge, or console his conscience with the thought that the description is exaggerated. God simply charges him with *forgetfulness.* This *resting place* is not prized nor used. It is forgotten. It is out of sight, out of mind, out of heart. This forgetfulness is strange and unaccountable. There are so many reasons why he should not forget it.

1. *It is so needful.* He cannot dispense with it. Other things *may* be, this *must* be. To a weary soul, what is so necessary as a resting place?

2. *It is so blessed.* It contains both rest and blessedness. It is not like sleep, or the insensibility produced by opiates. It is blessedness, as well as rest.

3. *It has been provided at such a cost.* God knew that man needed it, and how much he needed it, and He provided it at an infinite cost.

Yet in spite of all this the fact remains – he does forget it. How and why is this?

1. *He does not feel his need of it.* He thinks he can do without it. He has others. He has Abanah and Pharpar, which are to him better than Jordan (2 Kings 5:12).

2. *He does not know how blessed it would make him.* What a rest it

would be to him in his day of weariness. His thoughts of blessedness are all earthly and carnal.

3. *He hates the God that provided it.* The natural heart is full of this hatred. Hatred of God must lead men to seek to put all remembrance of the rest out of mind.

4. *He hates its provisions.* Its provisions are holy and righteous. They are all connected with God Himself. And therefore man's object is to close his eyes and ears against a rest whose provisions and characteristics are all holy and divine.

3. *Man's preference for other rests.* We ought not to call them *rests*, for they are not so. They are labor and weariness, sorrow and trouble. Israel wandered like lost sheep, from mountain to hill, in search of other rests, as if anything were better than God's. So does man. He wanders about seeking rest and finding none. But poor as the other rests are, man prefers them to that of the One in whom he has no delight. The sinner is weary, and he seeks rest. He seeks it for himself. He goes from place to place, from object to object, seeking rest. Each one is poor, but he prefers it to God and to God's rest. This preference of creatureobjects as the soul's rest is unspeakably sad and sinful, yet it is universal. There is hardly any object in creation that man has not tried, in preference, *deliberate* preference, to God. For it is all *deliberate*. It is not hasty, sudden, nor transient, but prolonged and resolute – thoroughly willful. It is this deliberate preference of other resting places for the soul that is the great aggravation of his apostasy.

4. *The evil of all this.* It is thoroughly evil; evil without mitigation or excuse; evil towards God, and evil to himself. It brings punishment with it. It leaves the soul unsatisfied.

1. *It brings punishment with it.* God avenges this forgetfulness, this preference of other objects; for God is jealous. He rebuked Israel; He does so to the sinner, both here and hereafter. God does not let us suppose that He overlooks the sin. He judges the sinner and will judge him hereafter. He shows us how He resents the

dishonor. Many sorrows of earth are God's stroke of vengeance because of this forgetfulness. And will not hell be the completed vengeance of Jehovah because of this? God sends blight here on man for this contempt of the resting place. But the eternal blight hereafter is infinitely terrible.

2. *It leaves the soul unsatisfied.* It fills no part of it. It does nothing to make it happy. It may drown the awful sense of emptiness for a while, but that is all. The weariness returns, and still the soul asks, *"Who will show us any good?"* (Psalm 4:6). No amount of pleasure, excitement, merrymaking, or business can remove the weariness. Rather, that weariness is increased the more it is tried to be removed.

Here are four questions for you to answer:

1. *Do you know that there is a resting place?* Have you not heard the report of it? There is such a thing as rest in a weary world. The goodness of it has gone abroad. Do not say then, "It is vain to think to be happy; rest is impossible here." There is a resting place.

2. *Do you know what and where that resting place is?* It is to be found in God and His Son Christ Jesus. It is not far away, but near. It is not inaccessible, but quite open and approachable. It is not costly, but free: *"Come to Me, . . . and I will give you rest"* (Matthew 11:28).

3. *Are you forgetting it and preferring other rests to it?* Most men are doing so. Are you? This is the way of the world. Is it your way? Are you a forgetter of the rest? You may not be an open sinner, but are you a forgetter of the rest?

4. *Do you know the peril of doing so?* It is misery here; it is woe hereafter. The wrath of God abides upon you. That soul of yours is sad even in the midst of pleasure. Your prospects are fearful in the extreme; for what but everlasting burnings are in store for those who forget God, or forget the resting place? Take the resting place as it is. It is sufficient for you. It will remove your weariness. Go then and rest.

Chapter 68

The Day That Will Right All Wrongs

"Oh, that You would bring the day which You have proclaimed." – Lamentations 1:21

This is the voice of faith; sorrowful faith, yet still faith – faith anticipating the coming day of right and truth. Jerusalem had fallen, her sons had gone into captivity, her walls and gates were in ruins, her streets were red with blood, her enemies were triumphant, and worse than all, her own sins had gone up to the heavens and brought down on her this terrible vengeance. In the midst of all this, Jeremiah sits and mourns. All around is dark. There is only one bright spot, and that is in the distant future; the arrival of the day that God had called or summoned. For he looks up to God as the righteous Judge, the avenger of the wrongs of Israel as well as the punisher of her sins. He comforts himself by the thought that God *"has fixed* [or called; that is, proclaimed] *a day in which He will judge the world in righteousness"* (Acts 17:31). This is Jeremiah's one hope, the solitary ray of light in the midst of utter gloom.

So it is with us now. We are troubled with the evil that surrounds us. The wicked triumph. The good are few, and their names are cast out as evil. Evil men and seducers grow worse and worse. We are helpless in the midst of all this sin, blasphemy, and defiance of God. What, then, is our consolation? That God will bring the day that He has *proclaimed;* that man's day and Satan's day will not last forever, but that God's day is at hand; for He that will come, *will come, and will not delay* (Hebrews 10:37). Having done our utmost to restrain the flood of iniquity, to maintain the cause of God, to lift up a banner for the truth, and feeling that we are wholly impotent against the powers of earth and hell, we call to mind the promise that God has appointed a day for setting all things right, and we fall back on this sure word, comforting ourselves with the thought that the cause is really God's, and not ours, and that He will vindicate it in due time. This enables us to possess our souls in patience.

God, by His prophet Amos, speaks of this day, and of those who look for it, in this way: *Alas, you who are longing for the day of the Lord, for what purpose will the day of the Lord be to you?* (Amos 5:18). It is as if he would say, "You know not what you are doing; why do you desire that day?" It is darkness, and not light. And this is, indeed, one awful aspect of the coming day. It is not to be desired but dreaded. But there is another aspect of it, so that it is a day to be desired, not dreaded. Let us speak of the reasons why a believing man should desire the judgment day and the judgment seat, and, looking up calmly, should say to God with a longing heart, *"Oh, that You would bring the day which You have proclaimed,"* and should respond to words of Christ regarding His arrival, with, *Amen. Come, Lord Jesus* (Revelation 22:20).

1. *God will no longer be shut out of His own world.* He is now excluded. Jehovah is not the God of this world. Man shuts Him out and has done so from the beginning. "Depart from us," is the world's all-but-unanimous voice. As far as the individual will, or the united will of humanity can do it, God has been shut out. But when the day that God has called arrives, God will intercede. He will come in and show Himself. He will take to Himself His great power and He will reign. What a world it will be when God will no longer be shut out! Men strive in vain to banish Him. They may do so for a little while, but the day of God is coming. He will force open the world's long-shut gates and enter triumphantly.

2. *Christ will no longer be denied and blasphemed.* The special hostility of the race has been directed against the Son, the Christ of God; against Him in whom God specially reveals Himself. It is *Him* that men deny

and blaspheme. A Christ in some shape they may acknowledge, but not the Christ of God. The Christ of Socinus, Strauss, Renan, or Colenso they will tolerate, but anything beyond this they scoff at and gnash their teeth. How often are our souls troubled, and our hearts all but broken, at the sounds of blasphemy, the utterances of hatred against Christ. Then we fall back on the promise regarding the coming day, when Christ will be exalted and His name honored! O day to be desired, when thus it will be! Lord, hasten the day that You have called.

3. *Evil will no longer prevail.* The will of God will be done on earth as it is in heaven. The world will no longer be what it now is. Satan will no longer have dominion as the god of this world, the prince of the power of the air. He will be dethroned and bound. Antichrist will no longer have power but will be struck down. Iniquity will no longer overflow. The curse will pass away, and creation will be delivered. The cry of the preacher (Ecclesiastes 1:2, 8) will no longer be heard: *All things are wearisome; "Vanity of vanities! All is vanity."* Man will not put light for darkness, or darkness for light, nor call evil good and good evil. The vile person will no longer be called liberal, nor the rude person said to be bountiful. The effects of the fall will disappear, and all things will be made new.

4. *Error will give place to truth.* The first sin was at once an error and a disobedience. Man allowed dark and untrue thoughts of God to come in. Since then, error has overflowed the earth like a deluge. It has spread, ramified, and multiplied. Out of God's book of truth men have (in perverse ways) drawn errors and falsehoods innumerable. Some of the worst untruths have been those *professedly* deduced from the book of truth. Indeed, and men glory in error, provided it is either clever or earnest. They call it speculation, philosophy, or free thought. Yet all error is sin. And we find error everywhere: in the world and in the church. God is dishonored by it. His Son is denied. His book is set aside or misinterpreted. But when man's day is over, and God's day comes, then error will depart and truth will flourish. False science, vain philosophy, and impure literature will not be known anymore. True knowledge will cover the earth and fill the souls of men. Truth will then be prized and exalted when He who is the truth and the true

One will reign. His throne will be the throne of truth; His crown the crown of truth. His light will put darkness to flight. Every falsehood and unreality will disappear. Everything will be real and true.

5. *The saints of God will no longer be maligned.* All along, hatred, contempt, and misrepresentation have been their portion. All manner of evil has been spoken and written concerning them, both in life and after death. They have been treated as the despised of all things. But when that day will come that God has called, this will be all reversed. Their lives will be all rewritten, and that by a divine hand; no misrepresentation, no falsehood there. The onesided or malevolent histories that have slandered them will vanish. God Himself will proclaim their true character and noble deeds or sacrifices that the world denied or sneered at. We will have new and noble volumes of "worthies," of saints and martyrs whose names the world never introduced into its histories. What a day of avenging injuries and righting the wronged will God's day be! Let us then be patient under the smearing of evil men. Let ungodly historians vilify our noblest men – our Reformers, our Covenanters. Let them slander Knox and Calvin, Melville and Rutherford, or Whitefield and the evangelists of his age. The day of reparation is coming. The falsehoods will not always lie upon their memories. God Himself will undertake their vindication, to the confusion of their slanderers. What a day for the clearing up of characters, and the placing of events, words, and deeds in their proper light. Then will the lie be answered, the accusation debunked before the universe. Then will the righteous shine as the sun in the kingdom of their Father.

Let us then rest in hope. Let us be patient. Let us meekly bear wrongs and reproaches. *"He who believes in it will not be disturbed"* (Isaiah 28:16). This is night, but the morning comes. Let us rejoice in the prospect of it and do our work regardless of present censure and reproach, anticipating the *"Well done"* of the great Master and Judge. He stands before the door.

Chapter 69

The Glory and the Love

Such was the appearance of the likeness of the glory of the Lord. – Ezekiel 1:28

The book of Ezekiel corresponds in many respects with the Apocalypse. These books begin and end much in the same way. Only the Old Testament prophet takes more the earthly aspects of things, while the New Testament prophet takes the heavenly. Ezekiel's first chapter is a description of the shekinah and the cherubim; the apostle John's first chapter is a description of Christ Himself. Ezekiel's last chapters relate to Israel and the earthly Jerusalem, and John's to the church and the heavenly Jerusalem.

Ezekiel's is the first full description we have of the shekinah and the cherubim. They are often alluded to in Jewish history. Isaiah especially mentions them, but only here are they *described*. Much about them was probably known to the Jews, for the high priest was permitted once a year to look upon them and would relate when he came out what he saw. We do not read that what he saw when he went in were among the unspeakable things *which a man is not permitted to speak* (2 Corinthians 12:4). But here the prophet is inspired to write down the details of the *marvelous sight* (Exodus 3:3) in the holy of holies.

God was about to remove the glory from Israel, but before doing so, He does two things. He *first* describes the glory, so that Israel might know what they were losing. *Secondly,* He gives His reasons for removing it (verse 12): the sins of Jerusalem and of Israel. This first chapter of Ezekiel is a description of the glory, the intermediate chapters contain the reasons for the withdrawal and God's judgments on those Gentile nations that were more or less in connection with Israel, while the concluding chapters contain a prediction of their return in greater splendor – never again to depart. Thus, the book of Ezekiel is connected in all its parts throughout: simple, yet complete in its object and execution.

Let us note the several words of our text – each of them full of meaning.

1. *The Lord.* That is, *Jehovah.* This is sometimes the name of the Godhead, but more frequently (and originally) it is Messiah's name. In the New Testament, *Lord* is almost always the name of Christ. Here in Ezekiel, it may be either or both. That which is seen there relates to God – to the Godhead – but then it is in Messiah, in the Word made flesh, that God comes into sight. So that while what the prophet saw relates to the Godhead, it does so in connection with Messiah as the manifestation or revelation of the Godhead.

2. *The glory.* Jehovah is the glorious One. To Him we ascribe the *glory,* that is, all-infinite perfection and excellence. That which we call His "perfections," Scripture calls His *glory*. It was this glory that Moses prayed to see, and it was this that God made known to him when He passed by and proclaimed His name (Exodus 33:22; 34:6-7). It was something infinitely admirable, perfect, lovable, solemn and awful, yet beautiful and attractive. It is the full glory of the Lord that we behold in Jesus.

3. *The likeness.* The word is the same as in Genesis 1:26: *"According to Our **likeness**"* (emphasis added), and occurs more frequently in Ezekiel than in all of Scripture. Man was originally God's *likeness,* but this being defaced, God makes another and more perfect likeness of Himself. The full development of this *likeness* is in Jesus Christ, the *exact representation of His nature* (Hebrews 1:3). There was, however, an imperfect foreshadowing of this in that which was placed in the tabernacle and the temple – that *is enthroned above the cherubim* (2 Samuel 6:2), or rather, that "inhabited the

cherubim." Every other *likeness,* or attempt to make a likeness, God has forbidden. For no one can reveal God except Himself.

4. *The appearance.* That is "the vision" that met the eye – the rays streaming from the glory; the brightness or *the radiance of His glory,* as Paul expresses it (Hebrews 1:3); *the Light of the knowledge of the glory of God in the face of Christ* (2 Corinthians 4:6). The "vision," or "appearance," or "visible form," was meant for man's eye to look upon – it was the visible representation of the invisible God, in such a way as should reveal the glory to creatures who otherwise cannot see God – *the King eternal, immortal,* **invisible** (1 Timothy 1:17, emphasis added).

Thus God gave to Israel a glorious discovery of Himself, a visible manifestation of His invisible perfections – a perfect embodiment to man's creaturesenses of God's character and excellencies, so that by looking to it man might know God, in His love, His greatness, His holiness, and His majesty. All this was gathered up later and embodied in the man Christ Jesus. Old Testament saints thus got glimpses of God and of His glory; enough to gladden them and produce happy confidence, but not enough to fully satisfy, for all these appearances said, "There is still something behind, something still to come"; and that something was nothing less than the only begotten of the Father. So is it said to us, "There is much yet to be revealed" – *good things to come* (Hebrews 9:11; 10:1).

The residence of this glory in the temple was the special mark of God's favor to Israel – His special honor bestowed on Jerusalem. For ages, that glory dwelt in that city, among that people. Its presence proclaimed the love of God and His desire that Israel should know Him. When, therefore, Israel had sinned beyond divine forbearance, God marked His condemnation and displeasure by removing the glory. But before He did so, He warned, threatened, and pleaded. Then, when He could no longer bear their sins, He sent His prophets to announce the departure of the glory. But even to the last, His longsuffering shows itself, just as when Jesus wept over Jerusalem. The glory first comes out from the sanctuary and lingers at the threshold – unwilling to leave. Then it takes its place over the city – lingering and unwilling to leave. Then it goes to the Mount of Olives – still fondly lingering, and desiring, if possible, to remain in the beloved city. Then at last, when every message is futile, it takes to itself wings and vanishes away.

What a lesson is here! What love, what pity, what long-suffering, what yearning! Truly the Lord *hate[s] divorce* (Malachi 2:16). He would gladly abide in the place of which He had said, *"This is My resting place"* (Psalm 132:14). Slowly, slowly He turns away from it and by that lingering slowness, invites them to ask Him to return – to lift the universal cry, "Stay, oh stay!" And He would have stayed, even at the last, but Israel would have none of Him. Rather did they pray for Him to depart out of their coasts.

Thus, God lingers over His wellbeloved world! Why this long delay of judgment? Why these ages of suspended wrath? Iniquity abounds, yet God does not strike. Men provoke Him to the uttermost, yet He yearns over them with His old, unwearied utterance of love: *How can I give you up?* He has not forgotten His threatenings. He is not trifling with sin, nor indifferent to the crimes of earth. But He is long-suffering toward us, *not wishing for any to perish but for all to come to repentance* (2 Peter 3:9). Yes! The meaning of the delay and the long-suffering is *salvation*. He has no pleasure in the death of the wicked. He would gladly spare even Sodom, much more Jerusalem. For God is love, and the last days of earth's apostasy will yet bear testimony to the sincerity of His messages – to the riches of divine grace, to the unquenched love of God.

Chapter 70

False Religion and Its Doom

"I will scatter your bones around your altars." - Ezekiel 6:5

It is about Israel's idolatries that the prophet is speaking: her false gods, her idol altars, her lying prophets and priests. Jehovah abhorred them, for He is a jealous God, and with Him there is but one religion, one creed, one Bible, one God. Men may speak of their right to believe as they please, and worship as they think fit. But God claims the right of deciding for us in these things. We are not under man in these, but we are under God. He will not tolerate falsehood, error, unbelief, superstition, or anything inconsistent with His revelation. Every false religion He will destroy, every false religionist He will condemn. The true and the false religion are in His eyes as far apart as east and west, as unlike as night and day. There can be no compromise, no fellowship of light with darkness, of Christ with Belial, of the believer with the infidel. *"God is not a man, that He should lie"* (Numbers 23:19), or that He should overlook the lies of others. If He is the *true* God, then let us follow Him, let us worship Him in spirit and in truth. Man says that he wants sincerity and earnestness, but what God asks for is *truth: the* truth, the one truth, the one religion that He has revealed. Mark these four things: (1) false religion, (2) its uselessness, (3) its hatefulness, and (4) its doom.

1. *False religion.* There is such a thing as *false* religion. It may be earnest and zealous, yet false. No amount of sincerity or zeal will make that true which is in itself false. False religion is the worship of a false god, or the false worship of the true God. In general, both are mixed, though in different proportions. To worship Baal or Molech would be to worship a false god. But do we not have, unconsciously, perhaps, many Baals and Molechs that we worship under the name of Jehovah, as the statue of Jupiter at Rome is adored as that of Peter? We worship a false god when we do not worship the very God and Father of our Lord Jesus Christ. We worship the true God untruly when we give Him only half a heart, half a soul, or when we go to Him with the doubt, and the gloom, and the unbelief that belong to Baal. Go to Baal with your uncertain and doubtful worship. Do not go to the living God, and do not think that uttering some true words or the expression of a little sentimental devotion is the true worship of the true God.

2. *Its uselessness.* It profits nothing and nobody, either here or hereafter. It is not acceptable to God. It will not be counted as a substitute for the true. It does not satisfy the conscience. It does not make the man happy. It does not fill the heart. It does not heal diseases nor remove burdens. It does not give a man a good hope toward God or brighten his prospects for eternity. It is irksome and unprofitable, only cheating the poor worshipper into the belief that he has felt or performed something good and worthy. It will not stand the fire. It is just wood, hay, and stubble. The judgment will sweep it all away. It does nothing for time nor eternity, nothing for earth nor heaven. It is so *unreal.*

3. *Its hatefulness.* God abhors it. It does not have one feature that is pleasing to Him. It is *outward,* it is *untrue,* it is *against His revelation,* it is *dishonoring,* it is *selfexalting.* Therefore, God abhors it. He wants the heart; it does not have that. He wants love, trust, peace, joy, childlike confidence, and reverence; it does not have any of these. It is deficient in every essential element that God expects in worship. Against false worship His prophets were commanded to speak. It was as smoke in His nostrils and abominable in His eyes. It is hateful in itself. It makes the worshipper hateful. It is pure mockery. It is rottenness and death.

It is a skeleton, not a thing of flesh and blood, but a mere mouthful of words, a handful of dust and ashes. Surely it is hateful to Him who is *true,* who *desire[s] truth in the innermost being* (Psalm 51:6).

4. *Its doom.* The worship will be destroyed and the worshipper covered with shame and everlasting contempt. The scattering of the bones of the worshippers around the altars (2 Kings 23:16), like that of mingling their blood with their sacrifices, was the indication of utter contempt as well as condemnation. It was vengeance extending even to the dust. It was *certain* condemnation, for God is to do it, and He will not lie. It was *utter* condemnation, for here is God's hand interceding to judge completely. It was *visible* condemnation, before men's eyes, in a visible and striking form, so that there may be no mistake, not in a corner but in open day before all. It was *expressive* condemnation, such as will mark the sin; not at random, nor general, but each man's sin will bear its own peculiar brand of punishment. It was *contemptuous* condemnation, mingling the worshipper and his worship in one common ruin. Both will perish – perish together, perish in the same doom; God will laugh at their calamity, and mock when their fear comes. It was *everlasting* condemnation. Their altars will never rise again. They and their false religion will perish forever. There will be no falsehoods in hell, no hollow religion amid the everlasting burnings.

See that your religion is *true,* your worship *real.* Beware of hollowness, falsehood, and externalism – of everything that will not stand the fan of the great Husbandman when He comes in His glory for sifting and for judgment.

Chapter 71

No Breath, No Life

And I looked, and behold, sinews were on them, and flesh grew and skin covered them; but there was no breath in them. – Ezekiel 37:8

This scene has two aspects (an event and a truth): (1) the prophetical, which specially points to Israel's restoration in the latter day; and (2) the spiritual, which points to the case of individual souls, churches, or congregations.

There are four stages presented to us: (1) the boneheaps in the valley, *very dry* (Ezekiel 37:2); (2) the gathering and reconstruction of these bones; (3) the clothing with flesh, sinews, and skin; and (4) the infusion of breath or life. It is through the *last* of these that the living man is constituted, and without it there is only the picture or statue of a man.

The *breath* is manifestly the "life," communicated by the spirit of life. This life may have different stages, but wherever it is there is a true and complete man. The disciples had life before our Lord breathed on them, but then they attained more. They had life before Pentecost, but then they obtained more. It was life that God communicated when He created man. It is life (of a higher kind) that the spirit of God communicates to the soul at conversion. The last Adam, as the possessor of the Holy Spirit, is thus an enlivening spirit.

Thus, a man may be very like a saint and yet not be one. A church or congregation may be very like a Christian one, with a fair appearance and compact organization; all in excellent bustling order, numerous, generous, united, earnest after a sort, yet lacking one thing that neutralizes and paralyses all the rest – the breath of life.

1. *Our creed may be sound, and yet we may not be Christians.* Balaam's creed seems to have been sound; also, that of Judas and Demas. It may be the creed of apostles and reformers, the creed of the Synod of Dort, or the Westminster Assembly, yet everything within may be wrong. It will form part of the bones, the sinews, or the flesh, but that is all it is. Indeed, its soundness may be the occasion of serious selfdeception. We may mistake orthodoxy for life – the correctness of our confession of faith for the *breath*. An inanimate, unproductive creed – What will it do for you in the day of the Lord? What will it do for you now? Does it give you real peace, real liberty, or real fellowship with God?

2. *Our religion may be externally complete, and yet we may not be Christians.* By *religion* I mean everything that pertains to the private or public worship and service of God: our praises, our prayers, our sanctuary services, our family worship. What are all these without the inward breath? What is routine without life? Mechanical religion may do for the gods of Greece and Rome, but not for the living and true God. Mechanical religion may do for those who imagine that religious performances are work done, or money paid, in order to ward off divine anger, and persuade God to keep them out of hell; but not for those who know that they are the channels of fellowship with God. Your sanctuary attendance may be regular and reverent, but what if there is no *breath* in it? Your prayers and praises may be punctual and beyond reproach, but what if there is no *breath* in them? Will God accept them? Will they satisfy you? Will they make you happy? Will they not be irksome and intolerable? And the more you multiply them, the more intolerable they will be.

3. *Our good works may be numerous and praiseworthy, yet we may not be Christians.* It is not the work that makes the Christian, but the Christian

that makes the work. This is a day of good works; of benevolent schemes; of societies great and small; of organizations for the relief of the poor, and the reformation of the wicked. Those who conduct them may be earnest and selfdenying men, but is the *breath* there? They often wonder why so much should be done with so little fruit. But is there not a cause? Is there breath or life in all this? Can statues, machines, or engines do the work of the living God? No! It is *life* that does real work. It is *life* that is successful. It is *life* that God honors, and by which He works. Let us see that in doing Christian work, we ourselves are Christians, or else we will be nothing but Noah's carpenters after all. We may do many good works, and yet not be Christians. Many will come in that day, saying, *"Lord, Lord, did we not prophesy in Your name?"* (Matthew 7:22). But the answer will be, *"I never knew you"* (Matthew 7:23).

4. *Our life may be exemplary, and yet we may not be Christians.* There may be bones, sinews, and flesh, and yet no breath, no life! There are many who mistake a fair external demeanor for Christian life. A man may be so like a Christian that another could not suppose that there was anything wrong, and yet there might not be any breath!

A life with *no breath* must be:

1. *A very imperfect life.* Many features lacking – even outward ones, but much more inward. The light will be dim; the salt will lack savor.

2. *A very unhappy life.* There is the secret feeling that everything is wrong. Everything is irksome, for lack of the divine internal reality.

3. *A very unsuccessful life.* It is not mere bustle, earnestness, or zeal that does the true work for God. If there is no *breath,* what are these? All the labor will be in vain.

There is *breath* for you, O sinner – in Him who has the Spirit, who is our breath. You will not be able to say, "I perished, or I was unhappy or useless, because God would not give me this breath."

Chapter 72

Every Christian a Teacher

"Those who have insight among the people will give understanding to the many." – Daniel 11:33

We do not receive knowledge for ourselves alone. We must share it with others. Like our Great High Priest, we must *have compassion on the ignorant* (Hebrews 5:2 KJV), and must remember Him who said, *"Learn from Me"* (Matthew 11:29).

In the days spoken of here by Daniel there will be some, it is said, *"who know their God"* (verse 32). These are *"those who have insight"*; for it is the knowledge of God that is alone regarded as understanding in the Bible. He who knows God is a man of understanding; he who does not know Him *lacks understanding* – he is *a fool*. For *"this is eternal life, that they may know You, the only true God, and Jesus Christ whom You have sent"* (John 17:3).

Those that have understanding are evidently few. They are described as *among the people,* as if they were a light in a dark place; a few who are of God, while the whole world lies in wickedness. *Not many wise* (1 Corinthians 1:26) are called, is the law of this age; indeed, not many of the world who become wise. To be wise in Christ is the privilege of few. In order to do this, they must become fools – fools in the eye of men – fools *so that [they] may become wise* (1 Corinthians 3:18), for the wisdom of God is foolishness with men. It is a great thing to know

God – to understand the things of God. Happy are they who thus know and understand.

Taking these words as applicable to every Christian man and woman, let us see what they teach us.

1. *A Christian is one among the people.* He is in the world, but not of it. He has been delivered out of it. He is of the same stock as the rest of mankind, just one of the people, one of Adam's race. He is one of a small band, not one of a multitude; one of those of whom our Lord spoke when He said, *"There are few who find it"* (Matthew 7:14). He was born of the flesh before he was born of the Spirit. He bore the image of the earthly before he bore the image of the heavenly.

2. *A Christian is one that has understanding.* It is this that especially marks him out from *the people*. He knows what they do not know. He has come to be of an understanding heart. He may not have much of earthly literature or human science, but he knows God – not only knows about Him but also knows Him. He does not have much to say for himself except this: that he knows God. The special distinctiveness of a Christian is that he is a man of understanding. He may be poor, obscure, unlearned, and untraveled, yet he understands what millions do not understand. He may not know the world and its wonders, but he knows Him who made all of these; he knows His greatness and His love.

3. *A Christian is one who does not keep his knowledge to himself.* He is not proud because he knows what others do not know. He pities others and longs to share his treasures; not to *divide* his inheritance, for that is impossible, but to impart what he possesses. He gives, yet he retains; he shares, yet he is none the poorer. He has a loving and unselfish heart as well as an understanding one. He becomes a liberal giver of what God has given. He is like the clouds, which cannot contain their water within themselves; like the sun, which cannot but shine; like the river, which cannot but scatter fertility; like the flower, which cannot but dispense fragrance.

4. *A Christian is an instructor.* He has been taught, and he becomes a teacher. He has found the preciousness of knowledge, and he seeks to impart it. He feels that what he formerly needed so much was *teaching*, that what the world still needs is *teaching*, and so he becomes a *teacher* – not as if setting himself up for superior powers or knowledge, but simply as one who has had a treasure imparted to him, and who therefore longs to impart to his poorer fellow creatures his divine gold and silver. He sees that the great need of humanity is teaching, true teaching, teaching in the things pertaining to the true God, and he sets himself fervently to *teaching* an untaught world. Christians, you must be *teachers*. This is your vocation, as those who have themselves been taught of God. Teach by your lives. Teach also in words. Lose no opportunity to instruct others, young or old. Let your lips keep knowledge for all. Live an *instructive* life.

5. *A Christian is an instructor of many.* He does not confine himself to a small inner circle, but he has his eye on everybody. He is not content with one or two. He remembers the words of commendation to Levi: *"He walked with Me in peace and uprightness, and he turned many back from iniquity"* (Malachi 2:6). *Many, many,* is his watchword. Like Joseph Alleine, he becomes "insatiably greedy of souls." *Many, many,* is the burden of his prayers. *Many, many,* is inscribed on all his plans. His spirit widens and widens, his eye and heart take in larger and larger circles. He remembers the multitudes whom his Master taught, the thousands in the early days of the church, and he seeks *many, many.*

Chapter 73

Work, Rest, and Recompense

"Go your way to the end; then you will enter into rest and rise again for your allotted portion at the end of the age." – Daniel 12:13

Daniel reminds us of John. The one was *a man greatly beloved* (Daniel 10:11, 19 KJV); the other was *the disciple whom Jesus loved* (John 21:20). The one had frequent revelations and visions, especially of the times and seasons; so had the other. The one fainted and was without strength at the sight of Messiah's glory. The other fell at Christ's feet as one dead. Both were comforted by the hand of Jesus laid upon them. Both were exiles in a Gentile land. Both were very aged men. In our text we are reminded of the last words of our Lord to John: *"Follow me!"* (John 21:19). To Daniel it is, *"Go your way to the end."*

Here we have three things for God's Daniels, God's saints, in these days: (1) a saint's present work, (2) a saint's coming rest, and (3) a saint's future glory.

1. *A saint's present work.* "Go your way to the end." This reminds us of Jesus' words, *"If I want him to remain until I come"* (John 21:22). These visions are not to make you remiss in duty, heedless of common things, or neglectful of daily work. No, go your way until the end comes – work while it is day. It was meant:

1. *To calm.* That which he had seen and heard was suitable to trouble, excite, and discompose. He had been in the presence of God, like Paul in the third heaven. He had been carried forward into the marvelous events of the latter day. He needed a *calming* word. And here it is, *"Go your way to the end."* Do your ordinary work. Walk in the simple way of common life. In the midst of this age's convulsions, storms, and heat; in the prospect of what is coming on the earth in the last days, we need calming words too. Let us listen to the calm, holy voice that speaks to us ever from heaven: *"Cease striving and know that I am God"* (Psalm 46:10); *"Do not let your heart be troubled"* (John 14:1, 27); *Keep yourselves in the love of God* (Jude v. 21); and *"What is that to you? You follow Me!"* (John 21:22).

2. *To exhort.* The words are those of command or exhortation, like those of Jesus: *"You follow Me!"* It is not that we are *permitted* to attend to our daily duties in the midst of all these vast events, present or future, but that we are *commanded* to do so; to work while it is day. Sow your seed. Do not be slothful in business. Be careful and scrupulous in filling up the common daily outline of life. Do the little things well, no less than the great things.

3. *To cheer.* The word speaks of *an end*. It is not perpetual toil, or endless weariness. There remains a rest. The end comes! It may not be long. Life will soon be done. Or the Lord may soon be here. Do not be weary or disheartened. Be of good cheer. What are a few years of toil in view of the eternal rest? How needful it is to keep in mind these words: *"Go your way to the end."* Let us not be turned aside from the plain path, troubled in mind, disconcerted in plans, nor led to slacken our diligence. Let us press on, fight on, work on, run on; steadfast and unmovable in the work of the Lord. We have a daily work to do in the sight of God. Let us do it well. Let us be faithful in all things; men in earnest; bent on doing the work that lies in our hand.

2. *A saint's coming rest.* There remains a *rest*! *"'Blessed are the dead who die in the Lord.'"* . . . *"Yes,"* says the Spirit, *"so that they may* **rest** *from*

their labors" (Revelation 14:13, emphasis added). The great rest is when the Lord comes. But there are two other rests. There is present rest in Jesus, and there is rest in the grave. And it is this rest in the grave that seems to be the one promised to Daniel, as to Abraham: *"You shall go to your fathers in peace"* (Genesis 15:15). He was to live long, but not always, and as soon as his time here was done, he was to *rest*. This rest is the same as that which is called "sleeping in Jesus." He that sleeps in Jesus *rests*. We are warranted, then, to set this rest before our eyes. Though death is our enemy, not our friend, and though death is different from the Lord's coming, still death does introduce the saints to rest. It is the "saint's rest," a pledge of the saint's everlasting rest when we will toil no more, be vexed no more, be weary no more, be pained no more, and be burdened no more. Work well, then, for the workday is not long, and the rest day comes! "You will rest" is God's promise to us as well as to Daniel.

3. *A saint's future glory.* "*You will . . . rise again for your allotted portion at the end of the age.*" Here we have:

1. *The days.* The days are those mentioned in the previous verses; the end of these days is the beginning of blessedness; *"How blessed is he who keeps waiting and attains to the 1,335 days!"* (Daniel 12:12). It seems indicated to Daniel that the end of these days is not to be in *his* lifetime. As for us, we do not know when the end will be, we do not know the times and seasons, and we do not know when the Lord will come.

2. *The rising.* To "stand" or "rise" are used synonymously. *Therefore the wicked will not stand in the judgment, nor sinners in the assembly of the righteous* (Psalm 1:5). This "standing" is evidently meant as "resurrection" in both passages, as in Daniel 12:2: *"Many of those who sleep in the dust of the ground will awake."* It is of resurrection that God speaks here to Daniel. He will arise! This is the great promise so often reiterated in the New Testament: *"You will be repaid at the resurrection of the righteous"* (Luke 14:14). Intermediate blessing is there; promises of intermediate rest abound; but the final glory is yet in reserve, both for Daniel and

for us. Resurrection. The first resurrection! Resurrection unto life! The better resurrection! Corruption exchanged for incorruption, dishonor for glory.

3. *The lot.* Daniel has a lot, portion, or special recompense of his own. To this he will arise after he has rested in the grave from his weary work on earth. There may be a twofold reference here:

   a. *General.* The first resurrection, resurrection of the just, resurrection from among the dead, resurrection unto everlasting life, or the better resurrection – these expressions refer to the saint's reward when the Lord comes. *Blessed and holy is the one who has a part in the first resurrection* (Revelation 20:6). This glorious resurrection is held before Daniel's eyes as his recompense. It is held before ours! *Your dead will live; their corpses will rise. You who lie in the dust, awake and shout for joy, for your dew is as the dew of the dawn, and the earth will give birth to the departed spirits* (Isaiah 26:19).

   b. *Special.* There seems to be something more special promised here to Daniel (as to Zerubbabel in Haggai 2:23), some personal and peculiar reward. What that may be, we do not know. *A prophet's reward* (Matthew 10:41) is referred to by our Lord as something special and great. Each saint will have his own crown, his own weight of glory, his own inheritance, *"**your** crown"* (Revelation 3:11, emphasis added).

The message, then, in these last days (days of excitement, change, and darkness), is: labor on – perseveringly, calmly, joyfully, and hopefully. The Lord is at hand. The resurrection comes. The glory of that day will be an ample recompense.

Chapter 74

Human Heedlessness and Divine Remembrance

And they do not consider in their hearts that I remember all their wickedness. – Hosea 7:2

Let me present this passage to you under these two topics: (1) human sin, and (2) the divine remembrance of it.

1. *Human sin.* What is sin? It is *not* (1) an accident, (2) an impoliteness, (3) a misfortune, (4) a disease, or (5) a weakness. It may be all of these, perhaps, but it is something beyond all of these; something of a more fatal and terrible character. It is something: (1) with which *law* has to do, (2) which *righteousness* abhors, (3) which the *Judge* condemns, and (4) which calls for the infliction of *punishment* from God. In other words, it is *guilt* – it is *crime*. Man's tendency is either to deny it or to excuse it. He either pleads not guilty or he smooths over the evil, giving it deceptive names. Or if he does not succeed in these, he casts the blame off of himself. He shifts the responsibility to his nature, his birth, his circumstances, his education, indeed, to God Himself. But human sin is not to be diluted or transformed into a shadow. It is infinitely *real* – true, deep, and terrible in the eyes of Him with whom we have to do. It is the transgression of law, and as such

it must be dealt with by God and felt by us. Let us not trifle with sin, either in the conscience or the intellect. Let us learn its true nature from the terribleness of the wrath and condemnation threatened by God against every sin, great or small.

2. *The divine remembrance of it.* God remembers. His memory does not fail in anything. Nothing escapes it, great or small. Nothing obliterates anything from it.

   a. *Time does not obliterate it.* Ages blot out nothing. The past is as clear and full as the present.

   b. *Other events do not obliterate it.* With man, one fact expels another; today's doings destroy the recollection of yesterday's doings. Not so with God.

   c. *Our own forgetfulness will not obliterate it.* Our memory and God's are very different. Our forgetfulness does not make Him forget.

God remembers! Nothing can make Him forget. He may seem to do so, but it is only seeming. He remembers the person; the time; the circumstances; the thing itself, public or secret, bad or good, and negative or positive. He remembers *sins*. Let no one say that He is too good to remember them. He cannot but do so. He would not be God if it were otherwise. God cannot forget anything; for memory is but the knowledge of the past, and He knows everything. It may be found hereafter that man forgets nothing either, and that the bitterness of a ruined eternity will lie in memory. But though man should forget, God remembers and He can call up sin to remembrance. It will and must come up at last. Men may try to forget it, to drown all thought of it, to obliterate all traces of it, but it will come up! As even Zophar said of Job, *His bones are full of the sin of his youth* (Job 20:11). For a season here men often succeed in forgetting sin. And having forgotten it they conclude that God has done the same. *They do not consider in their hearts that I remember all their wickedness.* They conceive that God's memory is as treacherous as their own. For this God reproves them. "*You thought that I was just like you; that My memory was as faithless as yours*" (Psalm 50:21). But the day is coming that will show how foolish, how criminal such a thought was! The opening of the books will show this if nothing else will.

But there is such a thing as *intentional forgetfulness* with God. *"I will remember their sins no more"* (Hebrews 8:12). This is the true oblivion; divine oblivion of sin; perfect and eternal oblivion. And how is this? The prophet in the Old Testament and the apostle in the New Testament tell us that this is one of the provisions and results of the new covenant; that covenant that has been sealed with the blood of the Son of God. It is the blood that enables God to forget sin; that blots out all sin of ours from His eternal memory, so that it becomes as if it had never been. But this oblivion is no accident, no mere result of time and intervening circumstances. It is *righteous* oblivion! Oblivion that righteousness constrains! O blessed oblivion that is the result of righteousness. Had it been accomplished in any other way, there would always have been the danger of reviving memory; memory rousing itself from dormancy and calling for vengeance after all. But where *righteousness* has produced the forgetfulness, all is well forever. Sin is buried beyond the possibility of resurrection.

But when does God cease to remember sin in my individual case? When I have accepted the covenant. When I have fixed my eyes upon the blood. When I have received the divine testimony to that great propitiation that has made it a righteous thing in God to remember my sins no more!

Is not this a description of our world? It is not the fool saying here, *"There is no God"* (Psalm 14:1). Nor is it men saying, "God has forgotten *us*." It is that God has forgotten our *sins*! Indifference to sin like their own, forgetfulness like their own, they ascribe to Him! "God does not remember sin" is this great world's motto. And so they neglect the sacrifice for sin and put away all fear of hell. *They do not consider in their hearts that I remember all their wickedness.* What will they say when the Judge arrives?

Chapter 75

Lies, the Food of Man

You have eaten the fruit of lies. – Hosea 10:13

The subject suggested by these words is "lies, their fruit, and man's eating it," or simply "lies and their fruit." The word *lies* is used in a twofold sense – a lie as to fact, and a lie as to doctrine; untrue reports and unsound teaching, false testimony, and false knowledge (or dogma). This falsity may be negative or positive, as in, *"You surely will not die!"* (Genesis 3:4), and, *"You will be like God"* (Genesis 3:5). The lie comes sometimes from man, sometimes from Satan, but never from God, for *"God is not a man, that He should lie"* (Numbers 23:19); it never comes from the works of God when rightly interpreted and understood.

By two great lies man was led away from God. By the same two lies the estrangement has been kept up. On these two lies the world has been feeding ever since the fall. Their fruit has been woe and death. These lies are those referred to above – the one a denial of Godheadperfection, the other an assertion of creatureperfection; the one saying there is no such thing as sin and punishment, the other saying that there is no such thing as creaturehood limitation and dependency. *"You surely will not die!" "You will be like God."*

God has written His Bible to contradict these two lies, for the whole divine Word is a refutation of them. But the special refutation is to be seen in the life and death of the Christ of God. His death, as the SinBearer, said,

"You surely will die"; and His life, as the dependent Son of Man, showed that no circumstances, no progress, or no knowledge could ever make man God, or make the creature the Creator; but the human, however blessed, holy, and wise, must ever be the human, and the Divine the Divine.

Israel's history, to which our passage refers, is the history of the fruit of lies. *They did not believe in God* (Psalm 78:22) is the accusation brought against them. They rejected the truth, they received the lie, and the fruit of this was judgment. Every sorrow that came on them was the fruit of a lie. Their last great sorrow, the ruin of Jerusalem, and the slaughter of its citizens, was the fruit of a lie. And are they not now, in their dispersion, eating the fruit of lies?

The world's history is the same. Our race has been eating the fruit of lies; not simply of *sin,* but also of *lies.* The sorrows, sighs, tears, and pains of our race are the fruit of lies – the original lie of Paradise, and a thousand such since then. The sweating toils of man, the labor pangs of woman, the cries of suffering infancy – what are they but the fruit of a lie? Yon tossing sickbed, yon weary deathbed ("The long day's dying," John Milton), yon swelling churchyard, yon shroud, yon coffin, yon funeral, yon open grave, what are they? The fruit of a lie. It is bitter, poisonous, longlasting fruit. And the world's last days are no improvement upon its first, for in them comes the *strong delusion, that they should believe a **lie*** (2 Thessalonians 2:11 KJV, emphasis added). What is every false religion but the belief in a lie, and the judgments with which God has visited its professing people but the eating the fruit of a lie. AntiChristianity is the special and preeminent exhibition of the belief in a lie, and the doom of Antichrist will be the special and awful exhibition of eating the fruit of lies.

Each soul's history resembles the above. It is the history of the belief in lies – in a thousand lies. We begin to believe lies as soon as we can believe anything at all, and we act daily upon believed lies. The two original satanic lies are continually coming up, and along with them myriads of others, all leading us astray. Each day brings forth the lie, the fruit, and the eating thereof. Satan, the world, the flesh, a friend, a book, or a scene whispers the lie. It is fair and hollow, and we believe it; it brings forth fruit, and we eat of it. The end is bitterness and disappointment. We "feed on lies."

What is pleasure, lust, or revelry? It is the belief in a lie, the feeding on a lie. What is worldliness, the love of merriment, the absorption of the heart in business? The belief in a lie, and the feeding on a lie. We persuade ourselves that this world is good, pleasant, and excellent, and so we pursue it in preference to the world to come. But the belief in the lie is quickly followed up by disappointment, and the sense of hollowness and dissatisfaction. God makes us thus eat of the fruit of lies, so that we may be torn from them and take ourselves to the truth.

What keeps us from Christ? A lie or lies! What makes us choose the broad way? A lie or lies! What is unbelief but the belief in a lie? Where do our doubts and fears come from but from the belief in lies in preference to the truth; indeed, from our making God a liar, in not believing the record that He has given of His Son? Where does backsliding or the loss of first love come from but from our returning to the lie that we had rejected?

God, in His gospel, meets *the* lie, and all the lies that have sprung up on earth. He sends us *the truth*. He sends us the true One. And while He meets the lie, He does it in His own divine way. He says, "Yes, you surely will not die." That deliverance, though, will not be in the way you think. Death is the wages of sin, yet I bring life to the sinner, everlasting life, life through the belief of the truth, even as death came through the belief in a lie. He says, "Yes, you will be like God," but not in your way. I will make you partakers of the divine nature, not by eating the forbidden tree, but by eating of Him whose flesh is meat indeed and whose blood is drink indeed.

What stress God lays on *truth,* and on our believing it! What sin He declares to be in a lie and in our believing it! All untruth, all error, all false doctrine, as well as false statement, has in it the nature of a lie. Men in our day think man is not responsible for the truth, and that there is no sin in the admission of error. God protests against this, and calls on men to receive truth, *His* truth, as expounded in His one revelation! Gloriously yet awfully will all this be manifested when He who is *the truth* will come the second time to vindicate both truth and righteousness!

Chapter 76

The Love and the Calling

When Israel was a youth I loved him, and out of Egypt I called My son. – Hosea 11:1

God's words to Israel by this prophet are hard and stern. Though intermixed with expressions of tenderness, such as, *How can I give you up?* (Hosea 11:8), this book is full of fearful things. In the midst of these God stops here and reminds them of His love – His first love – and the kindness of their youth, and the time of their betrothals to Him. It was sincere and deep. It had been so all along, and all of His messages by the prophets were no proof of hatred or hostility. He loved them in Abraham; He loved them in Jacob; He loved them when they went down to Egypt; He loved them in the days of their bondage; and He showed His love in calling him – even Israel His son, His firstborn – out of Egypt. The deliverance from Egypt was always in later ages the great standing proof to which God appealed, of His love: *When Israel was a youth I loved him, and out of Egypt I called My son.*

This calling out of Egypt was done more than once. The most marvelous calling out was that under Moses; but later, when they were carried into Egypt, God interceded and called them out again. Neither Egypt nor Babylon was to be the home of His people; only a sojourn, a place of exile, and nothing more. Out of it they must be called. They whom God did not love might remain there. They whom He loved could not be allowed to remain there. Servants or friends might, but not *sons*. For sons there was Canaan and Jerusalem – the land flowing with milk and honey.

The last fulfilling or "filling up" of these words was in the case of God's only begotten Son. Israel's history was the rehearsal of His. He was in certain points to tread in their steps, to go over their history in Himself. And what a closeness of connection, what a oneness between Him and them this implies! Thus in Him many words of the prophets received a filling up, a completion, an exhaustion, which makes everyone who reads feel how true, how accurate, how overflowingly full the words of God are. It is not by accommodation, allusion, or figure of speech that these words are applied to Christ. No, in Him they receive their last filling up, their perfect accomplishment. The last drop of the purposed metal is poured into the mold. It can contain no more; it needs no more. Then that was fulfilled that was spoken by the prophet: *Out of Egypt I called My son*. Egypt was not to be the home of Jesus, and yet it was to have the honor of sheltering Him. Yes, sheltering Him when Israel cast Him out. But out of it He must be called. God's purpose and God's Word demanded it. O marvelous fullness of the divine Word! O superhuman perfection of exactness in each announcement! Not one jot or tittle fails! Heaven and earth may pass; star after star may be broken or blotted out; but the divine Word remains unharmed and glorious amid the universal wreck. All that is on earth of beauty and excellence may come to nothing; *the grass withers, the flower fades, but the word of our God stands forever* (Isaiah 40:8).

In both these cases we see the Word literally fulfilled. The nation of God and the Son of God were called out of the land of Egypt and the house of bondage.

Why this calling? Could they not remain? Was not Goshen as fruitful as Canaan? In the case of the Son of God, the reason is obvious. It was in no sense His home or native land. He had fled to it for shelter, and it had received Him, even as it did Israel at first. But He had work to do elsewhere; work that could not be done in Egypt. It was to the lost sheep of the house of Israel that He was sent. In the case of Israel, we may say also, they could not remain. Though born in Egypt, it was not their true home. They were the heirs of another heritage, given by God Himself. They too had work to do that could not be done in Egypt. There was a purpose to be fulfilled in them by their settlement in Canaan. Too long of a connection with Egypt would have corrupted them with its idolatry, and worldliness, and pleasures. They had a testimony to bear in behalf of the true God that could not be borne in Egypt, so that even though they had never been oppressed, they could not have remained. It was to Jerusalem, to Canaan, to Zion, to Lebanon that they were bound. They are not to drink out of the Nile, but out of the Jordan. With streams from Lebanon, they are to quench their thirst. Whatever attractions Egypt might have (in the case of Moses it was riches, royalty, learning, and luxurious ease), they must not delay; nor look behind, like Lot's wife; nor sigh, as they did afterwards in the desert, for its carnal plenty.

But the Word is for us figuratively what it was for Israel literally. It is for us, for we are one with Israel, and one with the Son of God. Out of Egypt the church is called; each chosen one, each saint, each son, each Israelite indeed is called. Let us consider our history under the following: (1) our birthplace, (2) our calling, (3) our journey, and (4) our home.

1. *Our birthplace.* It is this Egypt world – *this present evil age* (Galatians 1:4). It is evil, yet it is fair to look upon, with its pleasures, elegancies, riches, glories, splendor, glitter, songs, and its magnificent palaces and gorgeous array. Egypt was one of the best specimens of the world. Into it were gathered all the world's wealth, art, science, philosophy, and splendor of every kind. It was a fascinating region; every object in it was magnetic to the natural man and intoxicating to the unregenerate heart. Everything was there but the true God. The world's religion was decked out there in its goodliness of temple, picture, statue, and image of every kind. The world's wisdom was all there; its astronomy, natural science, mechanical arts, architecture, and its skill in ornament, with all fascinations for the natural man, all stimulants for the lust of the flesh, the lust of the eyes, and the pride of life. All natural knowledge, beauty, and progress are here; intellect, power, greatness, magnificence, and splendor – all are here. Yet amid all these, the true God is not there. Human intellect is at its highest, religion at its lowest! The world by wisdom knows not God. All idolatry, of the vilest and most foolish

kind, is here. All sensuality, oppression, and wickedness are here! As was Egypt, so is this world! It is *this present evil age;* it *lies in the power of the evil one* (1 John 5:19); and it is our birthplace. Not Bethlehem, as in the case of the Son of God, nor Jerusalem, but Egypt is our birthplace. Children of wrath; sons of the Evil One; born in sin – these are the figures of speech that describe us. We are by nature men of Egypt.

2. *Our calling.* We did not rise and flee of ourselves. We would have remained there forever. We loved Egypt and delighted in its vanities. It was the home of our hearts. But God called us. He *called us with a holy calling* (2 Timothy 1:9). He called us as He did Abraham out of Ur; as He did Israel out of Egypt; as He did the fishermen out of their boats. With His own almighty voice, He called us. We could not but obey. It was irresistible. Therefore, He made us willing in the day of His power. Many voices within and without had called us. Conscience said, "Arise, and depart." The soul's deep longings after something higher said the same. Every pain, trial, disappointment, vexation, and bereavement said, "Arise, and depart." But all these failed. Then God spoke the word, and we found it irresistible; He spoke, and it was done. Then all those former voices that we had previously made light of gathered strength. Pain, grief, weariness, and affliction all spoke out now, and God spoke in them. Even the feeblest voice of all seemed irresistible. It was not so much one call as a thousand; each one irresistible. Yes, out of Egypt God called us. Blessed and holy calling!

3. *Our journey.* It is through the desert. Not at once into the kingdom; not at once to heaven; but circuitously. And this long round is not for smoothness, but for roughness! It is a *howling waste of a wilderness* (Deuteronomy 32:10); a land of barrenness, heat, thirst, hunger, and weariness. It is the *right* path, for God is our leader; it is *safe,* for God is our keeper; it is *blessed,* for God is our companion; but still, it is rough, dark, and dreary. Yet it is needful: (1) The *length* of it is needful, so that patience may have her perfect work. (2) The *roughness* of it is needful, so that we may be purified. (3) The *intricacies* of it are needful, so that God may have His opportunities for guiding us. (4) The *darkness* of it is needful, so that Christ may be realized as the sun. (5) The *sorrow* of

it is needful, so that the Holy Spirit may be known as the Comforter. How much less we would know of God and of ourselves if this journey were different! How much we would lose if we were taken at once into the kingdom, as there can be no second opportunity hereafter of going over the way again! Let us prize the journey in all its aspects.

4. *Our home.* Canaan is our promised land, and Jerusalem our city. For God has prepared for us both a land and a city, a home for eternity. Not merely better than the desert, but better than Egypt. A home that more than makes up for everything that we have left behind. It is eternal in the heavens, an incorruptible inheritance, the many mansions, God's home and ours, Christ's home and the church's forever. It is better than the earthly Jerusalem or the earthly paradise in which we will never be disturbed; from which we cannot be driven; in which we can neither be tempted nor sin; everlasting and glorious. It is to that we are bound, and we lay up our treasure there.

It is *love* that has done all this: *When Israel was a youth I loved him, and out of Egypt I called My son.* God's love has done it! It is love that *calls* us out and *draws* us out, the mighty love of God. It is love that takes us as we are, and that we are to take as it is. It is love like that shown to Abraham and to Israel. It is the love of the shepherd to his sheep; of the woman to her lost piece of silver; of the father to his lost son. It is love to which He Himself bears witness: *I loved him;* loved him even from the days of his childhood. It is love exhibited in the cross; love realized in the tens of thousands that have been called out of Egypt by it.

Chapter 77

The Anger and the Goodness

Who can stand before His indignation? Who can endure the burning of His anger? His wrath is poured out like fire and the rocks are broken up by Him. The Lord is good, a stronghold in the day of trouble, and He knows those who take refuge in Him. – Nahum 1:6-7

Throughout this chapter, and especially in these verses, let us note these two things: (1) Jehovah's anger, and (2) Jehovah's goodness. They stand out very strongly in this "burden."

1. *Jehovah's anger.*
    1. *It is real.* There is such a thing as anger in God. There are many expressions used concerning it, both in this chapter and elsewhere – jealousy, vengeance, fury, wrath; all to indicate its existence, and to show us that the human theories of divine universal benevolence are not true; they are being got up for a purpose. That purpose is to persuade the sinner's own conscience that he does not need to be alarmed because of his guilt; and that no one needs to dread the infliction of punishment, except perhaps a few of the most wicked of our race. But God's words are not exaggerations, nor words of methodology. There is a terrible truth contained

in these oft-repeated words of Scripture: *His anger was kindled* (Numbers 11:1). As loving and gracious as Jehovah is, His anger is real. When Jesus comes the second time, He comes to *"take vengeance"* (Jeremiah 50:15).

2. *It is righteous.* It is not the rage of selfishness, passion, or affront. It is judicial anger, the anger of the righteous Judge. It is anger against sin, and against the sinner; anger because of insulted law and dishonored righteousness. Nothing in it is unjust, cruel, or arbitrary. Then the condemned soul will be compelled hereafter to say it was right and just; it will be right and just to all eternity.

3. *It is terrible.* Though calm, it is unutterably awful; indeed, overwhelming. No power and no numbers will be able to stand before it. It will sweep everything before it like a whirlwind. The expulsion from Paradise, the flood, the ruin of Sodom are examples of its terribleness. The lost soul will be utterly overwhelmed.

4. *It is unstoppable.* Nothing will turn it aside or soften it when once it is kindled. *The punishment of eternal fire* (Jude v. 7); *their worm does not die, and the fire is not quenched* (Mark 9:44) – these are awful words. No bribery, argument, nor influence will prevail, nor pity to the poor soul. God will forget to be gracious. Repentance will be hidden from His eyes.

O anger of Jehovah, how real, how righteous, how terrible, how unstoppable! Yet, let me say one thing, if you should be one of the eternally lost, and if you should, in the course of your weary and tormented eternity, say to yourself, "Oh, that God were not so just." Then think what a wish that would be for yourself. Your security against unjust and overly severe punishment is that very justice against which you petition. Bad as your case may be at the hands of a *just* God, it would be unspeakably worse at the hands of an *unjust* God. The anger of a righteous God is no doubt terrible, but the unbridled fury of an unrighteous God is something too horrible even to think upon.

2. *Jehovah's goodness.* He *is* good, and He *does* good. He is kind to the unthankful and the unworthy. God is love. God loves the sinner.

THE ANGER AND THE GOODNESS

1. *His goodness is sincere.* He does not utter words of methodology, nor pretend to have feelings that are not in Him. His words mean just what they say. His deeds mean just what they indicate. The works of His hands have a most substantial and authentic expression of goodness. *"God is not a man, that He should lie"* (Numbers 23:19), either in His words of goodness or of anger.

2. *It is powerful.* It is almighty goodness. He is able to deliver those whom He loves. Their interests are safe in His hands. *The Lord is slow to anger and great in power* (Nahum 1:3). Who can withstand His love? *God is the one who justifies; who is the one who condemns?* (Romans 8:33-34).

3. *It is watchful.* His eye is on us at all times, especially in the day of trouble. His is a watchful goodness. His is the unsleeping eye, and the untiring hand. He is not weary of blessing. He delights in opportunities for pouring out His love; and our extremities are His opportunities.

4. *It is unchanging.* Like Himself, His goodness is without variableness; not ebbing and flowing, but always flowing. His heart is the heart of the unchangeable one. Not like the tides, or the seasons, but like the sky above us, always one calm arch of gentle, loving azure, embracing earth.

Such is the God with whom we have to do. He is righteous and cannot allow sin to go uncondemned and unpunished. Yet is He good and gracious, not willing to destroy or to take vengeance; a God before whom the sinner may tremble; a God in whom the chief of sinners may find forgiveness. I remind you of two passages that will form the practical improvement of all I have said.

1. *"The great day of their wrath has come, and who is able to stand?"* (Revelation 6:17). It has not come yet, but it is coming. Judgment does not linger, damnation does not slumber. It will be a day of terror for the sinner when the pentup wrath of God will pour itself out, not in seven vials, or seventy times seven, but in an eternity of vials without number.

2. *The Lord is . . . patient toward you, not wishing for any to perish but for all to come to repentance* (2 Peter 3:9). Such is His goodness now. He is rich in mercy. His patience is beyond all conception or measure. In His long-suffering there is salvation – salvation to the uttermost. He pities, yearns, pleads, implores, spares, prolongs the day of grace, and presents pardon, salvation, and life to the ungodliest, *freely.* Yes, freely to the last! Let this long-suffering goodness draw us, melt us, awaken confidence, and win us to love.

Chapter 78

Darkness Pursuing the Sinner

And will pursue His enemies into darkness. – Nahum 1:8

It is of Nineveh and Assyria that this prophet utters his fearful burden. That city and its inhabitants were to bear the judgments of Jehovah. *It* was to be swept from the earth, and *they* were to be driven out, pursued by destruction from the Lord. The Assyrian was Israel's great enemy, God's great enemy; a type of the church's great enemy in the last days. The capital city had been warned, had repented, and had returned like the dog to its vomit. Now the last blast of the prophetic trumpet is sounded, a warning to Nineveh, a consolation to Israel. Darkness has settled down on Nineveh from that day to this, and has pursued its dwellers – a type and pledge of the blackness of darkness forever.

Let us take Assyria as a specimen of sinners, and this prediction as a declaration of God's way of dealing with them.

1. *A sinner is an enemy to God.* This is a strong word, and worthy of solemn thought. It means much. Scripture speaks of the sinner as: (1) not loving God, (2) forgetting God, (3) disobeying God, and (4) departing from God. But this is more than all these; it is stronger, more decided, and more terrible. It means such things as the following:

1. *He hates God.* Hater of God is his name; hater of Christ also – hater of His whole being, His righteousness, His truth, His holiness, His power, and His sovereignty; indeed, His love.

2. *He tries to injure God.* He would gladly carry his hatred into effect by *injury*, in every way. He *robs* God, he *mocks* God, he tries to dethrone Him, and to oppose Him.

3. *He tries to do away with God.* Hostility, when it runs its course, ends in murder. So man, if he could, would take the life of God. When the fool says in his heart there is no God, he speaks as a murderer. When the Son of God came to earth, the Jews did not rest till they had killed Him. *"Crucify, crucify Him!"* (Luke 23:21) was the cry, the intensity of whose bitterness and viciousness arose from the suspicion in the hearts of the Jews that He was really the Son of God.

Thus, every sinner is an enemy of God, an injurer, a rebel, a robber, a murderer. All sin is the indication of this, and when fully carried out, it ends in this. And all unbelief is crucifixion of the Son of God.

2. *God means to deal with His enemies.* He is not indifferent to their hostility, He is not blind to it, and He does not mean to overlook it. But He is long-suffering, not willing that any should perish. He wishes to give them time to repent. He tries by this love of His to melt them; but, if all else fails, He will at length arise and deal with them. They will know His power and righteousness, His wrath and vengeance. Darkness will pursue His enemies. He does not use many words, nor strong language. The threat here is very decided, no doubt, but it is very calm; all the more terrible and certain from being so calm. It refers both to time and eternity; present darkness and eternal darkness.

1. *There is darkness in store for the sinner.* It is not fire or torment that is spoken of here, it is simply darkness. As such, it is the absence of everything that gives health, gladness, and life; for without light there is no life, verdure, nor bloom, either for man or man's earth. A world without a sun! How dismal! And it is the presence of that which produces gloom, uncertainty, perplexity,

terror, and despair. How cheerless is a cloudy day; how many more days of neverending cloud and darkness. No knowledge of the way, groping perpetually, exposure to dangers and enemies. How dismal would life be with nothing but darkness! Yet such is the portion of God's enemies! They have rejected the Light of the World, and darkness must be their lot, a common lot with him who is the Prince of Darkness.

2. *This darkness is from God.* It does not come by chance, from man, nor from natural causes. It is produced and sent by Him who has both light and darkness at His disposal. It comes as punishment – especially for their rejection of the Light. Darkness coming in any way is sad, but coming from God it is infinitely terrible. We must go astray, we must stumble, we must wander forever. O enemy of God, think what it will be, to be enveloped in darkness and followed by darkness forever.

3. *This darkness will pursue them.* It will be to them as an enemy, or as a beast of prey – ever following them, seeking their destruction. Wherever they go, this darkness will be upon their heels, and they will not escape. In vain will they seek for light; gross darkness will surround them. Eternal darkness will be their portion, the blackness of darkness forever. Darkness like a rushing whirlwind will sweep them before it – *they will be driven away into darkness* (Isaiah 8:22).

4. *Every enemy of God must expect this.* It is a certainty. It is not possible to be an enemy of God and yet escape the darkness. However swiftly they may flee, the darkness will overtake them like a tempest. Their hostility toward God must be avenged! For the darkness does not come at random. It follows in the track of the hostility. It marks the enemy and follows him. It finds him and pursues him.

Chapter 79

Jerusalem, the Center of the World's Peace

"'In this place I will give peace,' declares the Lord of hosts." – Haggai 2:9

It is to something still in the future that this whole passage refers to. Thus, Paul expounds it in Hebrews 12:26: *Now He has promised, saying, "Yet once more I will shake not only the earth, but also the heaven."* There was a shaking at Sinai. There is yet to be a greater and more universal shaking. There is to be the removal of the things that are shaken, so that those things that cannot be shaken may remain. Out of these shakings and removals – the successive dissolutions of the four Gentile monarchies – there comes the kingdom that cannot be moved, the *"everlasting dominion which will not pass away; and His kingdom is one which will not be destroyed"* (Daniel 7:14). This kingdom is the great "fifth monarchy" that will stand forever. There is to be a more stable kingdom than earth has ever seen, under the scepter of the righteous King. There is to be another Jerusalem, more firmly built than that of David and Solomon. There is to be another house more glorious than the temple of old. Both Israel and the church look for something more blessed, more excellent, and more enduring than eye has yet seen. For this it is that we must wait the advent of the great Melchizedek, with

His *royal priesthood* (1 Peter 2:9); the arrival of the new heavens and earth wherein dwells righteousness. *Then* will the words of our text be fulfilled: *"In this place I will give peace."* Here we learn: (1) Man needs peace; (2) peace is the gift of the Lord of Hosts; (3) peace is given in connection with Israel's temple; and (4) peace is to be especially given at the special time and place predicted here.

1. *Man needs peace.* He had it at first, but he flung away the pearl. Since then, everything has been trouble and conflict. God and he are not at peace. His fellows and he are not at peace. Discord, war, confusion, and hatred are everywhere. Yes, man needs peace; man's earth needs peace; creation needs peace; the animals on man's earth need peace. Israel needs peace; Israel's land needs peace. There is a cry for peace, often unconscious and inarticulate, everywhere. The whole creation groans. It cries for rest. For *unrest* is the condition into which sin has brought man and man's earth, with all that it contains. *There is no peace.* Yet man was made for peace; creation was made for peace. How sorely has this peace been needed! How deeply has the lack of it been felt these many ages – ages of unrest.

2. *Peace is the gift of the Lord of Hosts.* One of God's special names is *the God of peace* (Romans 16:20). Man can break the peace but cannot restore it. Peace seems a small thing, yet it is so great that only He whose name is "Jehovah of hosts" can give it. Man can neither make it nor purchase it. God must do both. "I create peace." *"Peace I leave with you; My peace I give to you"* (John 14:27). It is the free gift of the *Omnipotent*. It is the free gift of Him who, as the Lord of Hosts, the Captain of Jehovah's hosts, has fought our fight, overthrown our enemies, worked righteousness in our behalf, and secured peace for us. At His birth, "peace on earth" was proclaimed. He went about as the peacemaker. He died to make peace by the blood of His cross. He is our peace, who has made both one. For man, for Israel, for man's earth, for creation He has purchased peace; and this purchased peace He is still to *give*. Glorious gift for a weary, unrestful world! *"Peace, peace to him who is far and to him who is near"* (Isaiah 57:19). He gives it to His church now. He will give it to the whole earth before too long.

3. *Peace is given in connection with Israel's temple.* The place of peace was strictly the *altar.* Here the pacification was accomplished, for here the propitiation was made. From the beginning the *altar* was set up, and the blood was shed, in token of *peace.* Afterwards the altar was enclosed in a tabernacle, and again in a temple. From these came out the voice of peace from the Lord of Hosts. Then He showed Himself as the peacemaker. His peace was always in connection with His temple. No altar, no peace. No blood, no peace. These, of course, were symbols – figures – shadows of good things to come. In the fullness of time, *He* came who is temple, altar, sacrifice, and peace – all in one. He is our priest. He, as priest in His own house, gives peace. It is peace proceeding from Himself as the Lord of Hosts. It is royal and priestly peace; peace flowing from the righteous removal of all that had broken up our peace; peace that will never again be broken, because its foundations are stable and divine; peace unchangeable and everlasting.

4. *Peace is to be especially given at the time and in the place here signified.* Though peace has been secured (the work being done that pacifies – not to be done again), yet peace is so far just partially given. A few here and there are reconciled to God; that is all. The world still remains without peace. There is still distance, conflict, and controversy between man and God. There is still tumult, storm, and bitterness on earth. Man and man's earth, as a whole, are just what they were. But our text foretells a time when everything will be pacified. Then peace will be universal on earth; peace in Israel's land; peace in Jerusalem; peace issuing from the house of the Lord of Hosts. Creation will have peace. The curse will depart. Evil passions among men will cease. The beasts of field and forest will have peace as stated in Isaiah 11:6: *The wolf will dwell with the lamb, and the leopard will lie down with the young goat.* There will be nothing to hurt nor to destroy in all the holy mountain. The center and fountainhead of all this harmony, love, and peace will be Salem, the city of peace; and the house of Jehovah will be the dwelling place. Living waters, waters of health and peace, will go forth from Jerusalem; not only throughout the land, but also to the ends of the earth. That city will be earth's holy and blessed metropolis, from which all peace is to proceed. *"'In this place I will give peace,' declares the Lord of hosts."*

The Prince of Peace, the true Solomon, will be the giver and dispenser of that peace to a happy city, a happy land, a happy world, and a happy race. What a scene of order, rest, holiness, and beauty, when Jesus reigns, and all things are put under Him.

Thus, then we preach:

1. *Peace.* Not man's peace, manmade peace, nor churchmade peace; but divine peace, Godmade peace, the peace of God, peace from God, peace in God, peace from the God of peace. Receive the peaceproclaiming testimony – the gospel of peace – and be at peace.

2. *Peace through Jesus Christ.* It is from Him that all peace proceeds. He is the peacemaker, the peacepurchaser, and the peacegiver. It is with Him personally that we must deal in order to obtain it. Go to Him for it. It is free. Take it from His hand.

3. *Peace now.* Yes, we preach a present peace; immediate and sure; without working or waiting; simply in believing God's testimony to the work that has made peace; to the blood that has secured the reconciliation; to the love that has done all we need.

4. *Peace as the pledge of a worldwide peace.* As God is now giving peace to souls, so before long will He to give it to the whole earth. And we accept our *peace in believing* (Romans 15:13) as the pledge of a coming day of wider and more glorious peace. He who has given peace to us will, before long, give peace to the world. This is our hope, in the midst of convulsion, war, and tempest. Come, O Prince of Peace; set up Your kingdom of peace; reign in peace over this troubled world. Come, put on Your crown of peace. Earth has been without You for a long time, and without Your peace. Make haste; come Yourself; and bring with You Your everlasting peace.

Chapter 80

Jerusalem and Her King

Rejoice greatly, O daughter of Zion! Shout in triumph, O daughter of Jerusalem! Behold, your king is coming to you; He is just and endowed with salvation, humble, and mounted on a donkey, even on a colt, the foal of a donkey. I will cut off the chariot from Ephraim and the horse from Jerusalem; and the bow of war will be cut off. And He will speak peace to the nations; and His dominion will be from sea to sea, and from the River to the ends of the earth. – Zechariah 9:9-10

These two verses stretch over a wide span of time and history. They predict the scenes of Messiah's first and second comings. There is a long, long interval between the events of the ninth verse and those of the tenth. The former has been already fulfilled (and that how literally!) eighteen centuries ago; the latter still waits to be fulfilled. The former is a glimpse of Messiah's humiliation; the latter of His exaltation, power, and glory. He came the first time to be despised and rejected of men. He comes the second time to triumph and to reign. Jerusalem has seen His lowliness, it has yet to see His majesty. It has witnessed His cross; it has yet to behold His throne.

Let us note here: (1) Jerusalem's joy, (2) Jerusalem's King, and (3) Jerusalem's glory.

1. *Jerusalem's joy.* Zion and Jerusalem are the two different parts of the one city – the city of the great King. It is the inhabitants or daughters of this twofold city that are summoned here to "rejoicing" and "shouting," to "great" rejoicing, and to the loud utterance of it. To gladness and shouting is the city called by God. It is *the joyous city* (Isaiah 32:13 KJV). Babylon may mourn, but Zion must rejoice. Egypt may howl, but Jerusalem must shout. They who have received Messiah are inhabitants of no average city. To them belongs the heavenly Jerusalem, the everlasting Zion. Their citizenship is in heaven. They are not yet in the city, but they are looking for it. And the prospect of it is enough to make them rejoice and shout. O Christian, be glad. Do not have a heavy heart. He who believes that Jesus is the Christ is born of God and is the citizen of the joyous city.

2. *Jerusalem's King.* It is written in Psalm 149:2: *Let the sons of Zion rejoice in their King.* So it is here. Let us take each of the words relating to the King, in order, in Zechariah 9:9.

   1. *Behold.* It is the prophet speaking to his fellow citizens; it is the Holy Spirit turning our eyes to Jesus. "Behold!" See this great sight. What is there on earth to be compared to it?

   2. *Your king.* Jerusalem has a King. He is *the great King, King of Kings, King of Israel, King of nations, ruler of the kings of the earth*. His name is Jesus of Nazareth. He is *the Word [made] flesh* (John 1:14), Godman, *"Immanuel, . . . God with us"* (Matthew 1:23). She is now kingless. She has no David, no Solomon, no Hezekiah. Yet to her really belongs a King – greater than all the kings of earth, *your king* (emphasis added).

   3. *Is coming.* He was long "the coming One"; now He is "come." For four thousand years the promise spoke of His coming. Now He comes at length! He delays no longer. His feet tread our earth. His eyes look on our hills and skies. Bethlehem receives Him. Nazareth gives Him a home. Bethany welcomes Him. Jerusalem shouts, "Hosanna!" at His approach. But He has *left*! He is not here now. He is now "the coming One" again. And He may soon be here. Behold He comes!

4. *To you.* Yes, especially to *you.* Jerusalem is to reject Him, to crucify Him. He knows this, but He comes to *her.* O sinner, He comes to you and He bids you to come to Him. He does not stand afar off, He comes near.

5. *Just and endowed with salvation.* A just God and a Savior. Just and the Justifier. The Savior and the Justifier, *because He is the Just One.* He came with a righteous salvation for unrighteous men. He still presents that righteous salvation. It is salvation to the utmost. He is mighty to save, He is just to save! He came *"to seek and to save that which was lost"* (Luke 19:10). Oh, good news. The righteous One loves the unrighteous. Jesus Christ the righteous came into the world to save sinners.

6. *Humble, and mounted on a donkey, even on a colt, the foal of a donkey.* He is meek and lowly, or "humble"; and even when He comes to Jerusalem in triumph, He shows His meekness by the way in which He comes. No troops of soldiers, no guards, no procession, and no banners waving! No chariot, no warhorse! He rides upon a donkey, and alongside there is the colt, just as they were found, unprepared and unadorned. He is at once the loftiest and the lowliest of the sons of men. No one ever came from such a height or went down to such a depth. In birth, life, and death He was like the lowly One. May He not well say, then, "Come unto me," and "Learn of me"? He is distant to none. He repulses none. Even to the little ones He says, *"Permit the children to come to Me"* (Mark 10:14). In word, look, and action, He is infinitely attractive to all. No one needs to dread Him, nor to stand aloof in suspicion or distrust. O sinner, come and learn of this lowly One. He will give you rest. O Christian, trust Him more. Do not misinterpret Him or do Him injustice. Give Him your fullest confidence, in spite of all the evil, darkness, and folly that are in you. Always stay by His side. Look at Him, love Him, speak to Him, trust Him. Does He frown? Does He turn away? No, He bids you welcome. The more you deal with Him, the more welcome you are. He thus gets opportunities for bringing out His abundance.

3. *Jerusalem's glory.* The first feature of this glory is the cessation of war, and the destruction of all the implements of war – chariot, horse, and battlebow. No more of these. Jerusalem is now the city of peace, the true Salem. But there is peace to the heathen too. He speaks peace to them: *Peace to you who [are] far away* (Ephesians 2:17). The sound of peace goes out from Salem to the whole world. Jerusalem is now a quiet habitation; peace is in all her borders; the heathen share it; and universal dominion now belongs to Zion's King. The earth is His as well as Jerusalem. He is the King of Kings. As of yet this has not been fulfilled. Satan still roams and reigns. The kingdoms of this world are still unchristian or anti-Christian. But the vision will not lie. Jesus is coming the second time to fulfill these words. He fulfilled the ninth verse at His first coming; He is to fulfill the tenth verse at His second coming. He comes as King as well as Savior. He does not come only to judge, but also to reign. He comes to end all war, bind Satan, strike Antichrist, renew creation, rebuild Jerusalem, restore Israel, convert the nations, and reign in peace as earth's righteous King. His dominion will be as universal as it is everlasting. His kingdom is that which cannot be moved. Then will be the longexpected reign of righteousness and peace.

Chapter 81

Looking to the Pierced One

> *"They will look on Me whom they have pierced; and they will mourn for Him, as one mourns for an only son, and they will weep bitterly over Him like the bitter weeping over a firstborn."* – Zechariah 12:10

Let us take up this passage under the following topics, which will bring out all its parts: (1) the pierced one, (2) the piercers, (3) the lookers, and (4) the mourners.

1. *The pierced one.* Messiah – the seed of the woman; the man with the bruised heel. He is the pierced one. It is He Himself who speaks. He was pierced by the nails and by the spear; by the nails to effect His death, by the spear to prove it. Both of these are the exhibitions of man's hatred, before and after death. It is as the pierced one that we see Him in Psalm 23 and in Isaiah 53; as such on the cross; as such in heaven, the Lamb slain. Divine yet human; human yet divine; both of these perfectly: human, that He might be pierced; divine, that His piercing might be effective. *By His scourging we are healed* (Isaiah 53:5).

2. *The piercers.* These in the first place are the Jews and the Romans, at the cross. Jew and Gentile united in this act: the Jew the planner and counselor, the Gentile the executioner. It was the united hatred

of Jew and Gentile that did the deed. The crowd surrounding the cross, they are consenting and partaking – as are all to whom the proclamation of this piercing comes, who do not come out from the crowd and protest against the deed by believing in the pierced one. In this way it is that all the world is guilty of the deed.

3. *The lookers.* In one sense the first piercers were lookers. They looked and pierced; they pierced and looked. But that looking brought no change. They looked and hated all the more. Jew and Gentile then looked, but they remained the same. The lookers in our text are not those who surrounded the cross, but those who came afterwards, not looking at the actual cross, but listening to the story of the pierced one. How idly they talk who say, "Had we seen the cross we would have been melted down!" At Pentecost we find these lookers. In many places, times, and ages we find them. We still find them. In the latter day, our text is to be more fully verified to Jew and Gentile: *Behold, He is coming with the clouds, and every eye will see Him* (Revelation 1:7), that is, look upon Him. The whole world will be lookers then: *every eye*. In our day we may say that it is by the *ear* we look; it is the *record* that brings the cross before the eye and presents to us the pierced one. We preach the story of the cross and say, "Look!"

4. *The mourners.* The actual piercers at the cross did not mourn. They railed and wagged their heads. The sight of the pierced one then produced only hatred and mockery. A man might see the cross and remain hard-hearted. The cross and the crucifix in themselves can do nothing for a soul. Yet the pierced one is the object to which God turns our eye. It is of Him that the Holy Spirit makes use in breaking the hard heart and binding up the broken one. He does not work except in connection with the cross of Christ. He uses the cross for producing godly sorrow. Note:

   a. *The sorrow here referred to is very deep.* It is like mourning for an only son. It is like the bitterness of soul for a firstborn. It is not the sorrow of a moment or an hour, but prolonged; not surface sorrow, but deep sorrow; not sentimentalism, but genuine grief – the grief of the whole man.

b. *It is sorrow produced by the Holy Spirit.* His hand is in it; otherwise, we might look a thousand times over at the cross and remain unmoved. It is not the sorrow produced by pictures, statues, the sight of Sinai or Jerusalem, harrowing descriptions, sad poetry, plaintive music like the "Miserere" of Rome, or by the darkness of a gloomy chamber. These are artificial and mechanical ways of calling up *apparent* religious feeling. It is only the sorrow of the world that produces death, not godly sorrow working repentance unto life, nor is it even so deep as that of Judas when he said, *"I have sinned"* (Matthew 27:4). It is manmade conviction, if it is conviction at all, not the sorrow of the Holy Spirit.

c. *It is sorrow flowing from looking at the pierced one.* We do not first mourn and then look; we look and then mourn. Not the one without the other; and not the mourning *before* the looking. Many, in their selfrighteousness, would first mourn, and then carry their mourning to God as a recommendation. But there is no genuine sorrow except that which flows directly from looking at the pierced one. What do we see in this pierced one that produces such a result?

   i. *We see infinite love.* This melts the heart and draws tears from the eyes. It is love that is bleeding on that cross.

   ii. *We see our own rejection of that love.* We have long been rejecters and despisers of it. Our years of rejection come up before us and fill us with bitterness. What! So long despise such love?

   iii. *We see suffering.* It is suffering beyond all suffering of man. It is the suffering of love. The sufferer is love itself. He suffers because He loves. He loves and suffers!

   iv. *We see that suffering caused by ourselves.* We not only rejected the love, but we also nailed the loving sufferer to the tree. This is *sin*. This is *our* sin. We are the murderers. We hated, mocked, nailed, and killed. Oh, what sin is ours, and what must *sin* be! Yet hear His voice: *"Turn to Me and be saved"* (Isaiah 45:22).

Chapter 82

The Holiness of Common Things

In that day there will be inscribed on the bells of the horses, "HOLY TO THE LORD." And the cooking pots in the Lord's house will be like the bowls before the altar. Every cooking pot in Jerusalem and in Judah will be holy to the Lord of hosts; and all who sacrifice will come and take of them and boil in them. And there will no longer be a Canaanite in the house of the Lord of hosts in that day. – Zechariah 14:20-21

It is of *millennial* days that the prophet is speaking. Days when Paradise will be restored, and earth will be as heaven. Days when Israel will be restored, Jerusalem rebuilt, and the great kingdom set up that cannot be moved.

Of this period, it is the *holiness* that he especially points to, which is so unlike everything in Jerusalem or on the earth in preceding days. "*Holy, Holy, Holy is the Lord God, the Almighty*" (Revelation 4:8) will then be the burden of every song. Jerusalem will be *truly* what it is now, and has been up to this time, but in name: *the holy city.*

But it is the holiness of *common* things that he especially dwells on more. Not just holy men, holy service, holy songs, or holy Sabbaths, but also holy vessels of every kind, holy bells (or bridles), holy pots, holy bowls, with the holy use of all these, so that every sight and sound will proclaim holiness. On wall, gate, and bar, on houses, doors, posts, and lintels will be inscribed "holiness." On leaf and flower and tree will be holiness.

The following paraphrase will bring out the exact meaning of each clause. "In that day will there be even upon such common things as the horsebells, holiness unto the Lord; every vessel in the temple will be holy, and even the common boiling pots will be as sacred as the altar bowls; no, not the temple pots alone, but every pot in Jerusalem and throughout the land will be holiness to the Lord of Hosts; and all they that come from afar to sacrifice will make use of them; and there will be no more the Canaanite (like the present Muslim) in the house of the Lord of Hosts."

Thus, the most common of common things are selected to illustrate the great truth or fact of that day, namely, the *universality of consecration*. Nothing will be left unsanctified. Everything will be for God. Everything will glorify Him, exhibiting the full meaning of the text: *Whether, then, you eat or drink or whatever you do, do all to the glory of God* (1 Corinthians 10:31).

It is not then the *spiritual nature* of the things themselves that is needed for the consecration. The things named are evidently chosen to prevent that mistake. It is of the holiness of things that are not in themselves spiritual that the prophet speaks. We are to lift up these common things out of their low position – to ennoble and dignify them.

And how is this to be done? Not by changing their nature, not by spiritualizing them, but by the right use of them. By connecting them with God, and God with them. By refastening the link between the material and the spiritual, not by transforming the material into the spiritual. It is the right use of common things, in connection with God, that is the true consecration. They are not consecrated by some mysterious in-order process to their glorifying God, but the right use of them in the service of God is the true consecration.

God is dealing with us here about common daily things; common, daily, and as men would say, carnal duties. He wants *holiness in our common works and words;* our eating and drinking; our plowing, sowing, and reaping; holiness in the shop, holiness in the marketplace; holiness in each room of the house; in journeying and in resting; in buying and selling; holiness in the railway carriage, and upon the highway; holiness in our reading, our conversation, and our letter writing; holiness in our business, and our recreation; holiness in our merriment, in our feasts, in our ordinary interactions. All our common works are to be so done that God will be glorified in them. Many forget all this. They think that a religious life should *omit* as many as possible of common duties, whereas it is by the right doing of these that we are to exemplify true religion. A religious life is not a life by itself, the life of a recluse or a hermit. It is *common life sanctified*. Many say, "If I were a minister, with nothing to do but religious subjects and acts, it would be well." Ah, a minister does not have opportunities of glorifying God that others have. He does not have so many of life's everyday duties to discharge. Or they say, "If I had more time to spare, I could glorify God more." Ah, it is seldom the idle man, the man of leisure, who does this. A life of leisure is not so easily managed or sanctified as many think. Self comes in; irregularities come in; time is not properly valued; efforts are half-hearted. It needs much grace to regulate and lay out for God a life of leisure. There is much meaning in the words, *"Six days you shall labor"* (Exodus 20:9).

The little things of life are to be attended to: the common, menial, earthly things. In these Adam served God when he tilled the ground; Abel when he kept sheep; Amos when he gathered sycamore fruit; Joseph when he worked as a carpenter; Paul when he made tents. It is thus that we are to glorify God – inscribing *holiness to the* LORD (Isaiah 23:18 KJV) on everything we do; so transacting daily business that men will say of us, "They fear God"; so making our plans that in them God will always have a place; so speaking the little or common words of each hour, that men will recognize in us the servants of God. It is easy and it is good to hang up a text on the walls of our chamber, but let our words and deeds be a continual recognition of the Holy Lord God. This will be more effective. Let us make *ourselves* the texts. Regulate your house (with every room in it) so that it will speak of God. Make your family arrangements such that they will all speak of God. It is not at family worship, or in asking a blessing alone that God is to be seen. These are mockeries if He is left out of the rest of the day. Let Him be seen everywhere and felt. Do all to His glory. While consecrating *common* things, beware of profaning *holy* things. Reverence and godly fear suit us in dealing with everything that is divine.

Chapter 83

Wearying Jehovah with Our Words

You have wearied the Lord with your words. Yet you say, "How have we wearied Him?" In that you say, "Everyone who does evil is good in the sight of the Lord, and He delights in them," or, "Where is the God of justice?" – Malachi 2:17

The prophet's charge against Israel is of "wearying the Lord"; as Isaiah had long before said this to Ahaz: *Will ye weary my God also?* (Isaiah 7:13 KJV). And while God charged them with wearying Him, He solemnly denies having wearied them, and asks, *"How have I wearied you?"* (Micah 6:3).

The charge is not of "provoking," but of "wearying"; and is one of deeply touching emotion of pity, indicating sorrow, patience, long-suffering, love, the profound affection of a heart that yearns over unworthy objects, unwilling to abandon them to their deserved doom, that *bears all things, believes all things, hopes all things, endures all things* (1 Corinthians 13:7), and *is not easily provoked, thinketh no evil* (1 Corinthians 13:5 KJV).

There are many ways in which we weary God, such as by our:

1. *Carelessness.* Worldliness, love of self, vanity, and folly.

2. *Opposition.* Dislike of Himself, His law, and His gospel.

3. *Unteachableness.* Foolishness, hardness of heart, and perversity.

4. *Unbelief.* Distrust of Himself, and rejection of His love.

5. *Lack of zeal.* "This I did for you; what do you do for Me?"

6. *Inconsistency.* Life and creed at variance. A name, no more.

In many such ways we weary God continually. We vex, grieve, and resist the Father, Son, and Holy Spirit. To this wearying He might at once put an end and refuse to be so treated by us any longer. But He has long patience, He bears much before He intercedes in His wrath. Knowing the fearful consequences to us of His being worn out by us and allowing righteousness and vengeance to do their work, He waits, pities, pleads, and remonstrates with us to the end.

The prophet's words, *"If only you had paid attention to My commandments!"* (Isaiah 48:18) are expressive of this feeling. Our Lord's tears over Jerusalem are the indication at once of God's unutterable patience, and of the exhaustion of it at last.

But let us observe the particular kind of wearying to which the prophet points.

1. *It is wearying with words. You have wearied the Lord with your words.* Words in themselves do not weary God. They are pleasant sounds. He delights in listening to what His creatures say. All sights and sounds, coming from the works of His hands, are meant to be *good:* sunshine, starlight, earth's green, heaven's blue, ocean's brilliance, the music of birds, the voice of the wind, the roar of the thunder, the noise of many waters. These are among the things that He pronounced *good.* So it is with the human voice and human words. But when they are dissociated from the feeling within, so as not to be the expression of the heart but only of the lips, or when they are the utterance of error or falsehood, unmeaning and hollow, then they cease to be good; they displease Him. When they are repeated and reiterated, they weary Him. Talk, talk, mere talk, the talk of the lips – it may be respectable, religious talk, but if it is mere talk, it not only wearies man but also God. And think of the innumerable millions of words uttered every hour by the millions on earth, all of which go up to the ear of God! Think of the discords, dissonances, impurities, follies,

blasphemies, and hypocrisies that are heard hourly by God! Oh, how He must be wearied with the words of men! How He must be grieved with the sounds of earth!

2. *It is wearying by questions.* We say, "This is how we wearied Him?" Men do not like to be challenged by God, and yet they shrink from the denial of the charge. Instead of honest confession or bold denial, they speak like Cain, and ask, *"Am I my brother's keeper? How have I wearied Him?"* What more fitted to weary God than such a course of hypocritical questioning, judgmental questioning, faultfinding, or pretending surprise at what they could not but know that they were committing. O mockery of God! For men to look up in His face, and say, "How have we wearied You?"

3. *It is wearying by denial of the difference between good and evil.* One of the most explicit of all Bible teachings is about the difference between the evil person and the good person, the evil thing and the good thing, the evil opinion and the good opinion. Man often sees little of this difference, God sees it strongly. Man likes to erase or smooth over this difference; God keeps up the line, broad, deep, and clear – as between sea and land. He is wearied by man's earnest affirmations of the little difference between things and persons, and by man's attempts to obliterate moral and spiritual distinctions, to call light darkness and darkness light. Is not the present age wearying God in this way?

4. *It is wearying by disbelief of coming judgment.* "Where is the God of judgment?" is the infidel question, like that of the scoffer in the last days: *"Where is the promise of His coming?"* (2 Peter 3:4). No judgment, and no God of judgment, is the watchword of many. Every man is a judge to himself; a judge of all truth and error; the measurer of God; and the judge of his character and ways. This is not exactly the fool's saying, *"There is no God"* (Psalm 14:1), but it is close to it; for it means that there is no god but such a one as suits man's philosophy. God's noninterposition for so many ages, and His allowance of confusion and error, lead men to conclude that there is no God of judgment. This "wearies

God"; this semiatheism; this misinterpretation of His love and patience. God's long-suffering, instead of leading to repentance, leads to unbelief.

The Lord will come. He may come soon. Let us be ready. The Judge stands before the door.

Chapter 84

Dies Irae (Day of Wrath)

Malachi 4:1-6

This is a notable specimen of a double prophecy. It contains several distinct predictions – twice or more fulfilled; at first very partially, and then fully; at first almost apparently a failure, and then at last a perfect fulfillment. The center of these prophecies is Messiah Himself – Messiah in connection with Israel; Messiah both in His first and second comings; the things predicted having a partial and shadowy fulfillment at His first coming, and awaiting an exhaustive fulfillment at His second coming. By taking these both apart and united, we will have a clear insight into the meaning of this difficult prophecy.

In the previous chapter (Malachi 3) there is a *day* spoken of – a time of mingled wrath and grace. It is of this *day* that the present chapter is full. It is called *the day* (verse 1), and is described two times in this chapter: *"on the day which I am preparing"* (verse 3), or, *"that I will work"*; and *"the great and terrible day of the Lord"* (verse 5). It is the day of Christ – Messiah's day, as seen by the prophets, embracing both His first and second comings, and combining in one period the events of both of these.

"For behold." God calls men's heedless eyes to the events of the future. *"For behold, the day is coming"* (verse 1); yes, the day that will be *"burning like a furnace"* (verse 1); *the day of vengeance* (Isaiah 61:2; cf. 64:2; 66:15-16). Then will all *the proud* (Psalm 94:2), especially he *who opposes and exalts himself above every socalled god* (2 Thessalonians 2:4), *and every evildoer* (verse 1), the wicked one and all his hosts – be as *stubble* (Isaiah 47:14), and as *chaff* (Matthew 3:12) for the unquenchable fire. Yes, *"the day that is coming will set them ablaze," says the Lord of hosts, "so that it will leave them neither root nor branch"* (verse 1); *"and they will be completely burned with fire"* (2 Samuel 23:7). Such is *the day of the Lord [that] will come as a thief in the night* (2 Peter 3:10 KJV). John the Baptist referred to this day of fire and destruction when he began to preach repentance (Matthew 3:2-10), as if reminding the Jews of Malachi and his awful words.

In the midst of this fiery havoc there will be a "spared" remnant (Malachi 3:17), described by the expression, *"you who fear My name"* (verse 2). Yes, the fearers of Jehovah's name are (as in the case of Noah) to be spared in the fiery deluge that is coming. Indeed, on them a glorious morning is to dawn (2 Samuel 23:4). The Sun of Righteousness is to arise, not with destruction, but with *healing* in His rays or *wings* (verse 2), and under His sweet warmth and light, these fearers of the Lord will go forth as the flocks and herds to pasture. Blessed morning to *those who fear the Lord and who esteem His name* (Malachi 3:16), *"a morning without clouds"* (2 Samuel 23:4); ushered in by *"the bright morning star"* (Revelation 22:16). This was in a measure fulfilled when Jesus came as *"the Light of the world"* (John 8:12); but the full accomplishment is reserved for His second appearing.

Then (verse 3) will these fearers of the Lord accompany Him in executing His vengeance – *This is an honor for all His godly ones* (Psalm 149:9); for *"the Lord came with many thousands of His holy ones, to execute judgment upon all"* (Jude vv. 14-15). They come with their Lord to *"tread down the wicked"* (verse 3), to tread them in His anger, and trample them in His wrath (Isaiah 63:3; cf. Revelation 19:15). Yes, Antichrist and all his enemies, with all *who do not know God and to those who do not obey the gospel of our Lord Jesus* (2 Thessalonians 1:8), *will be chaff* under them in that day of fire (verse 1). Thus will the saints triumph. Victory will be theirs on that very earth where they were overcome and trodden on. They will be associated with the King of Kings in wielding the *rod of iron* (Psalm 2:9; Revelation 2:27). That day will be one of exaltation and triumph for the fearers of the Lord, *"But the saints of the Highest One will receive the kingdom"* (Daniel 7:18);

and then will the song of the redeemed be fulfilled: *"You have made them to be a kingdom and priests to our God; and they will reign upon the earth"* (Revelation 5:10).

In the fourth verse we have a statement which, while it refers mostly to Israel, applies to the world also: *"Remember the law of Moses."* It was probably to this that our Lord referred, when He said, *"Do not think that I came to abolish the Law or the Prophets; I did not come to abolish but to fulfill"* (Matthew 5:17). Throughout the whole dispensation that law was to be exhibited and magnified, as the law of laws, holy, just, and good. Christ Himself did this in life and in death; and God, even under this dispensation of grace, cannot allow one jot or tittle of that righteous law to be infringed. It will stand forever.

Then the forerunner is announced, before the great and dreadful day of the Lord; whether actually *before* it, or just *near* its commencement (for it is not a mere day of twentyfour hours), we do not know – *"I am going to send you Elijah the prophet"* (verse 5). As we find Joel's prophecy (2:31) receiving a faint and partial fulfillment at Pentecost, though it awaits a fuller one later, so we have a double Elijah – an Elijah of the first coming, and an Elijah of the second coming. The mission of both is alike – to call Israel to repentance, and to bring the whole nation – fathers and children – into happy unity before God; the warning being annexed, *"so that I will not come and smite the land* [earth] *with a curse"* (verse 6). John the Baptist was a burning and shining light – the vivid likeness of the Elijah the Tishbite, but his ministry did not accomplish the end specified. The heart of the nation was not turned, and instead of oneness, there was division and a sword (Luke 12:51-52); son against father, and father against son. They did not repent, and so they were struck; and not only they, but also their land, so that it remains a desolation and a curse until this day. But when the literal Elijah comes, at Messiah's second advent, then will be the blessing and not the curse. His mission will be effective. The heart of the nation will be turned; God will give them *"**one** heart"* (Ezekiel 11:19, emphasis added); *"all [the] people will be righteous"* (Isaiah 60:21); people and land alike will be blessed of the Lord; division and discord will cease; unity and love will overflow. Then will be the reign of peace, under the scepter of the Prince of Peace.

As the Old Testament ends with that awful word *curse,* the New

Testament begins and ends with blessing: *"Blessed are the poor in spirit"*; *"Blessed are the gentle"*; *"Blessed are the pure in heart"* (Matthew 5:3, 5, 8); and *the grace of the Lord Jesus be with all* (Revelation 22:21).

1. *The great warning* (verse 1). There is a day coming that will decide everything. All that God hates will be utterly swept away. Sinner, tremble and turn.

2. *The consolation of the faithful* (verse 2). There is a remnant; and the mark of this is that they *fear* God's name. What stress God lays on this *fear*. What honor He puts on those in whom it is found.

3. *The mighty victory* (verse 3). These "fearers" are "warriors" too. They fight, overcome, and triumph. The reward of victory is theirs: the victory and the crown.

4. *The unchangeable standard of holiness* (verse 4). God's law is perfect. It stands forever. In the last ages, as well as the first, it is the great rule. It tells what God loves and what He hates.

5. *The world's last sermon* (verses 5-6). It comes from revered lips; from one who has been nearly three thousand years in heaven. Elijah comes to give God's great message to Israel. The nation hears. The blessing comes.

To all this we are looking forward in these last days. When the great day will come, we do not know. It may be nearby. Let us look for its signs. Let us listen for its sounds of warning. The message has gone forth. *Watch. In such an hour as ye think not the Son of man cometh* (Matthew 24:44 KJV). *Children, it is the last hour* (1 John 2:18).

The world is not ready for its Judge. In the day when He comes, it will be dumb. *What wilt thou say when he shall punish thee?* asks the prophet (Jeremiah 13:21 KJV). Yes, the world is not ready. But this will not hinder His coming. *He who is coming will come, and will not delay* (Hebrews 10:37). As a thief He will come. As the lightning He will come. As a snare He will come. As a judge He will come. As an avenger He will come. As the wielder of the iron rod He will come. As King of Kings and Lord of Lords He will come.

O sons of men, take warning. When you are saying peace and safety, sudden destruction will come. When you are enjoying your lusts and pleasures – in the theater, the opera, the ballroom, the turf, or the gaming table – He, *the Judge of the living and the dead* (Acts 10:42), will come. Oh, before He comes to you, you come to Him! *Do homage to the Son, that He not become angry, and you perish in the way* (Psalm 2:12).

Make haste, for judgment does not linger, and damnation does not slumber. The time is short. But the gate is open, and He who has opened it bids you to enter. He pities you, He yearns over you, in the deep sincerity of divine compassion. *Not wishing for any to perish but for all to come to repentance.* While still then He lingers in His love – oh hasten to be saved. He may soon be here. The trumpet of the Judge may soon sound. The day that will burn as an oven may soon begin. Oh, turn, turn; why will you die?

Horatius Bonar – A Brief Biography

Born on December 19, 1808, Horatius Bonar was one of eleven children of James Bonar and Marjory Pyott Maitland Bonar. For several generations his ancestors had been ministers of the gospel.

Bonar graduated from the University of Edinburgh where Dr. Thomas Chalmers laid the foundation for solid learning, which continued through the years. This gave Bonar direction and strength during his most impressionable years. He was ordained in 1838 and accepted North Parish, Kelso, as his first parish. In addition to Dr. Chalmers, he allied himself with William C. Burns and Robert Murray McCheyne as spiritual mentors and friends.

As a young pastor, Bonar preached in villages and farmhouses throughout his district, for he saw evangelization in a different light from his other contemporaries. To him, Christ had to come first, not numbers of converts. In his house-to-house visitation, he proved himself as a comforter of the sorrowful and a guide for the confused. Colossians 3:23 was the verse he lived by: *Whatsoever ye do, do it heartily, as to the Lord, and not unto men.*

In 1843, he joined the Free Church of Scotland after the "Disruption." The old church with its civil service pastors had failed to arouse the faith of the nation. This disruption was a schism in the Church of Scotland where about 450 evangelical ministers broke away over an issue of the church's relationship with the state. There was disagreement about whether the church was sovereign within its own domain with Christ as Head or if the king was head. In this way, it was similar to the Lutheran Reformation.

Those who left forfeited their livelihood, pulpits, and aid from the established church to found and finance a new national church from scratch. They needed to train clergy and form a new college, which opened in 1843, with Dr. Chalmers as the first principal. Most of the protest principles were conceded by Parliament by 1929, which paved the way for reunification.

In 1843, Horatius Bonar married Jane Catharine Lundie. Together they had nine children, but five of them died before adulthood – three in infancy. One surviving daughter was later widowed with five children, so she moved back with her parents. Horatius said, "God took five children from life some years ago, and He has given me another five to bring up for Him in my old age."

In 1851, he wrote *Man: His Religion and His World* because he was concerned that pastors were diluting the gospel to make it pleasant and easier to accept. He always contended for the truth and never neglected pastoral work and preaching.

Horatius Bonar received an honorary degree of Doctor of Divinity from the University of Aberdeen and then visited Palestine on a mission to the Jews in 1856, which gave him the inspiration for the hymn "The Voice from Galilee," better known as "I Heard the Voice of Jesus Say." Revival had sprung up in Scotland while he was away, and he came back with a renewed interest in prophecy and a firm belief in the personal coming and reign of Jesus Christ. He did not believe that the world was getting better and civilization could save the world. Teachings of the coming of Christ, the tribulation, and the thousand-year reign had been lost, and the nineteenth-century preachers had to bring these doctrines back.

Bonar spoke as a dying man to dying men, resulting in many conversions. He wrote the *Kelso Tracts* to warn the careless, to present salvation simply, and to edify the saints. The tracts had wide circulation in Scotland, England, and America. In 1867, Bonar moved to Edinburgh to take over Chalmers' Memorial Church, and in 1883, he was elected moderator of the General Assembly of the Free Church of Scotland. Bonar continued to express his views in *Prophetical Landmarks* (1847) and served as editor of *The Quarterly Journal of Prophecy* (1848-1873) and the *Christian Treasury* (1859-1879). He even wrote biographies of ministers like *The Life of the Rev. John Milne of Perth* and *The Life and Works of the Rev. G. T. Dodds*.

Other books and tracts that bear his name are *Night of Weeping*, *The Everlasting Righteousness*, and *How Shall I Go to God?* Until his death, he warned about trends he saw creeping in and threatening the Christian church. In one of his last books – *Our Ministry: How It Touches the Questions of the Age* – he observed that "Man is now thinking out a Bible for himself, framing a religion in harmony with the development of liberal thought, constructing a worship on the principles of taste and culture, and shaping a God to suit the expanding aspirations of the age."

Horatius Bonar is best known as the principle hymn writer of Scotland. He was called the "prince of Scottish hymn writers." As he worked with young people, he realized they lacked enthusiasm. Even though he lacked an ear for music, he knew familiar tunes and wrote new words to them for the children. His experiment worked and the children became interested in the verses that were written for them personally. Because they were full of sound teaching, many adults loved to sing them also and requested to use them in other churches. He always granted permission for any church to use his hymns as long as they did not change his words.

He wrote more than six hundred hymns, and many hymnbooks carry these songs. Several are completely compiled from his hymns. The three volumes of *Hymns of Faith and Hope* contain a multitude of his hymns. While "I Heard the Voice of Jesus Say" and "My Redeemer Liveth" were two of the best known, he is largely remembered for his hymns that were based strongly on theology and doctrine, such as "Done is the Work That Saves" and "No Blood, No Altar Now." He wrote of justification, sanctification, the second coming, and the exaltation of Christ.

His hymns are childlike yet manly, hopeful but sympathetic. For many years they were mostly used by churches of other denominations but not his own. The Free Church of Scotland was opposed to singing at worship anything but metrical psalms and paraphrases.

Bonar believed "life is a journey, not a home; a road, not a city of habitation." He stated that "It is not the opinions that man needs; it is truth. It is not theology; it is God. It is not religion; it is Christ. It is not literature and science; but the knowledge of the free love of God in the gift of His only begotten Son." From the first day of his ministry until his last sermon, he closed with these words: "In such an hour as ye think not, the Son of Man cometh."

Other Similar Titles

Expository Thoughts on the Gospel of Matthew, Mark, Luke, and John
by J. C. Ryle

A Commentary Set

Wisdom, encouragement, and exhortation is contained in these pages. Not because of the author's brilliance, but because of the words of truth contained in the gospel of John. And just as the apostles didn't draw any attention to himself, so also J. C. Ryle clearly and wonderfully directs his words and our thoughts towards the inspired words of scripture. If we truly love God, we will love His word; and the more study His word, the more we will love God.

Available where books are sold.

Faithful to Christ,
by Charles H. Spurgeon

If there is a true faith, there must be a declaration of it. If you are a candle, and God has lit you, then let your light so shine before men that they may see your good works and glorify your Father who is in the heavens (Matthew 5:16). Soldiers of Christ must, like soldiers of our nation, wear their uniforms; and if they are ashamed of their uniforms, they ought to be drummed out of the army.

I believe that many Christians get into a lot of trouble by not being honest in their convictions. For instance, if a person goes into a workshop, or a soldier into a barracks, and if he does not fly his flag from the beginning, it will be very difficult for him to run it up afterwards. But if he immediately and boldly lets them know, "I am a Christian, and there are certain things that I cannot do to please you, and certain other things that I cannot help doing even though they might displease you" – when that is clearly understood, after a while the peculiarity of the thing will be gone, and the person will be let alone.
 – Charles H. Spurgeon

Available where books are sold.

Life in Christ,
by Charles H. Spurgeon

Volume 1-8

Men who were led by the hand or groped their way along the wall to reach Jesus were touched by his finger and went home without a guide, rejoicing that Jesus Christ had opened their eyes. Jesus is still able to perform such miracles. And, with the power of the Holy Spirit, his Word will be expounded and we'll watch for the signs to follow, expecting to see them at once. Why shouldn't those who read this be blessed with the light of heaven? This is my heart's inmost desire.

I can't put fine words together. I've never studied speech. In fact, my heart loathes the very thought of intentionally speaking with fine words when souls are in danger of eternal separation from God. No, I work to speak straight to your hearts and consciences, and if there is anyone with faith to receive, God will bless them with fresh revelation.

– Charles H. Spurgeon

Available where books are sold.

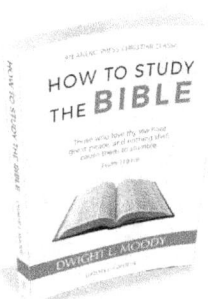

How to Study the Bible,
by Dwight L. Moody

There is no situation in life for which you cannot find some word of consolation in Scripture. If you are in affliction, if you are in adversity and trial, there is a promise for you. In joy and sorrow, in health and in sickness, in poverty and in riches, in every condition of life, God has a promise stored up in His Word for you.

This classic book by Dwight L. Moody brings to light the necessity of studying the Scriptures, presents methods which help stimulate excitement for the Scriptures, and offers tools to help you comprehend the difficult passages in the Scriptures. To live a victorious Christian life, you must read and understand what God is saying to you. Moody is a master of using stories to illustrate what he is saying, and you will be both inspired and convicted to pursue truth from the pages of God's Word.

Available where books are sold.

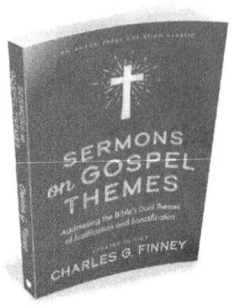

Sermons on Gospel Themes,
by Charles G. Finney

All Christians and sinners should understand that the whole plan is complete. They should understand that the whole of Christ – His character, His work, His atoning death, and His ever-living intercession – belongs to each and every person and simply needs to be accepted. There is a full ocean of it. There it is. You can just as well take it as not. You are invited and urged to drink, and to drink abundantly! This ocean supplies all your need. As the Scriptures say, He is of God made unto us wisdom, righteousness, sanctification, and redemption (1 Corinthians 1:30). What do you need? Wisdom? Here it is. Righteousness? Here it is. Sanctification? Here you have it. It is all in Christ. Can you possibly think of anything needful for your salvation, moral purity, or your usefulness that is not here in Christ? Nothing. All is provided here.

Available where books are sold.

Morning by Morning,
by Charles H. Spurgeon

Charles H. Spurgeon's devotionals Morning by Morning and Evening by Evening have inspired, encouraged, and challenged Christians for generations. Spurgeon, with his masterful hand, carefully selected his text from throughout the Bible and covered a broad range of topics, in order to present a well-balanced and fruitful daily devotional for readers both young and old.

Now updated into more-modern English for today's readers, and again separated into two volumes as originally published, with morning devotionals in one volume and evening devotionals in the second. We chose a 11-point font for the sake of legibility, and formatted the devotionals so each fits on a single page.

Available where books are sold.

www.ingramcontent.com/pod-product-compliance
Lightning Source LLC
Chambersburg PA
CBHW070442090526
44586CB00046B/1598